D1604162

# Rumsfeld's Wars

# Rumsfeld's Wars

## The Arrogance of Power

*Dale R. Herspring*

UNIVERSITY PRESS OF KANSAS

© 2008 by the University Press of Kansas

Published by the University Press of Kansas
(Lawrence, Kansas 66045), which was organized by
the Kansas Board of Regents and is operated and
funded by Emporia State University, Fort Hays State
University, Kansas State University, Pittsburg State
University, the University of Kansas, and Wichita
State University

Library of Congress Cataloging-in-Publication Data

Herspring, Dale R. (Dale Roy)
    Rumsfeld's wars : the arrogance of power /
Dale R. Herspring.
        p.   cm. — (Modern war studies)
    Includes bibliographical references and index.
    ISBN 978-0-7006-1587-2 (cloth : alk. paper)
    1. Rumsfeld, Donald, 1932– 2. United States.
Dept. of Defense—History—21st century.
3. United States. Dept. of Defense—Officials and
employees—Biography. 4. Cabinet officers—United
States—Biography. 5. United States—Military
policy—Decision making. 6. United States—Armed
Forces—Reorganization—History—21st century.
7. Military planning—United States—History—21st
century. 8. Afghan War, 2001– 9. Iraq War, 2003–
I. Title.
    UA23.6.H47 2008
    956.7044′3373—dc22                2008001344

British Library Cataloguing-in-Publication Data is
available.

Printed in the United States of America

10 9 8 7 6 5 4 3 2 1

The paper used in this publication is recycled and
contains 50 percent postconsumer waste. It is acid
free and meets the minimum requirements of the
American National Standard for Permanence of
Paper for Printed Library Materials Z39.48-1992.

*To General Eric Shinseki*
*Who had the moral courage to*
*speak out when it counted and*
*accept the consequences*
*Mahalo nui loa*

If a lion stands at the head of an army of lions, victory is assured.
If a lion stands at the head of an army of asses, the chances are fifty-fifty.
But if an ass stands at the head of an army of lions, you can call it quits.
—Russian General Alexandr Lebed, *On Leadership*

I don't think, if I had been president—on the basis of the facts as I saw them publicly—I don't think I would have ordered the Iraq War.
—Former President Gerald Ford

The Past was not predictable when it started.
—Donald Rumsfeld

I am reasonably certain that [the Iraqi people] will greet us as liberators; and that will help us to keep requirements down.
—Paul Wolfowitz

Guys, in a nutshell, it's not that we didn't plan. The problem is that we planned for the wrong contingency.
—Paul Bremer

The ultimate question policy makers have to determine is what standard of proof should be used before the United States decides to deploy force.
—George Tenet

Candidly, I have gotten somewhat nervous at some of the pronouncements Rumsfeld has made.
—General Norman Schwartzkopf

In my view, Rumsfeld is one of those most responsible for the current situation in Iraq. He rejected the advice given to him by his generals, while at the same time he discarded the detailed plans for the post-conflict period prepared by the State Department.
—British General Sir Mike Jackson

What David Halberstam said of Robert McNamara in *The Best and the Brightest* is true of those at OSD as well: they were brilliant, and they were fools.
—James Fallows

In the lead-up to the Iraq War and its later conduct, I saw at a minimum true dereliction, negligence and irresponsibility, and at worst, lying, incompetence and corruption.
—General Tony Zinni, U.S. Marine Corps,
former commander CENTCOM

# Contents

# Preface

This was a very difficult and painful book to write. Of all the books and articles I have put together over the years, none covered material more upsetting. Why? For the simple reason that I consider myself a conservative, and I voted for the Bush administration twice. Furthermore, in addition to spending over twenty years serving my country as a Foreign Service officer in the Department of State, I also spent thirty-two years in the U.S. Navy, going from a raw recruit to a captain. I supported the Bush administration when it called for an invasion of Iraq because I believed what it said: Iraq might use its weapons of mass destruction (WMD) against the United States and that there was a clear tie between Saddam Hussein and Osama bin Laden, the person behind the events of 9/11. As a retired naval officer, I felt I had no choice but to support my commander in chief.

However, the more I looked at the actions leading up to the invasion of Iraq in March 2003, as well as the process of military transformation in the U.S. armed forces, the more upset I became. I was not bothered by the president's concern over WMD. The rest of the world also believed Saddam had them. After all, he had used these weapons against his own people as well as the Iranians. I was, however, deeply upset and angered by what I learned about the supposed tie between Saddam and bin Laden. It soon became clear to me that this was an idea manufactured by the civilian leadership in the Pentagon to justify the war and that if Secretary of Defense Donald Rumsfeld and his subordinates had not manipulated data and convinced the president of the necessity of invading Iraq, the United States might not be there today. It is one thing to sound the alarm when the wolf is at the door. It is another to try to make someone believe the wolf is dangerous when it is really locked in a cage.

I also found myself increasingly agitated at the way Rumsfeld treated the uniformed military. He showed little respect to the top brass—men who had devoted more than thirty years of their lives to the military—and he did his best to force his own idea of military transformation, as well as military tactics and operational procedures, on the generals. Civilian control is the rule, yes, but to be most effective there must be mutual respect between a leader and his troops. Indeed, I am convinced that Rumsfeld's deep involvement in planning for the invasion was one of the main reasons why the United States was unprepared for the postcombat period. Instead of a quick withdrawal from Iraq, the United States has already spent five years trying to pacify Iraq and to create a stable government.

What to do? I decided I would write a book that would, as a serving officer put it, "help pull things together." I make no claim that this book includes original data. Instead, I have tried to make as thorough a search as possible of the unclassified information available to scholars in an effort to piece together what happened and why. Some of the issues discussed in this book, such as the proper role a military officer should assume in dealing with civilians, are complex and cannot be assigned a simple answer.

I decided to dedicate the book to General Eric Shinseki, U.S. Army (Ret.). I have never had the pleasure of meeting General Shinseki, but I have tremendous respect for him and the way he handled himself when testifying before the U.S. Senate Armed Services Committee in February 2003. I hope that if I am ever placed in a similar situation, I will show the same moral fortitude in standing up for what is right despite the consequences. I only wish more senior officers had acted similarly when talking to Congress concerning the military and its ability to carry out operations in Iraq.

In this undertaking I was lucky to have the help and criticism of a number of individuals. First, and foremost, I would note my editor, Michael Briggs of the University Press of Kansas. Dr. Charles Stevenson, my former colleague at the National War College and currently a professor at the Paul Nitze School of Advanced International Studies at the Johns Hopkins University, also provided helpful criticism and comments. I also want to thank Ann Robertson, whose magnificent editorial skills helped make this book far more readable than it was when she first encountered it. I should also mention that I was fortunate to have critical and insightful comments from several military officers who participated in various capacities in some of the events covered by this book. They have asked that their names not be used since they are still on active duty. General Tony Zinni, U.S. Marine Corps (Ret.) also kindly answered one of my questions, and General Richard Myers, U.S. Air Force (Ret.) provided answers to a series of questions I submitted to him. My faithful colleague Joe Aistrup was also helpful in commenting on the content of the book, as was my wife of forty-three years.

In the end, the views expressed here are my own. Likewise, I am solely responsible for any errors that may have crept into the text as I revised it.

*Manhattan, Kansas*

# List of Abbreviations

| | |
|---|---|
| AOR | Area of responsibility |
| CAS | Close Air Support |
| CENTCOM | Central Command |
| CEO | Chief Executive Officer |
| CIA | Central Intelligence Agency |
| CPA | Coalition Provisional Authority |
| DOD | Department of Defense |
| FCS | Future Combat Systems |
| FSO | Foreign Service Officers |
| MRAP | Mine Resistant Ambush Protected Vehicles |
| NATO | North Atlantic Treaty Organization |
| NCO | Non-commissioned officer |
| NCW | Network-centric warfare |
| NDP | National Defense Panel |
| NSC | National Security Council |
| OEO | Office of Economic Opportunity |
| OIF | Operation Iraqi Freedom |
| QDR | Quadrennial Defense Review |
| SALT | Strategic Arms Limitation Talks |
| SOCOM | Special Operations Command |
| TPFDD | Time-Phased Force and Deployment Data |
| WMD | Weapons of mass destruction |

# Introduction

A number of Donald Rumsfeld's posse of commissars with no first-hand
experience either of the military or the savage harshness of the world,
insisted that none of our generals or admirals or military veterans were
worth a damn and that civilians who had never tried on a combat boot
knew best how to wield our military.

    *Lieutenant Colonel Ralph Peters, U.S. Army (Ret.)*

## Why This Book?

On November 8, 2006, President George W. Bush announced that Donald Rumsfeld, the only man to serve twice as secretary of defense, was
stepping down. With Rumsfeld's departure, an important era in American
civil-military relations drew to a close. It was a contentious period, comparable to that of Lyndon Johnson and Robert McNamara in terms of conflict, distrust, and bureaucratic intrigue. As a direct result of Rumsfeld's
actions, the military had been demoralized and broken. Junior officers were
leaving the service in record numbers, while a number of retired senior officers had spoken out publicly against what they saw as Rumsfeld's heavy-
handed conduct and lack of respect for the country's armed forces. Indeed,
many senior officers believed Rumsfeld and his close associates had nothing
but scorn for them. To make matters worse, he put them through an ex-
cruciating process of military transformation that meant reliance on high-
tech weapons systems at the expense of fewer personnel for the army, navy,
Marines, and air force. He also undermined the military's merit-based promotion system by promoting officers of his choice, people he knew would
support him and his policies. Meanwhile, those who stood up to him soon
found themselves out of a job. Relations between Rumsfeld and the army,
in particular, quickly deteriorated.

If turning military structure, tactics, operations, and weapons systems up-
side down were not enough, Rumsfeld and his supporters successfully lobbied the administration and manipulated data to send the American armed
forces off to fight a war that many generals considered unnecessary. And

as the ultimate slap in the generals' faces, Rumsfeld dictated strategy and operations—on occasion even tactics. He wanted to use the war to prove his transformation theory—that high-tech weapons could compensate for numbers of troops. The result was a quagmire—the military was forced to fight a war in Iraq with too few troops, especially during Phase IV operations.

Predictably, Iraq has had a serious negative impact on both the army and the Marine Corps. Because of the casualties they have suffered, and the seemingly never-ending war they are fighting, both have begun to experience problems recruiting and retaining qualified officers and enlisted personnel. In addition, because of its heavy usage, their equipment is wearing out.

As the war dragged on and public support for it and the president constantly dropped, many in the United States, including those in uniform, began to wonder when Rumsfeld would leave. There were rumors that he would leave in late 2001, and then in April 2004 after the revelation of the mistreatment of prisoners at the Abu Ghraib prison. Bush repeatedly refused to fire his defense secretary, arguing that Rumsfeld was doing a magnificent job. Such loyalty, however, can have a very negative effect; most observers believe that Rumsfeld's mishandling of American operations in Iraq played a major role in the stunning Republican defeat in the November 2006 congressional elections. At that point, even Bush recognized that Rumsfeld had to go.

Rumsfeld's successor, Robert Gates, and the new chairman of the Joint Chiefs of Staff, Admiral Michael Mullen, faced the Herculean task of rebuilding the military, especially the army and Marine Corps, while at the same time trying to come up with a successful strategy in Iraq. In short, Rumsfeld left the Pentagon and the military services with major problems in personnel and equipment. This is not the first time that a departing secretary has left the military in disarray, and it took many years to rebuild it. The same was true of civil-military relations.

In retrospect, the deterioration of both the armed forces and civil-military relations during the Rumsfeld era was as unnecessary as it was unexpected. Rumsfeld was bright and had some very good ideas for changes in the way the military operated. Unlike many of his predecessors, he was prepared to question basic assumptions—assumptions that guided not only the kind of war the United States should fight, but also the kind of weapons it should purchase and how it should train its troops to use them. This was exactly the type of new thinking that the country's conservative military leadership needed to hear. Indeed, given his previous stint as defense secretary in the 1970s, his encyclopedic knowledge of the Washington bureaucracy, his strong work ethic, his formidable intellect, and his dedication to change, Rumsfeld seemed to be the right person for the job. The truth turned out to be otherwise.

## The Cast of Characters

This is a book about Donald Rumsfeld and the impact that he, and his inner circle of supporters, had on the senior leadership of the United States military during his second tour as secretary of defense from 2001 to 2006. Not since Robert McNamara in the 1960s has a secretary of defense been so hated by the military, nor has any secretary since McNamara played such a critical role in the formulation of national security policy. Rumsfeld was the only senior civilian decision maker who played a vital role both in the military transformation process and the invasion of Iraq. He was the driving force behind efforts to transform the U.S. military into smaller, more technologically sophisticated armed forces. He believed that greater reliance on high-tech weapons and equipment would compensate for its smaller size. He was convinced that the American military was still caught in the grip of the Cold War—that it had to think differently on how to fight a new kind of war. He planned to pay for it by diverting funds from one area to another and downsizing personnel.

Rumsfeld believed that the Iraq War provided a perfect opportunity to test his ideas on how to fight a war. This put him in potential conflict with the chairman of the Joint Chiefs of Staff. Theoretically, the 1986 Goldwater-Nichols Act made the chairman of the Joint Chiefs of Staff the primary adviser to the secretary of defense and the president on military affairs. Thus, the chairman has the right to go directly to the president if he disagrees with the secretary of defense. However, as soon as he had the chance, Rumsfeld found a chairman who would not go to the president "over his head." General Richard Myers was an excellent officer, but one who was prepared to play the game as Rumsfeld dictated.

In addition, Vice President Dick Cheney played a much bigger role in national security affairs during the Bush administration than had any other individual in his position since the beginning of World War II. Unfortunately, his actual role is difficult to document. Although there is no question that he was influential regarding American policy toward Iraq, he did not deal directly with the military—that was Rumsfeld's turf. Cheney often supported him, especially regarding the invasion of Iraq, but Rumsfeld was the one who set the standard for dealing with military culture.

There were also a number of other civilians who played important roles inside the Pentagon: Deputy Secretary of Defense Paul Wolfowitz, Under Secretary of Defense for Policy Douglas J. Feith, and Under Secretary of Defense for Intelligence Stephen A. Cambone. The important fact is that they carried out their duties as part of the Department of Defense under the supervision and control of Donald Rumsfeld. Since everything they did was in his name, and with his permission, he must assume responsibility for their actions. Rumsfeld set the tone for civil-military relations under President George W. Bush.

Given the type of issues discussed in this book, the primary focus will be on senior officers, specifically the Joint Chiefs of Staff as well as the combatant commanders—the military's most senior officers. After all, they were the focus of military transformation (especially the army) and they were the ones bearing the brunt of military operations in Iraq. Obviously, there would be occasions when other, lower-ranking generals would be the focus of attention, but that was a result of the issue at hand, not just because of their positions on transformation or Iraq.

## Civil-Military Relations

While the term "civil-military relations" is often used to describe relations between the military and its civilian leaders, it sometimes confuses two different but interrelated issues. One deals with how civilians like Rumsfeld interact with senior officers. The other issue is how military officers relate to civilians. Rumsfeld was not good with either.

Despite Rumsfeld's comments that he was "in control" of the military, even a cursory study of civil-military relations in the United States reveals that the U.S. military does not need to be "controlled." The idea of civilian control is deeply imbedded in the consciousness of everyone who wears the uniform. Only once has an officer openly defied political authority during the post–World War II era—General Douglas MacArthur—and President Harry S. Truman fired him for his insubordination, a decision that was supported by the Joint Chiefs of Staff.

Nevertheless, any civilian leader faces the sometimes daunting task of getting the military to change and evolve, which is much easier said than done. The military is a very conservative, cohesive, and, in some ways, closed organization; more often than not it resists change, especially if it is forced on it by outsiders. Yet change is always necessary.

In bringing about change, the secretary's approach in dealing with the military will play a major role in how effective he is. Rumsfeld wanted a military that was smaller, more high-tech, more flexible, more deployable—able to be sent halfway around the world at a minute's notice. Rumsfeld had several options. The key was to have a definable plan with clear objectives. He could have given the order, "I want it to be more flexible, more technologically sophisticated, and smaller," and left it up to the generals to figure out how to implement it. This approach has the advantage of avoiding what the military sees—and resists—as outside interference. It also shows a high degree of respect for the men and women leading the armed forces, a matter of considerable importance to the military.

Then there is the question of promotions. What amount of influence should the secretary have on promotions? Rumsfeld could have permitted the military promotion system to function the way the military believed it should operate. A promotion board, meeting in secret, selects officers for promotion on the basis of merit. True, politics inevitably plays a role, as some senior officers work hard to get officers they know and respect promoted. The generals expect that a person like Rumsfeld will limit his involvement to selecting a chairman of the Joint Chiefs and his deputy. Subordinates will lose respect for an officer if they believe he was promoted on political grounds rather than merit or, once in office, he does not appear to be standing up for their interests.

Rumsfeld realized that regardless of who occupied senior positions in the military, the armed services could take his order and bury it deep inside the infamous military bureaucracy. If subordinates did not like a proposal they could study a topic to death or file it away so that nothing is done. To counter such possibilities, Rumsfeld needed individuals who would function as liaison officers between the military and the Secretary's Office. To be most effective, Rumsfeld needed credible staff, men and women who understood the military at a level that would be respected by the armed forces. Selecting individuals who knew little or nothing about the military would undermine their effectiveness in pushing the military in any direction.

If Rumsfeld wanted to minimize conflict, he would include senior military officers in the decision-making process. Excluding them would only serve to embitter the generals and force them to circle the wagons, to be as obstructive as possible. Including them in the decision-making process also had the advantage of increasing the probability that the rest of their services would follow along. Such an approach would make the policy seem less alien. Finally, he would need to avoid becoming involved in tactical and operational matters. The generals and admirals expect the secretary to play a major role in strategic questions—but not to tell senior officers how to fight a war.

But if Rumsfeld wanted to upend the way the military is operating, to change the functions carried out by the various services and their missions, then conflict with the military was inevitable.

If, on the other hand, Rumsfeld's goal was to maximize conflict between the civilian Department of Defense and the armed services, he had several options. First, he would exclude the military from discussions about reforming the armed forces. Second, he would be vague on what it was that he wanted the military to do. Third, he would intervene in the promotion system to be sure that only officers who thought like him were promoted. Fourth, he would appoint civilians with little or no military experience to serve as the primary interface with the military. Fifth, he would interfere in military operations, not only at the strategic level, but at the operational and tactical levels as well. Finally, he would make few or no concessions to military culture—the attitudes and behavioral patterns that are unique to the armed forces.

## Rumsfeld's Agenda

Rumsfeld's number-one goal was to force the military to make changes, to significantly modify the way it did business. Change can take many forms, and it can mean many things. For example, personnel systems may be modified (e.g., the role of women or gays in the military). Similarly, some in the military may prefer to live and fight in a Cold War environment long after that war is over. In this case, it is important, indeed critical, that the military modify the way it approaches war to reflect the new environment. The military must introduce new weapons and weapons systems to keep up with the advance of modern technology. Failure to do so will significantly diminish the military's ability to deal with new and different threats. Take, for example, the issue of how to carry out combat operations. Should the army and the Marine Corps focus on conventional warfare or should they place primary emphasis on counterinsurgency? If the military is set up to focus on conventional warfare, how can the generals be persuaded to place emphasis on counterinsurgency, when they have spent most of their professional lives planning for a conventional war? Without external prompting, the military may not change its focus.

The essential question, as John Nagl has pointed out, is how to bring about military innovation or change.[1] Conservative senior officers must come to realize that the old way of fighting wars no longer suffices. There are three ways for this to occur. First, civilians like Rumsfeld, individuals who are outside the military organizational structure, can be the primary instigators of change. Second, forces inside the military, such as senior officers who see the need for change, can push for modifications in how the military goes to war. Third, it can occur as a result of interaction between civilian and military leaders.

The mode of change depends on the definition of change. If it is as radical as was Rumsfeld's idea of change, the secretary can expect problems, even if he can find senior officers who support his policy. That suggests that in such a case, he might be better off to just say "damn the torpedoes, full speed ahead." Break some china, if that is what it takes to get the job done. The problem is that secretaries like Rumsfeld are usually in office for eight years at most. Even if he is successful in overcoming the innate bureaucratic opposition that will accompany any effort to bring about change, he should keep in mind that many of the generals and admirals will still be around when he leaves. Furthermore, efforts to introduce radical change, may also undermine the efforts of senior military officers to make important but less radical changes by putting them on the defensive.

## Military-Civil Relations

One of the biggest myths in the United States is that the military is a unified entity made up of individuals who think alike as a result of their service in this closed and cohesive organization. To some degree that is true, but it is a tremendous overstatement.[2] While many military officers have traditionally identified themselves as politically conservative,[3] in reality the officer corps is a very diverse group. I have encountered military officers who are very conservative, but I also remember a navy captain who was about as liberal as many university faculty members.

Military officers adopt one of two different approaches to dealing with civilian authority. The first approach maintains that while military officers should never forget that they work for the civilians, it is in the country's national interest that military officers "talk straight" to their political masters. Relying on Colonel H. R. McMaster's now classic work, *Dereliction of Duty*,[4] officers in this category believe that "unqualified allegiance to the commander in chief" is an idea that "needs to be rethought."[5] General Colin Powell, for example, "vowed that when [their] time came to call the shots, [they] would not quietly acquiesce in half-hearted warfare for half-baked reasons."[6]

Members of this group believe that officers, like the chairman of the Joint Chiefs, should be prepared to tell the president and the secretary that they are wrong. If an officer believes the decisions reached by the civilians needlessly endanger their country and those they command, he should answer congressional questions honestly, and, if the officer cannot support policy, he has the option of resigning and then speaking out. The same is true for other senior officers who feel they cannot support the secretary or the president's policy. Such a decision should not be taken lightly. It should only happen if these senior officers are convinced that a critical mistake is being made. These officers believe that such an act should not be seen as mutiny or insubordination. Instead, sacrificing one's career in this way is an act of honor that could save the country and, more importantly, the lives of its troops.

The second approach argues that, like it or not, the president was elected by the American public, and senior officers must keep that fact foremost in mind. They have an obligation to provide the secretary with the best possible military advice. If he accepts it, fine. If not—they have done their job. Assuming the directive does not violate the Uniform Code of Military Justice, it is their task to salute and carry out the secretary's decision, regardless of how much they disapprove of it. If they disagree, they should make their dissatisfaction known privately, not publicly, even if they are retired. It is up to Congress and the American people to openly and publicly oppose decisions made by the president and the secretary, not the military. After all, there is a presidential election every four years. If the American people do not approve of the secretary's—and by extension the president's—national security policy, he can be voted out of office. If an officer, even a retired officer, speaks out against national policy, he is moving the apolitical military into the political sphere.

Rumsfeld's policies vis-à-vis the military created serious problems for the officer corps. There were good officers on both sides of the debate. In some cases, disagreements would lead to the resignation of officers, and public criticism of Rumsfeld by retired officers. In other cases, officers who found his policies objectionable, but believed they had an obligation not to criticize them publicly, risked the hostility and disrespect of those they commanded because the rank and file believed that the senior officers should have stood up to Rumsfeld on their behalf. Most importantly, neither of these situations was good for the armed forces.

## The Arrogance of Power

The term "arrogance of power" comes from a book that the late Senator William Fulbright (D-AR) wrote many years ago.[7] Its theme was that the United States was throwing its weight around the world, and acting like a bully. As used in this book, the term refers to a situation in which Rumsfeld and his associates ignored military advice on the implementation of security policy, believing they knew more about military matters than the professionals. This "superior" knowledge led them to ignore military advice on the type of weapons systems the generals and admirals believed the military should purchase and to attempt to force the military to adopt the civilians' preferred strategy for fighting wars. Such an approach for dealing with the military made sense as long as they were successful, as long as the weapons systems pushed by civilians worked, or as long as the civilian approach to fighting wars—whether at the strategic, operational, or tactical level—brought about victory.

Victory, of course, involved success not only in the operation of weapons and weapons systems in combat, it also required dominance in all four phases of combat as defined by the U.S. military. These four phases include: Phase I—Preparation; Phase II—Shaping the Battlefield; Phase III—Decisive Operations; and Phase IV—Post-Hostility Operations. In the case of the Bush administration and Iraq, Phase IV focused on creating a stable and democratic Iraq. Unfortunately for Rumsfeld, all four phases must be carried out successfully to declare a U.S. victory.

I do not mean to suggest that the professional military always knows what is right or best for the country. Generals and admirals also make mistakes, big and small. However, there is a tremendous difference between an honest mistake by a general, and a situation in which a civilian official blatantly ignores military advice, believing that he knows better. Generals and admirals can also be arrogant when it comes to decision making. However, in the United States at least, either the secretary of defense or the president has the last word. They can overrule the uniformed military if they so wish—and they did. Rumsfeld believed he knew best on two issues: reform and invading Iraq.

## Transforming the Military

The United States had a twentieth-century force in a twenty-first century world. Obviously, change was needed. One U.S. government source described army reconfiguration as an effort to "transform itself from a Cold War–oriented force into a more rapidly deployable and responsive force better able to meet the diverse defense challenges of the future."[8] This goal involved changing (sometimes radically) everything from personnel to force structure, including training and weapons systems. In this specific case, Rumsfeld wanted to turn the army on its head. He believed that the army was still focused on the idea of fighting a major ground war in Europe. His goal was to get the generals and admirals to look in another direction—to create a smaller, highly mobile force that could be deployed anywhere on short notice.

Transforming the military is a very complex process. It is not something that should be rushed into, although that is exactly what Rumsfeld did. In order to maintain an effective military, enough old weapons must be retained to fight any wars that may come up while the new ones are being developed and tested. Plans that jump a generation of weapons systems, as Rumsfeld's did, are almost guaranteed to face opposition from generals who believe they do not have enough troops to carry out their assigned missions. Yet Rumsfeld was simultaneously trying to cut back on personnel while ignoring weapons that might have helped with the transition from the old to the new.

## Iraq

The invasion of Iraq in March 2003 was a major military operation. It involved thousands of troops, plus hundreds of planes, tanks, and other types of combat equipment. Consequently, senior officers expected to play a major role in the planning and execution of this operation. The generals and admirals believe it is up to civilian authorities to determine the war's political goals, but they have the lives of their troops in their hands, and they expect to be consulted about their use. An operation like the invasion of Iraq is a very complex undertaking, not only in the preparation and implementation of the invasion plan, but in the postinvasion period as well. These are actions for which the generals and admirals have been training and preparing throughout their entire career. As experts in the management of violence, they believe they best understand the many logistical, tactical, and operational problems involved in a military operation. They are also trained to lead troops, especially when the mission involves troops from all the services. Getting soldiers, sailors, Marines, and airmen to cooperate in a military operation is not easy; but it is something that the military has been practicing and perfecting for years. Yet Rumsfeld opted not to consult with the military and take its views seriously. Instead, he forced his own ideas on how the war in Iraq should be fought on a reluctant military leadership.

Rumsfeld also ignored advice to take into account the local culture. Iraq has a very different culture from that of the United States, and both civilian and military officials must take that into consideration if they hope to succeed in conquering and pacifying it. This is a critical point, popularized by Samuel Huntington.[9] It requires careful consideration and preparation for a predominately Judeo-Christian, Western country like the United States to occupy an Islamic, Arab country like Iraq. According to Nagl, "Understanding tribal loyalties, political motivations, and family relationship[s] was essential to defeating the enemy we faced, a task more akin to breaking up a Mafia crime ring than dismantling a conventional enemy battalion or brigade. 'Link diagrams' depicting who talked with whom became a daily chore for a small intelligence staff more used to analyzing the ranges of enemy artillery systems."[10]

## Structure of the Book

The story of Rumsfeld and his dealings with the military unfolds chronologically, beginning with some background on Rumsfeld and his associates and placing the new policies favored by Rumsfeld in historical context. I then turn to Rumsfeld's efforts to force a policy of military transformation on the military in general, and the army, in particular. It should be kept in mind that this is a book about the politics of political-military decision making, not a technical manual on the complex process of transformation or the invasion of Iraq. As a result, I focus on interactions between Rumsfeld and his subordinates and how they worked to force their view of the world on the military leadership.

Next, I look at the decision to invade Iraq: how it was reached and who decided on operational strategy. Once the decision to invade was taken, how was it carried out and who made the key operational and tactical decisions? How was the post-invasion period handled and what role did Rumsfeld and his subordinates play in this critical period? Throughout the book, my primary focus is the politics of the relationship between Rumsfeld and the senior military leadership.

The occupation of Iraq has lasted more than five years, which raises the question of how decisions on the ground were taken. Was it the Pentagon or the State Department that was calling the shots in Iraq, or was it the generals on the ground who were in control of the situation? Someone must be held responsible for the mess in Iraq.

Finally, I draw some lessons from Rumsfeld's handling of the military in both of these cases. In brief, he failed to respect the military. He considered many of them to be Neanderthals, hopelessly behind events in the modern world. Even more important, is it possible to determine what impact Rumsfeld's leadership style had on long-term developments in military transformation and in Iraq? Does his behavior provide a useful lesson on how a secretary of defense should or should not handle the military?

## Sources

This study relies on a variety of sources. Major U.S. newspapers, such as the *New York Times, Washington Post, Washington Times, Los Angeles Times, Christian Science Monitor, Wall Street Journal,* and *Chicago Tribune,* from 2001 to the present, were consulted. Other newspapers were included as appropriate. The same is true of congressional testimony and U.S. government reports or other documents.

A scholar working on this topic is lucky because of the numerous, journalistic-like studies that have been written to date. These include the works by Michael Gordon and Bernard Trainor, Bob Woodward, Thomas Ricks, Michael Isikoff and David Corn, Rajiv Chandrasekaran, Bing West, James Fallows, Andrew Cockburn, and Tom Clancy and Tony Zinni.[11] The best analytical study of the Iraq war and its impact on that country was written by one of the participants on the Iraqi side: interim prime minister Iyad A. Allawi.[12] One of the best studies of the military transformation process is by Frederick W. Kagan.[13] There are also a number of memoirs of varying quality: L. Paul Bremer, Tommy Franks, David Phillips, Peter W. Galbraith, Michael DeLong, George Tenet, and Larry Diamond.[14] There are other books of value, for example, Karen DeYoung's biography of General Powell, which was very useful.[15] Finally, I had numerous discussions with a wide variety of uniformed military officers. Since the vast majority of them are still serving, they have asked that their names not be used in this study. I have honored that request. One exception was General Richard B. Myers, the former chairman of the Joint Chiefs, who kindly agreed to answer a list of questions I prepared and sent to him.

# The New Administration and Military Transformation

One should be skeptical of any military strategist who claims certainty in the future of warfare, especially those who assert that technology changes the fundamental nature of war.

*General Gordon Sullivan and Lieutenant Colonel James Dubik*

No one in the George W. Bush administration played a more important role in dealing with the U.S. military than the new secretary of defense, Donald Rumsfeld. He would be in charge of the armed forces from 2001 to 2006 and did his best to force them to change their force structure, personnel, and war-fighting procedures. Indeed, no post–World War II defense secretary, including Robert McNamara, had such a major impact on this critical institution. Unfortunately, in terms of civil-military relations, Rumsfeld's tenure would be a disaster.

## The Early Years

Donald Henry Rumsfeld was born in the Chicago suburbs in 1932 to a family of modest means. His father was in real estate. Rumsfeld's primary passion in high school and later at Princeton University was wrestling. It suited his rather short stature, and it matched his personality. It was combat to the end. He either out-pointed or pinned the other guy or lost. The skills, mindset, and approach to life that he learned in wrestling would mark him the rest of his life. "He brought his longtime obsessions with fitness, fast maneuver, and domination of opponents to the E-Ring of the Pentagon."[1]

1

*On the Hill*

After college, Rumsfeld joined the navy, went to flight school, and became a flight instructor, eventually moving up to the position of instructor for instructors. Unfortunately, this was not a leadership position that would require him to embrace a team approach to dealing with military problems. Upon leaving the navy, he went to Capitol Hill, where he spent three years as a congressional aide, an experience that taught him how the Hill worked. In 1962 he seized a political opportunity when the incumbent representative for the 13th Congressional District in Illinois decided not to run for reelection. Rumsfeld left Washington to run a spirited and successful campaign for that seat. While in Congress, he served on the House Committee on Science and Astronautics, an experience that helped convince him of the importance and promise of high-tech programs.

Rumsfeld's formidable bureaucratic skills were especially evident in the role he played in a coup against the Republican House leadership to replace minority leader Charles A. Halleck with an obscure congressman from Michigan, Gerald R. Ford. In the process Rumsfeld managed to alienate some Republican conservatives, but he was successful in impressing the one who would later count most—Ford. Rumsfeld eventually grew tired of the battles on the Hill, and in 1968 he decided to leave Congress.

*Nixon Appointee*

At that point President Richard M. Nixon asked him to head the Office of Economic Opportunity (OEO), the agency that President Lyndon B. Johnson had created to fight poverty. Most people expected Rumsfeld to sit back and permit the organization to collapse, but instead he worked to streamline the OEO and make it more efficient. While at OEO Rumsfeld made a hiring decision that would have a major impact on his future: he took on a young graduate student and staff aide, Richard Cheney. The two men complemented each other—Rumsfeld was driven, while Cheney was more laid back. They would work together for the next seven years, through the Nixon and Ford administrations, and indeed, far beyond. During the George W. Bush administration, for example, they worked as a unit to oppose Secretary of State Colin Powell and National Security Adviser (and later Secretary of State) Condoleezza Rice on a variety of policies.

After his success at OEO, Rumsfeld was summoned to the White House in 1970, where he was given the position of counselor. The post provided him frequent contact with Nixon. Then in 1973 he had a major stroke of luck—Nixon decided to send him to NATO as U.S. ambassador. Rumsfeld not only enjoyed the lower-stress job; it also meant that he was not in Washington or the White House when the Watergate scandal broke.

The ensuing events unexpectedly landed Vice President Gerald Ford in the White House.[2] Now Rumsfeld's work for Ford began to pay off. Ford recalled him from NATO and asked him to help reorganize the White House. As chief of staff Rumsfeld held one of the most important positions in Washington; he controlled access to the president. Indeed, that job was perhaps the second-most important position in the White House, because he who controls access can in many ways control policy. Rumsfeld immediately began to build a reputation as a "cold-blooded back-room-operator."[3] He was more than prepared to do whatever was necessary to get a job done. Cheney became his deputy and would later succeed him.

Rumsfeld earned his reputation as a skilled politico with the so-called Halloween Massacre, a major reorganization of Ford's cabinet announced on November 4, 1975. Rumsfeld, the argument went, had been conspiring for months against others in the administration, so that when Ford decided to reorganize his administration, he was able to take advantage of the situation.

> In short order the White House announced that [Vice President Nelson] Rockefeller had 'voluntarily withdrawn from the 1976 ticket, Henry Kissinger had lost his post as national security adviser, CIA chief William Colby had been fired, as had defense secretary James Schlesinger. Colby was replaced by George [H. W.] Bush then serving as ambassador to China. Replacing Schlesinger at the Pentagon was Rumsfeld, at forty-three, the youngest man ever to hold the job.[4]

## Pentagon, Take One

During his first stint at the Pentagon, Rumsfeld seemed to get along relatively well with the military. He was a Cold Warrior, with an attitude toward the Soviet Union shared by many in uniform at that time. But at the same time, Rumsfeld made it very clear—in case there were any doubts—that he was the boss. For example, when General George Brown, chairman of the Joint Chiefs, made highly controversial comments on Israel, Great Britain, and the Shah's Iran, Rumsfeld forced him to write a two-page letter of apology.[5] Consequently, it should have been obvious when he took over the Defense Department for a second time in 2001 that he would not only be a strong taskmaster, he would go out of his way again to show that he was in charge. In one episode from his first term as secretary, Rumsfeld and his staff were convinced that the M-1 main battle tank had a serious flaw.

"The American tank was equipped with a 105 millimeter gun; but the British and German tanks had 120 millimeter guns. . . . He ordered the tank contract delayed and dispatched Norman R. Augustine, then secretary of the army, to negotiate a deal with the allies to build a tank to accommodate either gun."[6] Senior army officers and members of Congress whose districts included the factories making the 105 millimeter gun protested strongly, but Rumsfeld held his ground. He was proven right in Desert Storm, when the 120 mm cannon outranged the Iraqi tanks.

From a substantive standpoint, Rumsfeld believed that his primary task at the Defense Department was to ensure that the United States was prepared to engage and defeat the Soviet Union on the strategic level, if necessary. Accordingly, he pushed a number of strategic weapons systems designed to counter the Soviets, including the B-1 bomber, the Trident nuclear submarine program, the MX missile, the land-based ICBM, and the cruise missile. However, Rumsfeld did not believe that arms control agreements were in the national interest. In fact, he worked hard to undermine them. To wit, in 1976 Secretary of State Henry Kissinger went to Moscow to negotiate a second SALT Treaty. Kissinger held a press conference in Moscow, assuming it would undermine his opponents at home and make his treaty with the Soviets a "done deal." However, Rumsfeld and the Joint Chiefs refused to go along, putting Ford in a difficult position. As a consequence, a very embarrassed Kissinger had to disavow the treaty that he had worked so hard to achieve. Amazingly, according to one report, Rumsfeld "had stage-managed the outcome without even having attended the National Security Council meeting." The same source called Rumsfeld's undermining of the treaty "the most clever and forceful power play by Mr. Rumsfeld in his [first] tenure as secretary of defense."[7] In addition to subverting the second SALT treaty, Rumsfeld also succeeded in winning a larger defense budget, and he managed to convince many in Washington of the strategic danger presented by the Soviet Union. Similarly, he argued effectively regarding the need for the United States to ensure that the Soviets did not get ahead in nuclear forces.

*Private Sector*

In 1977 Rumsfeld decided that fourteen months as defense secretary was enough. He accepted a lucrative offer to become president and chief executive officer of G. D. Searle & Company. Searle was one of America's leading pharmaceutical companies, but it was in serious financial trouble: "The stock price had fallen from $110 a share to $12, earnings had dropped 23 percent the previous year, and the Food and Drug Administration was investigating it to see if the company had misreported the results of testing for new drugs."[8]

Rumsfeld quickly turned the company's fortunes around. Not surprisingly, given his hard-charging personality, some of his changes were brutal to the people concerned. For example, Rumsfeld decided that the company's major problems were that it had become far too centralized and that the staff had taken their eyes off of research into pharmaceuticals. To remedy the situation he fired "150 employees outright and transferred 150 others from the corporate staff to the various groups that were actually in charge of producing and selling Searle's product line."[9] Next, he turned his attention to the Food and Drug Administration (FDA). The FDA had banned aspartame, the key ingredient in NutraSweet and a major product for the company. Starting on January 21, 1981, the day after Ronald Reagan took office, Rumsfeld made good use of his Republican political connections. He had Searle reapply to the FDA for approval to use aspartame in its artificial sweetener. Reagan's new FDA commissioner appointed a five-person board to review the application. In short order, it became clear that Searle would lose 3–2. So another person was added to the panel. This committee became deadlocked 3–3. As a result, the commissioner himself cast a vote breaking the tie 4–3. Searle was now back in business with what would become one of its most important and profitable products.

## Defense Adviser

Meanwhile, Rumsfeld maintained his ties to the Department of Defense. In 1997 Congress asked him to chair the Commission to Assess the Ballistic Missile Threat to the United States. Rumsfeld's first priority was to gain unquestioned control of the Commission. Thus, he made sure that he would have a major input into its policy recommendations. He also worked overtime to ensure that the Commission would have a significant impact on U.S. national security thinking. Its report, which was widely circulated and read in Washington, argued, "Certain hostile regimes could have missiles that could hit the United States within five years (ten for Iraq), far sooner than the existing intelligence reports indicated."[10] The Commission called for a reassessment of U.S. intelligence-gathering abilities as well as the creation of a national missile-defense shield. The Commission's report catapulted Rumsfeld back to the center of the debate over national security strategy and would ensure that when the new Republican administration came to office in 2001, his name would be high on the list of those tapped to deal with national security matters. The report reinforced his belief in the superiority of technology. The missiles studied were high-tech weapons that could only be countered by the creation of even more complex high-tech defensive missile systems.

## Secretary and CEO

In late December 2000 president-elect George W. Bush announced that he had selected Donald Rumsfeld to be his secretary of defense. Interestingly, when Bush made the announcement he echoed a number of Rumsfeld's main ideas, especially military transformation. "We must work to change our military to meet the threats of a new century. And so one of Secretary Rumsfeld's first tasks will be to challenge the status quo in the Pentagon, to develop a strategy necessary to have a force equipped for warfare of the twenty-first century."[11] Rumsfeld went to the Pentagon to shake things up in the military. Bush knew this would not be an easy task, but many believed Rumsfeld to be a first-rate manager. His time as President Ford's chief of staff, his time in the Pentagon, and the way he turned Searle around had convinced many that he would be the perfect person for the job. "Ironically," noted a USA Today editorial, "Rumsfeld was tapped for a second stint as defense secretary not because of his skills as a warrior or public spokesman but for his prowess as a manager."[12]

One interesting aspect of the Rumsfeld reign at the Department of Defense is that despite his close association with individuals such as Paul Wolfowitz and Douglas Feith, he did not share their ideological commitment to democratic regime change. However, as a good bureaucrat, he understood that with Bush's election, individuals like Wolfowitz and Feith had become the new power in town. Accordingly, Rumsfeld hitched his star to them. For example, one biographer argued that Rumsfeld was especially impressed with Richard Perle, who had long played a major role in conservative Republican circles.[13] In fact, Rumsfeld purportedly offered Perle the position of undersecretary for policy, the third-most important policy position in the department. Perle refused, supposedly because his primary goal at that time was to make money. However, according to a general who had access to Rumsfeld's office, Perle became "one of Rumsfeld's principal military advisors."[14] Furthermore, the new vice president, Rumsfeld's old pal Dick Cheney, tended to agree with him on most issues. This meant that Rumsfeld had a good political foundation that would help push through his agenda.

Rumsfeld believed that civilian control of the military had eroded during the Clinton administration. Because President Bill Clinton was so uninformed and weak on military-related issues, Rumsfeld believed that the generals and admirals had filled the vacuum and become increasingly powerful. As Rumsfeld saw it, most of the military—and especially the army—was hidebound. The services were still fighting the Cold War. They were smaller than they had been during the Gulf War, for example, but they had not substantially changed their structure. In his mind, this meant that one of his first tasks would be to show the generals and admirals who was boss. This could only be done by jolting them out of their complacency.

Despite his criticisms, Rumsfeld was not antimilitary. To the contrary, Rumsfeld felt comfortable in advocating the use of military power, especially air power. He did oppose using ground troops as peacekeepers. He also remained infatuated with intelligence, space weapons, and missile defense. His goal was not to weaken the military; indeed, it was just the opposite.

Rumsfeld's primary defining characteristic while at the Pentagon was his arrogance. He was rude, abrasive, and relied heavily on a small group of advisers, in many cases with few or no military officers present. He had no compunction about either ignoring or "getting in the faces" of generals and admirals. While there is no excuse for a senior military officer to come to a meeting unprepared and while military officers are tough enough to live with almost any personality or approach on the part of civilian authorities, members of the professional military consider abrasive or rude behavior to be unacceptable. It goes against the canons of military culture. As far as Rumsfeld was concerned, he did not care whether senior military officers liked his approach or not. His blunt response to criticism that he was rude to his subordinates was to comment, "The Constitution calls for civilian control of this department, and I am a civilian."[15] He was the boss, just like at Searle.

Furthermore, Rumsfeld would do his best to keep senior officers and others off balance with his "constant blizzard of dictated memos—known as 'snowflakes' inside the Pentagon and 'Rummygrams' elsewhere—asking questions and proposing new policies. . . . 'What are you doing about this? How long is it going to take?'"[16] referring to the kind of changes he wanted to introduce in the military. To achieve these ends, he would need the support of a loyal staff, and that included allies outside of the Defense Department.

## Rumsfeld's Team

*Vice President Cheney*

The most important person on Rumsfeld's team was clearly the vice president. The two had worked closely together in the past, and they would continue that effective working relationship throughout Rumsfeld's time at the Defense Department. Indeed, Cheney's position as vice president would turn out to be one of Rumsfeld's most important assets.

Throughout postwar U.S. history, vice presidents have occupied a somewhat nebulous position. Formally, their first and most important qualification is to be ready to assume the presidency if the president should be incapacitated or die. Often they have been kept out of policy matters; Harry

Truman did not even know about the Manhattan Project—the effort to develop a nuclear bomb—until after he became president. The U.S. government is hierarchical, with the president sitting at the top of the pyramid (in military terms, a six-star general). The vice president comes next (a five-star general), and then come the national security adviser and cabinet secretaries, including the chairman of the Joint Chiefs (four-star generals).

The executive branch of the U.S. government is not a democratic organization—rank matters and can be strategically wielded. Unlike past vice presidents, Cheney personally attended the principals' meetings at Bush's request. During the Clinton administration, Vice President Al Gore usually sent his national security adviser, Leon Fuerth, to represent him at meetings of principals. Cheney's mere presence made it difficult for people like National Security Adviser Condoleezza Rice, who chaired the meetings, because he could outvote the cabinet secretaries. As CIA Director George Tenet put it, "The vice president's presence may have had an unintended chilling effect on the free flow of views as important policy matters were debated."[17] Furthermore, by siding with one faction (in this case, Rumsfeld), Cheney could gently push matters in that direction. The bottom line was that unlike his predecessors, Cheney became a major player in policy debates—especially those concerning military and foreign policy.

Cheney was one of the most conservative members of the new Bush administration. Regarding the collapse of the Soviet Union, former national security adviser Brent Scowcroft commented about Cheney as follows: "Cheney was the most skeptical, holding the view that the changes [in Moscow] were primarily cosmetic and we should essentially do nothing."[18] It was not until August 1990—after the fall of the Berlin Wall—that Cheney accepted the fact that the USSR was on its way toward collapse. But even then, he later warned, "We may well find ourselves ten or fifteen years from now faced with a Soviet military that's smaller, but that is far more capable, more lethal than it is today in terms of its modern capabilities."[19]

Cheney was a hardliner on foreign policy. He agreed with Rumsfeld about the utility of military force. Diplomacy was fine, but the world is a very dangerous place, and occasionally force might be necessary to protect the United States. Indeed, it might become necessary to use military force frequently; but that was the price that a nuclear superpower might have to pay to protect itself in a very dangerous world.

## Deputy Secretary of Defense Paul Wolfowitz

Aside from Richard Perle, Paul Wolfowitz could claim to be the number-one conservative ideologue in the Pentagon. He had spent most of his life in the government or academia, and he was convinced that the United States had a new "civilizing" calling—a modern form of "Manifest Destiny," which meant the introduction of new governments based on democratic principles. Such governments would mark a major change from the past, as local officials and the populace made good use of this new, freer type of government. There may be some transitional problems, but they were manageable. Within a year of the introduction of a democratic polity, support for the new democratic institutions would be strong. As a result, Wolfowitz became one of the administration's strongest proponents of regime change, especially in the case of Saddam Hussein and Iraq. By 1997, for example, he was calling "directly and unequivocally for the use of military force to oust Saddam Hussein from power. 'Overthrow him,'" he argued, a theme that became his watchword from that point on.[20] Wolfowitz lobbied for U.S. government support for the Iraqi opposition and continually blasted Saddam Hussein as a war criminal. While Bush wanted Wolfowitz at the State Department, Secretary of State Powell said no; instead, Rumsfeld selected him to be deputy secretary of defense. He was the strongest and most senior proponent in the U.S. government for invading Iraq. When this did occur in 2003, Wolfowitz's reputation became even more closely tied to the Iraq War.

Key to Wolfowitz's approach was the assumption that Western democratic political culture (its history, language, and culture—the result of hundreds if not thousands of years), could be transplanted to an Arab country with a very different type of political culture. Unfortunately, this approach assumed that Iraqi or any other society was a cultural *tabula rasa*. It naively assumed that Arabs in the Middle East were just waiting for the chance to discard their centuries-old tribal, religious, ethnic, authoritarian systems so they could behave like Americans and Europeans. It assumed that countries in the Middle East were just like Japan or Germany at the end of World War II. Aside from the fact that both of those countries were totally defeated in a war and—most importantly—had accepted that fact, neither faced the problem of religiously or ethnically inspired opposition and both had functioning institutions when the Americans arrived. Instead, Iraq's institutions collapsed, and the United States faced fundamentalist religious ideas that were incompatible with the secularist, democratic system Wolfowitz favored.

## Under Secretary for Policy Douglas Feith

Douglas Feith was primarily responsible for implementing Pentagon policy toward Iraq.[21] While he had a law degree, Feith came to focus on national security issues and the Middle East. He began by working on the National Security Council (NSC) staff for his mentor Richard Pipes, then moved to the Pentagon where he stayed until 1986. Feith then left the Pentagon to practice law and became very active as a member of a conservative group that produced a report entitled "A Clean Break: A New Strategy for Securing the Realm"[22] for the newly elected Israeli Prime Minister Benjamin Netanyahu. In 1999 Feith was one a group of former U.S. officials who signed an open letter to President Bill Clinton calling for the ouster of Saddam Hussein. In addition to his staunch support for Israel, Feith promoted U.S.-Israeli cooperation, and he wrote numerous articles and op-ed pieces articulating his political views. There have been charges that his religion and his support for Israel affected his recommendations to Rumsfeld, but he has denied such allegations.[23]

Rumsfeld considered Feith very bright; indeed, he called him "one of the brightest people you or I will ever come across. He's diligent, very well read, and insightful."[24] Feith is highly regarded for his ability to understand abstract issues, but his main critics were those who dealt with him on practical matters. For example, Army General Tommy Franks, commander of CENT-COM, called him "the fucking stupidest guy on the face of the earth."[25]

It was Feith's responsibility to ensure that the policies advocated by Rumsfeld and Wolfowitz were implemented. In many cases, this would involve playing Machiavellian games with other segments of the U.S. government. It would be an understatement to note that his actions did not endear him to places like the State Department, the CIA, or the military. Indeed, there would be numerous charges that he was acting duplicitously when dealing with others. In some instances this would not be his fault, because he was simply carrying out orders from Rumsfeld and Wolfowitz. But in other instances, he would have no one to blame but himself.

*Under Secretary for Intelligence Stephen Cambone*

Starting in 1982, Stephen Cambone, who holds a Ph.D. in political science, served in a number of national security positions before joining Rumsfeld's Defense Department in 2001. These positions included some in the government and some in academic think tanks. He was reportedly very close to Rumsfeld when serving as special assistant to the secretary of defense and as the deputy secretary from January to July 2001. He went on to become director of program analysis and evaluation. Finally, in 2003 he won Senate confirmation as principal deputy under secretary for intelligence, a new position Rumsfeld had sought because he was very skeptical of what the CIA reported. Although Cambone had never served in the military, he played an important role in helping with the justification or implementation of Rumsfeld's policies, especially toward Iraq.

## Others

While the list of civilians who interacted with the military during Rumsfeld's time in office could go on and on, only two more will be mentioned here. First, NSC Adviser—and later Secretary of State—Condoleezza Rice and her predecessor as secretary of state, Colin Powell. Neither individual was a supporter of Rumsfeld and the way he treated the military. Furthermore, unlike the individuals noted above, neither was dogmatic or ideological when it came to the problems facing the United States. Both were pragmatic diplomats. Rice was in the unenviable position of being asked to coordinate matters within the U.S. government at a time when Rumsfeld and his supporters were doing their best to cut agencies like the CIA and the State Department "out of the action." As a retired general, Powell often found himself siding with the generals against Rumsfeld.

## Rumsfeld Recruits Reformers

Many senior ranks of the Republican Party believed Rumsfeld had exactly the right kind of skills to run the Pentagon. He had extensive government experience—including working in the White House and fourteen months in the Pentagon, which, they argued, meant that he understood the military and the games that senior officers play to get their way with "uninformed" civilians. Furthermore, he had been a hard-nosed CEO of a failing firm, and, through his strength of character and commitment, he had turned it around by imposing efficiencies and cutting back on unnecessary personnel. He was tough and took no prisoners, just the kind of individual the country needed—or at least so Bush believed. Rumsfeld would make it clear to the generals and admirals who was running the country and in the process move them into the twenty-first century.

## The Clinton Legacy

Meanwhile, the military was still living in the Clinton era, which meant that it essentially ran itself. The secretary of defense was in charge of the Department of Defense, while the civilian service secretaries had been cut out of the action, in many cases leaving it to the uniformed officers to run the services. To them, the president and Congress were where the real action was.

After all, the chairman of the Joint Chiefs had a direct line to the president through the Goldwater-Nichols Act of 1986.[26] However, Rumsfeld would change matters.

From Rumsfeld's standpoint, the Clinton administration's refusal to stand up to the generals was especially evident when it came to the question of military transformation. The generals, and especially the army, gave transformation verbal support, but were happy with incremental changes. Clinton had said he was dedicated to modernizing the military and wanted it to make greater use of modern technology, but it was all talk. As Tomes put it, "The Clinton administration did not make transformation a priority in terms of leadership attention, a willingness to expend political capital to influence service decisions, or a clear vision for change conjoined with "sticks" to induce compliance."[27] Then, to make matters worse, the pace of military operations during the Clinton administration was overwhelming. Some segment of the military always seemed to be deployed somewhere— Somalia, Haiti, Bosnia, Kosovo, etc. In addition, because of the extensive deployments abroad, the money earmarked for transformation was used up maintaining military operations: "The future was mortgaged to pay for current operations, a reality that was also true in the intelligence community."[28]

Rumsfeld got off to a quick start. He called a meeting in his office for January 21, 2001—the day after Bush's inauguration.[29] However, the meeting *excluded* military officers. Instead, he met with the civilians that he had worked with throughout his career. The only individual present who would go on to play a major role in the Rumsfeld era was Paul Wolfowitz. The focus of the meeting was "how Rumsfeld could gain control of the Pentagon bureaucracy in order to pursue the major goal of his administration: the reform, or transformation, of the U.S. military."[30] The topics reportedly discussed included an overhaul of the military personnel system, the need to promote joint operations and the need to close some bases in the United States. Translated into plain English, Rumsfeld planned to tame the senior military leadership and, to a lesser degree, the civilians working in the Pentagon. The key was how to make absolutely sure that they understood he was the boss.

## Controlling Promotions

Next, he fired his military assistant, a one-star admiral, and replaced him with a three-star admiral, Edmund Giambastiani, a nuclear power submariner. Rumsfeld wanted someone who would be able to "crack the whip" over the rest of the military community and, given how rank conscious the armed forces are, a one-star was simply too junior. He followed that up with bringing his eighty-five-year-old former military aide, Staser Holcomb, out of retirement. Holcomb, who had been a Navy admiral, was assigned to look over the current crop of generals and admirals. He began interviewing all three- and four-star officers. It was made clear that Rumsfeld himself would play the key role in selecting new generals and admirals. Indeed, he participated in many interviews with these senior officers. And if he did not like a senior officer's political views or approach to leadership, the officer was doomed to retirement. On many occasions Rumsfeld participated in the selection of officers at the two-star level.

While the secretary of defense and the president generally have the final say when it comes to the chairman and vice chairman of the Joint Chiefs of Staff, other senior positions are normally the prerogative of the chairman (of the Joint Staff) or the service heads. When asked if his actions involving the appointment of senior officers meant he was "stepping on the toes of the service chiefs by getting involved in the selection of two- and three-star generals, Rumsfeld grinned and laughed, but said nothing."[31] It was a clear violation of military culture. Not only was Rumsfeld directly involved in this process at the beginning of his time at the Pentagon, he continued doing it. For example, when he became chairman, Richard Myers informed Rumsfeld that he intended to appoint Lieutenant General Ronald E. Keyes to be the next director of operations, or J-3. "'Not so fast,' said Rumsfeld. 'Give me someone else,' Rumsfeld told Myers after twice interviewing Keys."[32] He eventually accepted Air Force Lieutenant General Norton A. Schwartz.

By 2003 Rumsfeld had issued an order stating that he must approve all three- or four-star promotions. Needless to say, this infuriated the top brass. As Andrew Krepinevich, a former army officer and an insider in dealing with the Pentagon, put it, "He wanted people who believed in transformation so they could carry on after he was gone. But those decisions have typically been the prerogative of the military services. And if you really want to make someone angry, fool around with who is to have what job."[33] The bottom line was that Rumsfeld made certain no one was appointed to a key position without his approval. He might back down if Myers objected; but if Rumsfeld objected the individual was not promoted. "He insisted on a veto over the choice assignments."[34]

Rumsfeld's interference in the promotion process sent a clear message throughout the military: either play ball with Rumsfeld or face the prospect of not being promoted. As time passed, that rule would include not only Rumsfeld, but his subordinates, because they could always go back to the secretary and tell him that they were doing their best to implement a particular policy, but "General X" refused to cooperate. As a former defense official who attended many such meetings put it, "I remember going to my first meeting with Rumsfeld and the Chiefs. I was astonished to find all the chiefs sitting there quiet as mice, not speaking unless spoken to."[35] This was no isolated event; as late as 2005 there were reports that Rumsfeld "routinely reaches down to interview one-star and two-star officers for important jobs, a practice some officers deride as a politically motivated 'Rumsfeld Sniff Test'."[36]

## Taming the Joint Chiefs

As if controlling officer promotions were not enough, Rumsfeld took on the Joint Staff, a group primarily of military officers who support the chairman and his deputy. The chairman may be called upon to testify on Capitol Hill on Somalia on Monday and joint U.S.-Canadian cooperation on Tuesday, only to be expected to give a speech on Iraq on Wednesday. These officers must back the chairman up by preparing talking points, speeches, or testimony. Furthermore, the Joint Chiefs may be asked to create new strategies for several parts of the world at the same time. That process is carried out by the 1,200 officers on the Joint Staff.

One of the main reasons for Rumsfeld's effort to reorganize the Joint Staff was an incident on February 16, 2001. On that day two dozen U.S. and British aircraft struck 20 radar and command centers inside Iraq. While a general from the Joint Staff had briefed NSC Adviser Rice beforehand and she then told the president, unfortunately, no one bothered to tell Rumsfeld what was going on. The uniformed services were talking to the president (through Rice), and Rumsfeld was out of the loop. Big mistake.

> Rumsfeld, furious, declared that the chain of command had been subverted. By law, military command ran from the president to him as secretary of defense to General Franks at CENTCOM. The Joint Chief's role, again by law, was advice, communications and oversight. He should be the one to deal with the White House and the president on operational matters. Period. "I'm the secretary of defense," he reminded one officer. "I'm in the chain of command."[37]

Rumsfeld believed the Joint Staff—and everyone else in the Pentagon—worked for him. He accused the Joint Staff of specializing "in thick studies that took months or more, didn't cut to the essential issues and were basically unreadable. 'I can't get a product out of these guys'."[38] He dismissed them as just a group of people spinning their wheels.

Rumsfeld's battle with the Joint Staff continued throughout his time in office. On January 3, 2003, for example, he sent a private memo to his civilian aide, Larry Di Rita, a former navy officer, asking him to compile a list of the reports produced by the Joint Chiefs.[39] The memo criticized the Joint Chiefs of Staff for preparing unnecessary and poorly written papers. Rumsfeld wanted to combine the civilian and military staffs in order to avoid a duplication of work. Eliminating this "waste" would also mean that he controlled what was produced. There would not be an independent military point of view for the chairman or the president. Not surprisingly, officers' reaction was not positive.

> But some staffers are taking Mr. Rumsfeld's memo as an insult. They say the Joint Staff works hard to produce papers so that General Myers can better advise Mr. Rumsfeld and President Bush on everything from the size of units to the war in Iraq.
>
> "It's an indication of what he really thinks of us and the work we do and quality of it."[40]

### Busy Work

However, the Joint Staff's job expands beyond supporting the chairman. It was also required by law to produce a variety of reports on topics such as personnel, force structure, roles, and missions, as well as pay and benefits. Also, Congress deals directly with the Joint Staff on issues that require reports or certifications from the Joint Staff.

As mentioned, another one of Rumsfeld's techniques for getting control of the military was his "snowflakes." If he couldn't get rid of the officers who stood in his way as he tried to gain control of the Department of Defense, he would keep them so busy they would not be able to upset his plans. Perhaps one day a good idea would come back. The memos flew over the building, asking questions such as, "provide more detail on issue X, explain what was meant in memo Y, or why hasn't job Z been completed by now? When will it be finished?" Not only did they keep the bureaucracy busy, they carried deniability if they were leaked. Rumsfeld never signed them, but everyone knew they represented orders or questions from Rumsfeld.

> Rumsfeld either scribbled out his notes or dictated them, and Delonie Henry, his confidential assistant, then typed them out. Rear Admiral J. J. Quinn, the new military assistant, became the keeper of the snowflakes. There were roughly three kinds—administrative ("call and arrange a lunch with Fed Chairman Alan Greenspan"—an old Rumsfeld friend from the Ford days), simple thoughts or personal reflections, and calls for information and action. Some were quite broad and asked a lot. Quinn delivered them, often by hand

if they were urgent and important. Rumsfeld kept copies of the snowflakes on his desk. He had a file for Shelton, another for Quinn, one for Cambone, and others for his top aides.[41]

In the beginning some staffers—military and civilian—would stay up all night putting together an answer. But over time, it became obvious to those in the Pentagon that Rumsfeld was not serious about getting answers to all of them. As one staffer put it, "Then I started letting it slide for a week, and no one seemed to notice." Eventually, this staffer said he stopped responding altogether—and still no one seemed to notice.[42] Often the snowflakes were only busy work.

*Outside Advice*

Rumsfeld also appointed eighteen review panels, staffed almost entirely by civilians or retired military officers, to take a careful look at the armed forces. Theoretically, the purpose of these panels was to stimulate thinking on how better to respond to the demands of the twenty-first century. He was not about to put up with the "old thinking" that he was convinced afflicted the military in general, and the army in particular.

With the idea of transformation foremost in mind, the key task for these review panels was to identify what changes needed to be introduced to bring the U.S. military into the twenty-first century. How could the U.S. military skip a whole generation of technology so that no other nation on the planet could stand up to it in combat? This review panel approach was not unprecedented. When he first took over as secretary of defense, Robert McNamara did the same thing, relying on his "whiz kids," civilians experts from places like the Rand Corporation, to come up with new and different ways for the military to approach the multifaceted problems it faced. Needless to say, McNamara's action deeply infuriated and alienated the U.S. military, as it implied that a group of college professors or civilian specialists knew as much about how to develop and use complex weapons systems as did the professionals.[43]

From the military's standpoint, Rumsfeld and his assistants might have known theory, but the generals and admirals had designed and implemented strategy during their thirty-plus years of military service. "Above all, some members of the military would later tell interviewers, they feared that the future of the institution to which they had devoted their lives was being shaped without seriously consulting them."[44] And it was not only senior military officers whose access to these studies was restricted, Rumsfeld also restricted congressional and industry access as well.[45] Even worse,

Rumsfeld ordered that the review be completed by March 2001, only two months away. From the generals' standpoint, this was a clear violation of military culture. Senior military officers, individuals who were up to date on the latest developments, not to mention the complexity of the problems, should be involved.

### Waiting Out Shelton

When Rumsfeld came to power, Army General Hugh Shelton was chairman of the Joint Chiefs of Staff. But Shelton, following the 1986 Goldwater–Nichols Act, believed that the chairman of the Joint Chiefs of Staff was an independent adviser to the president, making a clash with Rumsfeld inevitable. Rumsfeld insisted that the secretary of defense advise the president, while Shelton was just as determined to provide the president with his own, independent advice. As Woodward explains, "Rumsfeld was suggesting that Shelton should give his military advice to the president through Rumsfeld. Shelton reiterated that since Title X made him the 'principal military advisor' to the president, he didn't see how that could work. He had to give his advice directly."[46]

Shelton was not prepared to capitulate to Rumsfeld's pressure to subordinate himself to the secretary of defense. Indeed, the general had already shown his independence by taking more than a week to respond to Rumsfeld's request for "the military's plan for a U.S. response to an Iranian sponsored terror attack. The plan that Shelton eventually produced three weeks later called for a invasion of Iran by half a million men following a six month buildup, a scheme Rumsfeld derided as ludicrously ponderous, firming his conviction that the military were absolutely incapable of inventive thought."[47] However, Rumsfeld could not simply fire Shelton. He had no choice but to wait him out, as Shelton's term ended in October of 2001. That would give him an opportunity to appoint an officer who understood the world the way he did; an officer who was as committed to the creation of a high-tech military as he was.

## The Lure of Technology

During the 1990s, there was talk about a "revolution in military affairs," a seismic shift that, in many minds, changed the way wars would be fought. Instead of masses of soldiers, new, high-tech weapons would transform the battlefield. The United States would now be able to see and evaluate what was happening on the battlefield as a result of advances in computers and information systems to the point where U.S. superiority would have "no peer competitor until [at least] 2020."⁴⁸

There were, however, a number of problems with this heavy reliance on high-tech weapons systems. It made war too precise and too predictable. It removed human, cultural, social, and political factors from the conduct of war. While technology can play an important role in combat operations, the human factor remains critically important. The problem with war and technology is that war, by definition, is unpredictable. "Indeed, what some refer to as the moral domain of war involve [sic] psychological and emotional dynamics that defy quantification or prediction."⁴⁹ How does one see into the minds of the enemy? Perfect intelligence would tell the United States who was on what side among the ruling elite, how important ethnic factors or religion will be in a conflict, as well as providing a good understanding of the kinds of weapons systems and their capabilities. But our knowledge of the battlefield is always imperfect, regardless of how much high-tech material we may possess.

## Rumsfeld and Military Transformation

Everyone who dealt with Rumsfeld noted his intelligence and especially his debating skills. He was enamored with technology, especially missiles, but he understood that technology did not supply all the answers to fighting a war. This is why he would emphasize the importance of getting officers to think differently about warfare—he was convinced that how they thought and fought would make a major difference. The officer corps had to be taught how to think flexibly, how to anticipate the unexpected. But, when he had the opportunity to test his theories in Iraq, Rumsfeld focused almost entirely on technology and ignored the political, ethnic, economic, and religious aspects of war.

Rumsfeld began his quest to transform the military with the idea of quantity. Technology made the need to rely on mass armies—so much a part of the past—irrelevant. In the future, the armed forces would rely "on high-technology weapons systems rather than on soldiers. He has continued to pursue this program even as the armed forces were being stretched thinner and thinner."⁵⁰

Another aspect of Rumsfeld's thinking was the idea that air power, in particular cruise missiles, would enable the United States to destroy targets from thousands of miles away. The missiles would be widely dispersed, incredibly accurate, and be able to attack enemy targets at a minute's notice. This kind of warfare relies heavily on accurate information in the form of intelligence—the United States would need exact and detailed information on the opponent while the latter would need to have no idea what was about to happen. Furthermore, the United States would possess the high-tech weapons systems needed to strike enemy targets while the enemy was unsure of what is happening. Such a situation would require superiority in what the military calls "battlespace knowledge." To quote another specialist, "By integrating a system of systems, a picture of the battlespace measuring 200 miles on each side could be created. Linking command, control, communications, computers, intelligence, surveillance and reconnaissance (C4SIR) system can provide information superiority—or dominant battlespace knowledge."[51] In short, the enemy's weapons systems would be destroyed before he could use them, while his communications system was disrupted. The United States would be able to win its wars before the other side knew what hit him.

Because of his respect for technology and his belief that fewer soldiers would be needed, Rumsfeld argued in favor of homogenizing the services as Kagan argued. "No longer will each service bring unique capabilities to the table, but all will now provide the same capability—the capability to identify and attack with PGMs [precision-guided missiles] at great distances."[52] In other words, air power would reign supreme. America would no longer need a large army or Marine Corps. Everything would be funneled into this common area.

This model would do away with the careful balance in the U.S. armed forces—the Marines are primarily set up as a light expeditionary force, with limited staying power, while the army possesses the heavy units with considerable staying power. The result would be a military focused on carrying out one mission and one mission only. Instead of having heavy army divisions, the U.S. would only have light-infantry divisions, presumably to be used as a small, highly flexible, expeditionary force. The war would quickly be over for all practical purposes, so it would only be necessary to "mop up" after air power has won the war. This is one of the reasons Rumsfeld favored the Marines. "The Marines have fared better in Rumsfeld's personnel choices. Rumsfeld's aides made it known that they found most of the army's top generals not innovative enough for the demands of the 21st century warfare, but thought the Marine Corps top officers intellectually nimble."[53]

Doing away with balance, however, could have a very negative impact on the military. In essence, it meant putting all the eggs in one basket. It assumed that there was really only one function for the military to perform and that was fine as long as a high-tech war was the only matter of concern. Specifically, "The Rumsfeld vision of military transformation, therefore, is completely unbalanced. It will provide the U.S. with armed forces that will do one thing only, even if it is superbly well."[54] The one thing it provided was the ability to destroy enemy targets far away with minimal losses to the United States. But what if the other side made a technological breakthrough that caused Washington to lose its superiority in this area? It could then overwhelm the U.S. in other, more traditional spheres or branches of military force—such as infantry or armor, or even partisan warfare, for that matter.

In retrospect, it is clear that despite his aides' efforts, Rumsfeld did not have a good definition for the term "military transformation." In fact, at times he was contradictory. For example, he was quite intrigued by the use of horses and special operations forces in Afghanistan. Clearly, that had little or nothing to do with high-tech weapons. As the assistant director of the Office of Force Transformation explained, "Transformation should be viewed as a continuing process rather than a set of platforms or new organizations to be deployed by certain dates. The process is continuous in part because adversaries adapt as they identify U.S. vulnerabilities."[55] Rumsfeld preferred high-tech systems, but if the term would be helpful to explain another policy, he was prepared to stretch it to cover that situation. It meant change and innovation, but in whatever direction Rumsfeld felt was most promising or most desirable.

Transformation also meant getting those in uniform to change how they thought—to be open to new ideas for fighting a war. If the army was too wedded to the use of mass force on the battlefield, soldiers would have to change their minds, perhaps by putting greater emphasis on technology and special operations forces. The one thing Rumsfeld would not abide was senior officers who refused to change their old way of thinking, not just regarding doctrine, but also the weapons they pushed for every budgetary cycle. Not surprisingly, this kind of "meddling" by a civilian, even if he was the secretary of defense—was not welcome among the generals and admirals in high places in the Pentagon.[56]

Rumsfeld's primary method to achieve military transformation was to bring high-tech systems into the military. In every case that he argued for new weapons, Rumsfeld opted for the most modern, most technologically superior weapon he could find. He stretched the definition of military transformation to include things like horses in Afghanistan because he believed that if officers could be pushed to accept Special Forces soldiers on horseback, they would be more open to new, innovative forms of high-tech weapons.

## Conclusion

From the military's standpoint, Rumsfeld was throwing them a curve ball. He and the president claimed to respect the military and what it represented, yet the secretary of defense (presumably with the president's concurrence), violated one aspect of military culture after another. Rumsfeld seemed to believe that the Department of Defense was just another corporation to reorganize, like Searle. He seemed to believe he could toss subordinates around at will, even interfering in the promotion process, a realm considered sacred by the upper ranks of all the services. They believed it was up to them to decide who would get a second, third, or fourth star. And here was this outsider interviewing candidates—even for one star. His only concern seemed to be whether or not they supported his current idea of military transformation. Such an action was bound to have a serious impact on the future of the officer corps—producing "yes men," individuals who were prepared to support him. Their qualifications as military officers per se, were no longer the primary criteria for getting ahead in the military.

Rumsfeld clearly did not respect the military and was not interested in working with the armed forces. A common front would still have disagreements, but both sides would be able to put their cards on the table. They could work out compromises—thereby keeping an amiable relationship between the two sides. But Rumsfeld gave the impression that he did *not* want compromises. He wanted to be in sole charge, and they had better get used to the idea that they would be doing things his way.

This was clearly a recipe for intensified conflict, not the kind of give-and-take that should be part of the civil-military relationship. The military brass knew that Rumsfeld was the boss and that he had the final say on critical issues. Still, they had hoped he would meet them halfway, listen to their concerns and ideas, and take them into account. But he made it clear that he was not interested in what they had to say. The first year of Rumsfeld's tenure at the Defense Department was neither quiet nor a model of healthy civil-military relations.

# 2 Rumsfeld Pushes Transformation

You look at Rumsfeld, and beyond all the rationale, spoken and unspoken, he just dislikes the army. It's just palpable. . . . You always have to wonder if when Rumsfeld was a Navy lieutenant junior grade whether an army officer stole his girlfriend.

*Lieutenant Colonel Ralph Peters, U.S. Army (Ret.)*

George W. Bush was concerned with the status of the military transformation even before he became president. During his 2000 election campaign he had suggested that he would put far more money into the military than Bill Clinton had, at least that is what most in uniform understood by the comment he and his running mate made—"Help is on the way."[1] Second, he was critical of the situation the armed forces found themselves in under Clinton, and he promised to reform and modernize them to make them capable of fighting wars in the twenty-first century. As he put it in a stump speech at the Citadel in 1999, "Our military is still organized more for Cold War threats than the challenges of the century—for industrial age operations, rather than information battles."[2] Toward that end, Bush promised that he would act on the military from the first day he was in office. After a "comprehensive review of the military," he would "replace existing programs with new technologies and strategies" that would skip forward to a new "generation of technology."[3] This latter concept would play a major role in Rumsfeld's efforts to transform the armed forces. With the president's words ringing in his ears, he decided he was not interested in the next generation fighter plane, ship, or tank. Rumsfeld was dedicated to finding and harnessing the technology necessary to go beyond the weapons currently available to the U.S. military. Marginal improvements—such as putting a new, more effective weapon on a preexisting platform—would no longer be acceptable. Advanced technology would make the United States untouchable in the twenty-first century.

Bush understood that transforming the military would not be cheap, and he made it clear during the campaign that he was prepared to pay for it. For example, he stated, "He would add $20 billion over five years for the scientific research and development of better weapons systems, and that he would demand that 20 percent of the military procurement budget be devoted to new technologies."[4] After all, the United States was now the world's only superpower, so Washington had the time necessary to jump a generation of weapons before any other country became a significant threat. Bush added an important cautionary note, however. He warned in January 2001, "We cannot let the effectiveness of our military forces to degrade while we are modernizing and transforming."[5] In other words, while it was in the U.S. national interest to make a generational jump in weapons, it was important for the Pentagon to ensure that it was capable of meeting any threats that might arise in the meantime, a warning that Rumsfeld would ignore.

Rumsfeld believed his primary task was to implement Bush's vision, a job he took very seriously. Given the approach he and Bush adopted, however, a major blowup with the military brass was inevitable. By February 10 an unidentified officer was already stating, "I'm not ready to say I'm yearning for life under [the Clinton Administration], but it certainly was less nerve racking."[6] Three days later, the president announced that he had no intention of going along with "Pentagon Orthodoxy." Instead, he stated that he was out to create "a new architecture for the defense of America and our allies." He stressed that he intended to invest in new technologies and weapons systems, not spend money for "marginal improvements" in weapons.[7] He seemed to have reversed his earlier position, arguing that the United States was prepared to ignore existing weapons systems—if that were necessary—in order to focus on new technologies. The president went on to note, "We do not know yet the exact shape of our future military, but we know the direction we must begin to travel. On land, our heavy forces will be lighter. Our light forces will be more lethal. All will be easier to deploy and sustain. In the air, we'll be able to strike across the world with pinpoint accuracy, using both manned and unmanned systems."[8] Bush also expressed his support for Rumsfeld's planned comprehensive review of Pentagon operations. Bush's remarks made it very clear to the chiefs that Rumsfeld had his full backing. He also put Congress and the defense industry on notice that their lobbying efforts would have little or no impact.

## Rumsfeld's Thinking Evolves

Rumsfeld was not the first to think about transforming the American military. When he was chairman of the Joint Chiefs, Colin Powell created the Base Force plan, which established a minimum troop level adequate for the Pentagon to handle two large-scale conflicts at the same time, not just the most current threat. Existing forces could always be moved to meet a threat, as was the case in the Gulf War.

In 1993, President Clinton ordered a "bottom-up review." The Cold War was over and many believed that the U.S. did not need the large-scale armed forces required to counter the Soviet threat. Little was accomplished under Clinton, however. The military's heart was not in it, and Clinton was not about to pick a fight with the generals and admirals over something he knew very little about. Reviews were undertaken, but the result was always the same. A smaller military was recommended, but nothing was done fundamentally to change its organization or structure.

On May 24, 1995, the Congressional Commission on Roles and Missions of the Armed Forces released its report, "Directions for Peace." While it made some suggestions for organizational changes, the document did not focus directly on issues such as strategy or operations. The most important recommendation was that Congress should create a "Quadrennial Defense Review" (QDR), which would routinely assess the state of the U.S. military at the beginning of each administration to confirm that the Pentagon was looking seriously and systematically at the future of the U.S. military. The report required the secretary of defense and chairman of the Joint Chiefs to conduct a comprehensive assessment "with a view toward determining and expressing the defense strategy of the United States and establishing a defense program for the next 20 years."[9] The report was sent to the Armed Services Committees of both the Senate and House of Representatives. The Pentagon was to address fifteen separate areas.

From the military standpoint, the outcome was confusing, because while the QDR recognized that the tasks facing the armed forces were increasing, it actually recommended

> cutting overall U.S. force structure by a total of 60,000 active duty, 55,000 reserve, and 89,000 civilian personnel. It proposed making cuts primarily by slashing 'overhead' in headquarters and support structures while keeping the same number of units available in the active army. It did propose to move an Air Force wing from the active component to the reserve and to reduce the number of Navy combatants from programmed 131–116.[10]

On the other hand, the Commission did not recommend canceling any major weapons systems currently planned or under production. But most of these weapons, either planned or in production, were created for use against a Soviet Union that no longer existed. The Commission recommended cutbacks in two high-technology jet fighters: the air force's F-22 fighters would be cut from 438 to 339, while the navy would have to absorb a cut in F/A-18E/F fighters from 1,000 to 548.[11]

Later in 1997 the congressionally mandated review of the QDR by the National Defense Panel (NDP) resulted in a report. The commission that reviewed the QDR was chaired by Philip Odeen, a senior national security aide to Nixon, and composed of four retired senior officers and four civilians, including Richard Armitage and Andrew Krepinevich. The report made two points. First, it questioned the wisdom of basing U.S. military planning on the assumption that two wars will occur at the same time. That assumption was being used to justify weapons programs, but it might not be relevant. Second, it argued that U.S. weapons, doctrine, and training should focus on the future. There was no doubt that dangers such as North Korea, Iran, and Iraq existed, but "our current forces, with the support of allies, should be capable of dealing with both contingencies."[12] The important point was reflected in the title of the report—"Transforming Defense: National Security in the 21st Century." "Transformation" had become a buzzword. The NDP estimated that transformation would cost $5–10 billion. While it would be nice if the government would add that amount of money to the budget, the NDP recognized that would not happen, so it suggested that the size of American forces should be reduced, the two-war idea scrapped, certain weapons systems cancelled, and the money saved should be used to pay for modernizing the military.

The NDP proposed a novel approach toward transformation. Rather than merely "upgrading" older, legacy systems, it proposed that the military "jump" a generation. For example, instead of upgrading the weapons and other systems on the M-1 tank, the military should create an all-new twenty-first century tank. Like Rumsfeld, the NDP emphasized that reform was most critical for the army, because the army must "become more expeditionary: fast, shock-exploiting forces, with greater urban operations capability." It also called for systems that were more mobile. In short, "Speed had become all."[13]

This report was important, because it presaged Rumsfeld's thinking. Congress appointed another commission in January 1998 to assess the danger the U.S. faced from ballistic missiles. This one was chaired by Rumsfeld, and Paul Wolfowitz was a member. The commission looked at two questions:

"How widely was missile technology actually being disseminated, and second, given the United States' own technological superiority in this field, just how great a danger to us was there from the missile programs in the less advanced nations."[14] The commission concluded that missiles from countries like Iraq, North Korea, and Pakistan could be upgraded and pose a serious threat to the United States. Russia would also continue to pose a threat. Foreshadowing Rumsfeld's view of war, the report concluded, "The key to this revolution are [sic] precision-guided munitions, stealth technology and space-based equipment for command and control, communications, surveillance and reconnaissance—along with computer based capacity to make these things work together."[15] In short, one of the policies that this commission—and Rumsfeld—stressed was the need for a missile defense system.

The other concept discussed during the 1990s was network-centric warfare. Key to this concept is the idea that warfare and the economy are tied together. Indeed, one of network-centric's main tenets was that the information revolution had fundamentally changed both business and war, and the two were intimately linked. As Admiral Arthur Cebrowski put it, "Nations make war the same way they make wealth."[16] Just as success in business depends on the ability to circulate information, the same is true of armies. The winning army is the one that obtains the most accurate information. This approach is therefore premised upon the speed of command. That concept can be further broken down into three components: "information superiority, the concentration of effects rather than of forces, and the ability to ensure the 'rapid foreclosure of enemy courses of action and the shock of closely coupled events.'"[17] Network-centric warfare can be a confusing concept. But the goal was to confuse and disorient an enemy, so that his ability to conduct military operations quickly disintegrates. Indeed, the concept could be summarized as: "Shock and awe are achieved not simply as a function of the number of targets destroyed, but as a result of the destruction or neutralization of significant numbers of critical targets within a short period of time and/or the successful targeting of the right target at the right time."[18] Rumsfeld became an avid supporter of network-centric warfare. It became one of channels of reform that he would introduce in the Pentagon. "He believed enthusiastically in the Network-Centric Warfare model then being propounded, and he went even further. Determined to transform the military in accord with NCW ideas, Mr. Rumsfeld was also determined to do it at the lowest possible cost. He adopted a business approach to that problem as well."[19] For the U.S. military that meant emphasizing the area where the United States had its greatest comparative advantage—high-tech weaponry, especially the ability to deliver ordnance from far away, using cruise missiles or manned bombers.

There is, however, a serious problem with both NDP and network-centric warfare. Both of them are purely military concepts, but war is also deeply political, as noted above. Cultural factors may make the enemy respond in unexpected ways. Some countries may quickly surrender, like the Japanese after enduring two atomic bombs, while others spurred on by religious or nationalistic fanaticism may fight to the martyr's death in what may appear to be a hopeless struggle. But Rumsfeld ignored these possibilities, because his mind was focused elsewhere—on transforming the American military as quickly as possible.

By the turn of the century, Rumsfeld was convinced that the future of military force was in the world of space and technology. The human warrior would remain important, but, in his mind, the difference between the American military and other militaries was its ability to rely on high-tech weapons. Furthermore, as the National Defense Panel had argued, it was time for the United States to pause weapons production in order to make the jump in generations the revolution in military affairs promised.

## The Army Considers Its Own Needs

Contrary to Rumsfeld's opinion, the army was not oblivious to technological innovation. It also realized that change was necessary. For example, in 1993 General Gordon Sullivan (Ret.) and Lieutenant Colonel James Dubik released a manuscript that looked into the need for reform in the army.[20] The authors argued that, given advances in technology, the U.S. Army would have to change the way it operated. Among the recommendations, for example, it must become more mobile, and it must have better communication systems. The army's twenty-first century forces would have to maneuver more quickly and learn how to fight from greater distances. These changes would affect every aspect of army operations. "This trend," they predicted, "will place a great premium on the commander's ability to make decisions quickly, the staff's requirement to synchronize the movements of dispersed units, and the subordinate leader's responsibility to make on-the-spot decisions within a senior commander's intent."[21]

While recognizing the importance of technology, the authors went out of their way to impress on the reader that there would be some things that would not change.

> First, the future will differ little from the past with regard to the root causes of war. People—whether political leaders of a nation state or leaders of some other kind of organization—still fight wars as a result of fear, hatred, greed,

ambition, revenge, and a host of other quite human ever-present ambitions. They still fight when they perceive that they can accomplish their objectives by resorting to force, or that they have no other alternative, or that honor or pride or principle of "the gods" demand it. In other words, they fight for what are to them fundamental reasons, even if others do not share or understand their rationale. Therefore, strategists must clearly and completely think through the use of countervailing force and its possible unintended consequences.[22]

Sullivan and Dubik argued that mastering modern technology is only part of the solution. "Prosecuting war requires both science and art, judgment, trust, cohesion, creativity, flexibility, and just plain guts also are absolutely necessary."[23] For those who thought that technology was a "cure-all" for fighting a war, they added, "Those who seek 'silver bullets' must first acknowledge that land warfare under Napoleon, Grant, Pershing, Patton, Ridgeway, Westmoreland, Thurman, Schwarzkopf, and Hoar is surprisingly similar. War is a matter of heart and will first; weaponry and technology second."[24] They stressed that the military is changing due to modern technology, especially the communications and computer revolutions, but some things do not change, and any battle plan must consider them, including the nature of the enemy, his culture, how (and how long) he will fight, as well as the kind of American forces that will be necessary to win both the war and the peace.

Although leaders now recognized the need to modify the army's force structure, efforts faced bureaucratic resistance. Following the collapse of the Soviet Union and the Gulf War in 1991, the army, like the other services, downsized, but it did not make any major structural or organizational changes. It is easier to recognize the need for change than to convince people in an organization to both change and, in some cases, eliminate their positions.

In 1994 the army established the Force XXI project to "digitalize the army" with computerization and communication systems. These systems would then link "the most senior general to the most junior lieutenant."[25] This would tie the increasingly scattered army units together while providing the war planners with "the best possible understanding of the 'battlespace.'"[26] Everyone in the army would have a computer—a hand-held one for the infantrymen, and others mounted in tanks, trucks, APCs, and other vehicles.

Colonel Douglas MacGregor, an officer who had demonstrated his willingness to think "outside the bubble" in the past, took matters a step further in his 1997 book, *Breaking the Phalanx*, arguing that because of the increased availability of information and technology, there was no reason why the army could not get rid of divisions in favor of armored brigades.[27] This would eliminate two levels of command and accelerate decision-making. The brigade commander would report to a front or task-force commander. These brigades would be self-sufficient and not require reinforcements to be effective in combat. The result would be a much faster, more mobile unit that could respond immediately to threats. Once again, the military bureaucracy resisted change—getting rid of the traditional corps and battalions went against history and tradition. But regardless of how brilliant it might have been, the logic of this argument did not carry the day in the army's bureaucracy.

In 1999 the army discovered that it could no longer ignore its organizational problems. It ran into a major problem during the conflict in Kosovo. General Wesley Clark requested the deployment of Black Hawk helicopters; however, in order to deploy them, the army would have to send an additional 5,000 support troops. The idea of having the helicopters operate independently was never seriously considered, and, given the structure and organization of the army at that time, there was no easy way to solve the problem. Something had to be done if the army expected to be able to respond to Kosovo-like contingencies in the future.

## General Eric Shinseki Pursues Reform

The task fell to General Eric Shinseki, who had become chief of staff of the army in 1999. He had the authority to launch an army transformation, but he was worried that it was too late. He had recognized the need for transformation when he commanded the Implementation Force (IFOR) in Bosnia. He understood that the army must improve the timetable for deployment or run the risk of becoming militarily irrelevant. Nobody wanted an army that took weeks or months to deploy, which had happened in the Gulf War. If the army could not be deployed in a reasonable time, other services might play the key role in conflicts, leaving the army to pick up the pieces. After all, both the navy and the air force were already high-tech services, and the Marines were highly mobile. Shinseki wanted his legacy to be a transformed army that met the demands of the twenty-first century.

On October 12, 1999, Shinseki delivered a speech to the Association of the U.S. Army in which he recognized the transformation problem and outlined how he planned to deal with it:

> With the right technological solutions, we intend to transform the Army, all components, into a standard design with internetted C41SR packages that

allow us to put a combat capable brigade anywhere in the world in 96 hours once we have received executive liftoff, a division on the ground in 120 hours, and five divisions in 30 days. Being able to do so gives the National Command Authority a genuine deterrent capability—when ordered, we intend to get to trouble spots faster than our adversaries can complicate the crisis.[28]

In a press conference following the luncheon, Shinseki argued that the army was well-suited to take on major threats anywhere in the world. The problem came with lesser threats, which meant getting high-tech material that "will help us get smaller, lighter platforms."[29] This reasoning gave rise to the army's "Transformation Plan."

Undertaking such a transformation program presented a number of problems. First, the military needed to maintain its combat readiness during the process. Shinseki began by categorizing the weapons and equipment that the army already had as the "legacy" force; i.e., the heavy tanks and mechanized divisions. Some of these could be modernized to improve their utility in combat, others would become irrelevant. As one specialist writing in 2001 noted, "The army has already restructured five major programs and cancelled seven others in order to free $16 billion for the transformation effort."[30]

Next, Shinseki planned for the army to move to an "interim force." It would be a transitional force working to create "lighter and more mobile brigades and divisions,"[31] and it would provide the army with time to integrate both new and old weapons. Gradually, the army would transition to an "objective force," which would include the so-called army future combat system. While the details were vague, Shinseki had in mind a new group of fast, armored vehicles. However, they had to weigh less than 20 tons to assure that they could be moved quickly by air. Shinseki expected them to begin to appear in the army by 2010. However, he believed the process had to be carefully managed both in terms of equipment and people. Priorities had to be set and plans carefully considered. Eliminating a weapons system before its new high-tech replacement had been tested and accepted by the army would be foolish. Similarly, it made no sense to put soldiers in Objective Force weapons systems until they had been fully trained.

Shinseki devoted considerable time to preparing the groundwork for these changes. For example, following his 1999 speech he traveled to every "pre-command course to speak to the rising generation of officers, and their spouses, about army transformation, and the quality-of-life issues that concern them."[32] In addition, he also ordered changes in the way the army assigned and trained its soldiers.[33] He pushed the army bureaucracy hard, driving the army at a "fanatical pace to ensure the force evolved rapidly yet logically."[34] Shinseki also ordered the production of a replacement for the army's Operational Directive (FM 3-10 Operations) in the summer of 2001. The directive discussed how the army would fight traditional wars, and it also dealt with the full spectrum of operations for "prompt sustained army force operations on land as a member of a joint or multinational force."[35] The army was not waiting around for something to happen. Instead, "The army is arguably the most aggressive service pursuing transformation."[36]

On March 1, 2001, Shinseki reiterated his dedication to transformation, arguing again that if it did not have an effective force in the field by 2010, the army risked losing its relevance. As he put it, "This is about speed."[37] The key to the Objective Force would be the integrated future combat system (FCS), which focused on weight—the army needed weapons between 16 and 18 tons so they could fit into a C-130 transport plane. The army had to be light and mobile in order to respond to the increasing number of peacekeeping operations, not to mention small-scale insurgencies that fell to the army to deal with. Furthermore, it was becoming clear to Shinseki that the battlefields of the future would be cellular, not linear. Instead of the front lines that marked World War II and the Korean War, for example, the bad guys would be intermingled with U.S. forces. They might be in front of or behind the Americans, but they would be a new kind of enemy.

## Rumsfeld Ignores Shinseki

Shinseki seemed to be exactly the kind of military leader Rumsfeld was seeking. The general understood the importance of technology and was working hard to integrate it into the army, just as Rumsfeld wished. Unfortunately, the two men would turn out to be bitter enemies. "To the new Defense Secretary," *Los Angeles Times* reporter Frank Gibney wrote in 2004, "transformation meant greater reliance on technology, not troops, to achieve goals; to Shinseki, it meant more intensified training, featuring highly mobile medium light brigades of mechanized infantry capable of a variety of missions."[38] Shinseki believed that the U.S. fighting man was the key, just as Sullivan and Dubik had argued in their study. But for Rumsfeld, the future belonged not to the GI slogging it out in a foxhole, but weapons from space and more use of air power. The army did not figure high in his plans. In fact, Rumsfeld wanted to save money by cutting army programs so he would have more funds to devote to space and air power. In Rumfeld's mind, close combat, the army's raison d'etre, was a thing of the past. Future wars would be conducted by missiles and other technological tools—areas where the United States had a clear advantage.

The situation between the two men worsened when Rumsfeld initially refused to even meet with Shinseki. Like every chief of staff of the army, Shinseki was accustomed to getting a meeting with the secretary of defense when he requested it. Consequently, early on in the administration, Shinseki asked to meet with Rumsfeld in order to iron out any differences they had. Rather than meet with him, Rumsfeld told him to wait. He waited, and according to his aides, as of May, 2001 "he [was] still waiting."[39] The military considered this kind of behavior to be reprehensible, as it shows no respect for the chief of staff and, by extrapolation, the army itself. To say that it was violation of military culture would be an understatement.

The relationship between Rumsfeld and the army would get so bad that by 2002 army officers referred to Rumsfeld and his aides as "the enemy."[40] In return, Rumsfeld's office leaked Shinseki's successor's name fourteen months prior to the end of Shinseki's tour as chief of staff of the army: "At a Saturday-morning meeting with Rumsfeld and Wolfowitz at the Pentagon early in April 2002, Steve Herbits, a special assistant to Rumsfeld, proposed undercutting the obstructive chief of staff by leaking the name of his successor. As all of them knew, Shinseki was not due to retire for over a year."[41] Such an action was unheard of, and while Rumsfeld would deny reports that he was behind it, he and/or his aides clearly hoped Shinseki would retire—so he could put someone more sympathetic to his ideas in that position. Shinseki, however, refused to take the easy way out, and instead decided to finish out his term as chief of staff.

## Crunching Numbers at the Pentagon

In an effort to get a leg up on the incoming administration, at the end of 2000 General Hugh Shelton, chairman of the Joint Chiefs, publicly stated that the military did not have enough money. He argued that it faced "'an insatiable burden' caused by aging equipment, shrinking forces, and the pace of military operations."[42] Shelton did not cite a specific budgetary figure; rather, he cited a Congressional Budget Office study that called for increasing spending on weapons to $90 billion.

Rumsfeld not only upset the military brass, but the defense contractors and their supporters on the Hill were probably even more irritated—an especially unsettling development considering that many of those most upset on the Hill were Republicans. "If anything, Rumsfeld's relations with Capitol Hill have been even more tumultuous. The military, after all, ultimately will follow orders. But Congress expects to have a big say in the orders."[43] From a military standpoint, planners had to be certain that it could safely develop these kinds of weapons while ignoring the current inventory.

Soon Rumsfeld's relations with the armed forces deteriorated even further. In early February, one of Bush's top advisers purportedly commented, "The only way to reform the Pentagon is 'to fire a few generals.'"[44] Then in March Rumsfeld gave a few more details about his planned restructuring of the armed forces. Whether intended or not, rumors soon began leaking out of the Pentagon suggesting that major changes were coming, especially with regard to which weapons the military buys and how it looks at future warfare. One source predicted that Rumsfeld would tell the navy to stop building aircraft carriers "and start designing a new, smaller carrier that is less vulnerable to missiles. 'The big loser is the carrier,' said one person familiar with the review."[45] The air force would not be spared either. One rumor had it that Rumsfeld would tell it to purchase fewer F-22s. When he returned to the Pentagon, Rumsfeld briefed senior military officers.

According to press reports, Andrew Marshall, Rumsfeld's senior adviser and long-time head of the Pentagon's Office of Net Assessment, made a number of points at this meeting. First, the Pacific will be the key area of operations, as China becomes more powerful. Second, the United States will need to pay greater attention to "long-range power projection." Third, the United States must be able to sustain itself, especially when it is far from its bases. Fourth, U.S. systems should have "stealth" capabilities because of the spread of missiles and weapons of mass destruction. Finally, as expected, "The armed forces should cut spending on older weapons systems that they are likely to stop using within the next 10 years or so."[46]

Whether Rumsfeld knew it or not, this meeting probably did more harm than good. First, Chairman Shelton was in South America and thus did not attend. From a military standpoint, the chief should be present whenever the secretary of defense makes a major pronouncement on weapons acquisitions and military strategy. Rumsfeld's impatience was a clear lack of courtesy toward the chairman. Indeed, given his lack of respect for military culture, the idea of waiting for Shelton may never have occurred to him. Second, one general who was present during the meeting later commented that Rumsfeld was "brusque" when he spoke to the generals and admirals. As he commented, "It is clear that there is a very different management style at the top." His appraisal was backed by a civilian official who commented, "The uniformed military is only beginning to recognize the extent of reform that Rumsfeld intends to seek at the Pentagon. They want this to be collegial, and Rumsfeld is about change."[47]

The military was clearly concerned about this new secretary and how to deal with him. They were not opposed to the review process—they knew that the world had changed and they had to adapt. The problem was the way Rumsfeld approached change. In May, for example, there was a report that the Joint Chiefs of Staff had held a closed-door meeting in the "tank," the secure facility they have to prevent eavesdropping. They reportedly "posed scathing questions about Rumsfeld's intentions on strategy and possible cuts to the army."[48] General Sullivan, a leader in the army reform effort, gave a speech blasting Rumsfeld's actions as "impudent."[49] To make matters worse, the generals complained that talking to him was a waste of time. Rumsfeld "takes a lot in, but he doesn't give anything back. . . . You go and brief him and it's just blank."[50]

Senior officers began their counterattack in May. They quietly spoke with members of Congress, outlining what Rumsfeld was doing and how he was leaving the uniformed military out of the process. Not only were many members of Congress concerned, the generals made effective use of the media to ensure that their complaints were heard. Rumsfeld responded by meeting with Congress. He denied that he failed to consult the military. A former Senate defense adviser recalled, "He had his staff tally the numbers and then bragged about them. 'I've met with Shelton about 1.3 times per day.' And he boasted of 170 meetings with 44 different generals and flag officers in his first four months in office, as well as 70 meetings with 115 members of Congress."[51] The difficulty was that just meeting with generals and flag officers is not significant unless it involves a two-way conversation. Calling individuals in and then acting arrogant or failing to listen to what they say—especially given their importance and the seriousness of the topic under discussion—often was worse than not meeting with them at all.

The chatter in the Pentagon corridors soon focused on Rumsfeld's transformation process. Some blasted him for his "imperious" way of dealing with people,[52] while others mocked his policies, calling them "a martial version of Hillary Rodham Clinton's health care plan, which failed spectacularly in 1994 when it was offered up to Congress."[53] Senior officers shared these views, with one contrasting Rumsfeld with General Colin Powell at the State Department. "Mr. Powell is very inclusive, and Mr. Rumsfeld is the opposite." "We've been kept out of the loop." "We've been disenfranchised."[54] General Gordon Sullivan again blasted Rumsfeld, stating that he "seemed headed toward 'the easy but erroneous conclusion that by spending hundreds of billions of dollars weaponizing space, developing a national missile defense, and buying long-range precision weapons, we can avoid the ugly realities of conflict."[55]

Bush used a May 25, 2001, address to the graduating class of the U.S. Naval Academy to call for more creativity in military thinking. He indirectly reiterated his support for Rumsfeld, calling on the graduating seniors to help "Change the course of a mighty ship." He continued, "I'm committed to building a future force that is defined less by size and more by stealth, precision weaponry and information technologies." Finally, he suggested downsizing the military, "suggesting that the active force could shrink. At 1.4 million, it is 33% below the level of 2.1 million in uniform near the end of the Cold War."[56]

In June David Gompert, a vice president of the Rand Corporation, gave a briefing on the future of conventional warfare. He spoke about the importance of "long-range, precision-strike bombs and missiles that airplanes can fire at faraway targets." His comments were along the lines of the NDP, and the army was hardly mentioned. Given Rand's importance in the military planning system, the generals were right to be concerned. Even a think tank like Rand had received the message—forget the army and focus on space and long-range missiles.[57] In fact, the Rand review suggested that the army's 70 ton M1-A2 Abrams battle tank—a weapon that soldiers believed was critical in any major conflict and was so successful in Operation Desert Storm—was marginal or even irrelevant.

Later that month, Rumsfeld announced the fiscal 2002 defense budget. The budget gave priority to people, calling for significant increases in personnel-related accounts. The biggest single increase was in military health care, and there was also an across-the-board pay raise of 5 percent. At the same time, it included some provisions the military brass undoubtedly rejected. For example, the army faced cuts in flying time for helicopters and driving time for tanks. "Pentagon Comptroller Dov S. Zakheim called the reduction in tank driving time 'a minor risk' and explained that 'they have to make life a little more livable for the troops.'"[58] Turning to changes in force structure and individual weapons systems, Rumsfeld said, "I will be . . . reviewing the weapons systems and putting them in the context of the strategy and putting them in the context of how we see the total funds available over the period ahead and making these decisions."[59] That meant that weapons such as the B-2 bomber, the F-22 fighter, and the DD-21 destroyer were still on the chopping block. Rumsfeld left open the possibility that he would cancel one or all of them—in addition to other weapons that did not fit into his idea of a twenty-first century military.

By mid-July, the two sides were deadlocked. On July 19, Rumsfeld announced that he was rejecting a review that was critical for the upcoming Quadrennial Defense Review. He referred to the document—that reportedly called for a total of thirty-four aircraft carriers to project power around the world—as a "joke."[60] Both civilians and military officers stated that the review process was not working. The projected budget would not be enough to pay for the weapons the Clinton administration had ordered—let alone the new high-tech weapons Rumsfeld had in mind, leading one official to call the review process a "reality free zone."[61]

Rumsfeld's arrogance and refusal to pay attention to the generals had alienated them. In a certain sense, he had burned his bridges with many senior military officers. Indeed, in the review cited above, Rumsfeld and Wolfowitz made clear it "is the civilian leadership's responsibility to undertake the review—with the military playing a supporting role."[62] Senior officers were fed up with him and his review. "Several said in interviews, on the condition their names not be used, that the review has been disorganized and is being rushed to meet Congress's deadline. Many complain that they were frozen out of Rumsfeld's reviews for the first four months of his tenure and now are being consulted with little time to shape a plan."[63] Rumsfeld's supporters blamed everything on the military and warned that the "floor is going to run red with military blood."[64] Indeed, the situation was so serious that General Shelton reportedly "expressed concern . . . to Rumsfeld about the defense secretary's review of the military."[65]

Rumsfeld admitted that there were significant problems with his military review process. He openly stated that he found recommendations by a panel of senior officers unacceptable, and he told them to "go back" and try again, dismissing their concerns because "Anytime any change is made, somebody's not going to like it."[66] In the meantime, Rumsfeld expressed optimism that the process would ultimately succeed, noting, "I feel that while it's a tough challenge, that we're making very good progress on it."[67] He gave them a deadline of September 30, which was the date Congress had set for the QDR report to be finished.

The military was not as confident that agreement would be reached by the end of September. One unidentified general commented that Rumsfeld had privately told the chiefs and other senior officials that "we have a problem." He reported, "Things are on hold until the Joint Staff and [Rumsfeld's aides] figure out the way ahead . . . There is a huge rift between the Joint Staff and [Rumsfeld's aides] over this."[68] Krepinevich suggested that the chiefs should come back to Rumsfeld saying, "You can get any kind of military you want, as long as it's the one we're already building."[69]

The situation was worsened by the way civilians approached senior officers. For example, there was a widely reported incident involving Steven Cambone, who was Rumsfeld's point man on transformation at that time. According to one report, Cambone walked into a room full of "three stars" a half hour late on a Saturday morning to discuss transformation and the QDR. He began the meeting by saying, "So guys, . . . what's transformation?" He walked around the table asking each officer what he thought—in a military context—treating them "like morons." When they met a week later, they all refused to say anything—instead remaining mute. Furious, Cambone left. One three-star was so infuriated by Cambone's disdainful behavior that he reportedly said, "If we were being overrun by the enemy and I had one round left, I'd save it for Stephen Cambone."[70] On another occasion, Cambone attempted to get military leaders to "think creatively," which meant to go along with the approach advocated by the secretary. Finally, in frustration, he turned to the military brass and said, "Can't you come up with anything new?"[71] Needless to say, Cambone's effort to get the military brass "on board" was unsuccessful. They did not respect him and found his comments banal, to say the least.

The heart of the debate revolved around a classified document Rumsfeld and Cambone had developed earlier that summer, the "Terms of Reference," to guide Pentagon planners who were preparing for the QDR. It was an integral part of Rumsfeld's desire to change the existing two-war strategy. "This [existing] approach had served us well in the immediate post–Cold War period," the secretary said, "but it now threatened to leave us over-prepared for two specific conflicts and under-prepared for unexpected contingencies and twenty-first century challenges."[72] It was time for change. The chiefs agreed that the two-war option made little sense any more. As one of Rumsfeld's aides noted, "He really locked them in. . . . He got them to agree that the world had changed."[73]

Under Rumsfeld's new strategy, the military was assigned four tasks. First, it must defend U.S. territory. Second, it must deter hostile actions in Europe, the Middle East, Southwest Asia, Northeast Asia, and the East Asian rim. Third, it must be able to "win decisively" in one major conflict. Finally, it must be capable of conducting a number of small-scale operations in other parts of the world.[74] In essence, the new strategy meant that Rumsfeld expected the military to do everything it was doing then. But he also wanted the services to develop new capabilities in space, intelligence, and information warfare and to experiment with new technologies. Then, to make matters even more difficult, he argued that the military should create task forces that would respond to crises around the world, quickly and decisively.

Changing strategy on paper was the easy part. The hard part came in operationalizing it. Strategies determine force structures, and the two-war strategy justified the existing force structure. Consequently, if the United States has a new strategy, it should change its force mixture to match it. That normally meant that one or two services might lose weapons systems while others gain them. Not surprisingly, the chiefs were very protective of what they considered their services' prerogatives. They were more than prepared to fight to maintain their piece of the force structure pie. Rumsfeld's new strategy would have a major impact on the army, which was already at battle stations over what it saw as Rumsfeld's attempt to reduce—if not castrate—it as a fighting force. The army believed that Rumsfeld's main objection to the two-war strategy was that it required a large ground force—about 1.4 million ground troops on active duty. Out of this the army needed four corps, not to mention logistical support. But the army was not the only branch that was upset; the navy worried about its ships and aircraft. Everyone was concerned that Rumsfeld was primarily interested in finding money for his high-tech favorites: missile defense, space, and intelligence. Indeed, there is one report that Rumsfeld had bluntly told senior generals, "We've got to find a way to de-emphasize conventional programs to pay for strategic defense."[75] The military fought back with leaks to the media and by taking their cases to Capitol Hill.[76] The generals were fighting to save critical parts of their forces; therefore, everything was in play, even if that meant going behind the secretary's back.

A Pentagon panel responded to Rumsfeld's proposals, but not with the answer he sought. Instead of agreeing with him, the panel reiterated the military's position, arguing that Rumsfeld was cutting back on force structure, but not their assigned missions. To the contrary, he was expanding them. If he wanted to cut back the size of the military, he needed to cut back U.S. commitments. In order to do all of the things he had in mind—and have the forces needed to deal with a crisis—the panel said he would have to increase the size of the military, not only in terms of personnel, but he would need more aircraft carriers and fighter wings as well.[77]

By August there were increased signs that Congress was stiffening its opposition to the new military strategy. For example, a majority of members on the House Armed Services Committee sent a letter warning Rumsfeld "against trying to cut the size of the army."[78] The letter followed a vote by the Republican-controlled committee against the Pentagon's plan to cut the number of B-1 bombers.

On August 4 Rumsfeld met with the service secretaries and four-star generals. He quickly discovered that the two groups were standing together shoulder-to-shoulder. They opposed a further reduction in active-duty personnel—they had already been cut by a million since the end of the Cold War. The meeting was contentious, or as one army officer put it, "It did not go well, and it ended early." Secretary of the Army Thomas White reiterated the army's position—that army commitments had not been reduced, yet the secretary wanted a smaller force. Jim Roche, secretary of the air force, opposed any cuts in fighter squadrons. Cambone did not help Rumsfeld's case, as he continued to find it difficult to understand the relationship between force cuts and the resultant threat to regional stability.[79] The army dug its feet in as White argued adamantly against a two-division cut unless he got "firm commitments to curtail missions." His soldiers, he argued, were already stretched thin around the globe. "In fact, just last month Mr. White and General Eric Shinseki told the Armed Services Committee that they may need another 40,000 soldiers"[80] just to carry out the missions currently assigned to them.

By mid-August Rumsfeld had two plans to consider. One, drafted by Cambone's Office of Program Analysis and Evaluation, argued for a reduction in the armed forces by more than 10 percent. The army would lose two of its ten active-duty divisions; the air force would lose sixteen of its sixty-one fighter squadrons; and the navy would have to give up two of its twelve carrier battle groups. The other proposal, from the Joint Chiefs, maintained that the military must remain at its present size.[81]

Left with this political standoff, the secretary backed off. Instead of telling the services which weapons systems to cancel or field, he decided to limit himself to describing "only missions, military requirements, and budget items, and leave to the services the hard and contentious task of deciding how many people to put into uniform, how many weapons to field, and what kind of weapons those should be."[82] As Rumsfeld himself put it, "This is a big organization. The services make a lot of decisions. It would be foolhardy to micromanage from the top . . . every aspect of everything that is going on."[83] To most observers, it looked like Rumsfeld was backing down. "It appears that the first thing the new Pentagon team is doing is to downsize their own expectations. . . . Apparently, instead of making hard choices, they are going to defer to the services. Where's the revolution here?" asked analyst Loren B. Thompson.[84] In fact, Rumsfeld did seem to be backing down. The classified budget guidelines went from "pulling 15,000 troops from Europe and cutting two army National Guard divisions," to the point where it only called for a 15 percent reduction in headquarters units.[85] Altogether, there were three reviews under way—the White House-led national security strategy review, which set overall goals in military policy; the QDR, which set the Pentagon's strategy; and the budget review, which would propose funds to pay for the armed forces.

One of the fiercest battles raged between Rumsfeld and the air force over the fate of the B-2 bomber. The air force adamantly opposed restarting production of the most expensive aircraft in history. Instead, the air force wanted to use the money to purchase the F-22 Raptor, a stealth fighter. Supporters of the B-2 believed that because of its long range and its ability to deliver satellite- and laser-guided bombs, it should remain in the U.S. inventory. This was precisely the kind of weapon that "could transform the way the United States wages war."[86]

## Replacing Shelton

In the middle of his battle with the services, Rumsfeld faced the need to name a new chairman of the Joint Chiefs. Shelton's tour was up, and the secretary had no intention of reappointing him. The general was a Clinton holdover, and—even worse—from the army. Furthermore, Shelton did not hesitate to stand up to the secretary when he believed he was wrong.

After interviewing a number of candidates, Rumsfeld narrowed the selection process to two candidates; the vice chairman of the Joint Chiefs, Air Force General Richard Myers, and Admiral Vern Clark, the chief of naval operations. Rumsfeld was impressed with the navy, Clark was familiar with the secretary's high-tech world, and Shelton recommended him. But according to Bob Woodward, Clark made it very clear from the first time he spoke with Rumsfeld about the job that he took Goldwater–Nichols, and the chairman's right to provide independent advice to the president, very seriously.[87] Rumsfeld was clearly nonplussed by the idea of having a chairman as independent as Admiral Clark.

Myers got along with Rumsfeld, and on occasion he would disagree with him, but as Woodward put it, "He had the Myers way of softening the blow by agreeing."[88] After all, before becoming the vice chief he had been commander of the North American Aerospace Defense Command and commander of the U.S. Space Command for four years, so he was more than up to speed on many of the items that were of interest to the secretary. As far as his independence is concerned, Myers carefully followed Rumsfeld's lead. White House Chief of Staff Andrew Card had told Woodward that when Myers spoke, "It was an echo, and he could not recall an instance when the chairman's advice challenged Rumsfeld's."[89] Another source called him "pliable,"[90] while a third stated: "Myers' term as chairman of the Joint Chiefs was characterized by an extraordinary deference to Rumsfeld. He let himself be overruled on issues such as picking his own staffers for the Joint Staff. Inside the military, he was widely regarded as the best kind of uniformed yes-man—smart, hard-working, but wary of independent thought."[91]

Finally, as a result of Rumsfeld's bullying, Myers became known "as 'an abused puppy,' the 'sycophant to end all sycophants' who shrank from backing up to his master, though his visceral hatred of [Douglas] Feith would occasionally erupt during meetings."[92]

Shelton reportedly was disappointed. "The selection meant that when it came to the hardest decisions there would be no one in the uniformed military positioned and supported by law to provide alternative advice to the president and stand up to Rumsfeld."[93] The secretary had what he wanted—a chairman who would quibble with him over details, but one who believed in the interpretation of civil control that meant that his job was to give the secretary his advice, and if he did not accept it, that was it. Outside of Rumsfeld's office he did not disagree with him on issues of substance or say anything to the president that he had not previously approved.[94] His deputy was Marine General Peter Pace, who was also viewed within the military as a Rumsfeld "yes-man." In fact, according to Ricks, Pace was seen "as even more pliable, especially to fellow Marines."[95] Myers and Pace assumed their new posts on October 1, 2001, only three weeks after the terrorist attacks on 9/11. Rumsfeld had his kind of senior officers in place.

## 9/11 Saves Rumsfeld

By September 2001 relations between Rumsfeld and the military had not improved. One general called him even worse than Les Aspin, Clinton's first secretary of defense.[96] In fact, there was talk about Rumsfeld's replacement—Senator Richard Lugar's name was being floated. On September 8, the Senate Armed Services Committee cut $3.1 billion from Bush's proposed missile-defense program. The Hill seemed as opposed to Rumsfeld and his plans as were the country's senior generals and admirals. To many, his departure seemed to be only a matter of time.

Rumsfeld's standing dropped even further on September 10, when he blasted the Pentagon way of doing things. The occasion was the Defense Department's Acquisition and Logistics Excellence Week. His focus was the process—not the people. As he put it, "The adversary's closer to home. It's the Pentagon bureaucracy. Not the people, but the processes. Not the civilians, but the systems. Not the men and women in uniform, but the uniformity of thought that we too often impose on them."[97] The secretary's problem was that, given the way he had treated the bureaucracy and the military, most listeners could be excused if they took his comments personally. Rumsfeld then announced that the Senior Executive Council, made up of Under Secretary Pete Aldridge, Army Secretary Thomas White, Navy Secretary Gordon England, and Air Force Secretary Jim Roche, would now oversee efforts to improve the Pentagon's work.

The terrorist attacks on September 11, 2001, changed everything. Rumsfeld's image actually benefited from the tragedy. Not only was he pictured on the evening news helping to save those injured at the Pentagon, defense became a matter of major concern to the country, and the idea of changing the secretary of defense at such a critical time was unthinkable.

## The 2001 Quadrennial Defense Review

Although 9/11 upended traditional thinking at the Pentagon, the much-anticipated QDR continued apace. Rumsfeld wrote a foreword to the report, finally published at the end of September, claiming that it had been completed prior to 9/11. He disingenuously asserted, "The attacks confirm the strategic direction and planning principles that resulted from this review."[98]

The QDR approached the question of the two-war scenario by not solving it at all. For example, it read: "The new force-sizing construct specifically shapes forces to: Defend the United States; Deter aggression and coercion forward in critical regions; Swiftly defeat aggression in overlapping major conflicts while preserving for the President the option to call for a decisive victory in one of those conflicts—including the possibility of a regime change or occupation; and Conduct a limited number of smaller-scale contingency operations."[99]

One important aspect of this formulation was that it ignored things like peacekeeping, instead placing primary emphasis on the high end of the scale of possible conflict. Other tasks were mentioned, but the primary goal was to defeat a foe "decisively." However, the QDR did not commit the military to win two major wars decisively, as in the past. Presumably, the authors had in mind a scenario in which the military would engage in a holding action in one case, while winning decisively in the other. This was a change—now the United States did not have to win *decisively* in both. However, the main import of the 2001 QDR was that it did not change matters significantly. As Kagan put it, "Despite all the discussions about how revolutionary the new force-sizing construct was, however, the QDR did not actually recommend *any* significant changes in the actual size, composition, or organization of the U.S. military."[100]

The QDR did announce the creation of a Pentagon Office of Force Transformation, whose director would report directly to the secretary or deputy secretary. This office would oversee transformation efforts, and the services were ordered to develop a number of broad operational goals. If these ends were to be realized, this office would have its hands full monitoring and recommending steps to be taken to integrate transformation activities. "Politically, the QDR placed transformation at the center of U.S. defense planning."[101] This meant that while important questions remained unanswered and unsettled, the issue of transformation would constantly be in the forefront of any discussion. In this sense, it was a partial victory for Rumsfeld, because, if nothing else, it put the military on the defensive. The generals and admirals would constantly find it necessary to explain to the Office of

Transformation why their planned weapons systems or force structure did or did not fit into overall military transformation.

## Going to War and Transformation

Anyone in uniform who hoped that the war in Afghanistan[102] would place military transformation on the back burner would be sadly disappointed. On December 11, 2001, Bush told cadets at the Citadel that the six-week-old war in Afghanistan had shown the need for military transformation. As he put it, "Afghanistan has been a proving ground for this new approach."[103] Then he renewed his commitment to reform, citing "a sense of urgency" based on "the need to build this future force while fighting a present war." He admitted that this would not be easy, likening it to "overhauling an engine while you're going eighty miles an hour." In short, the commander in chief remained a strong supporter of Rumsfeld's transformation policy.

The Pentagon also got into the act when it sent its *Annual Report to the President and the Congress* at the end of 2001. According to one observer, "The language of the report implied an accelerated pace and broadened scope, although the administration announced it would delay making significant programmatic changes until all the commissioned transformation studies were completed, fully analyzed, and utilized to inform a new defense transformation strategy."[104] Despite military opposition and ongoing operations, there was no doubt that Rumsfeld—and Bush—were determined to see this policy implemented.

## Conclusion

Throughout his first year as secretary of defense, Rumsfeld had one overriding policy—military transformation. He sought to turn the military into a twenty-first-century armed force. However, senior military officers resisted, using almost every tool available to them. They went to their friends on the Hill, got others in the defense industries to weigh in, and leaked material to the press to help their cause.

While the military is conservative by nature and often resistant to change, one of the major problems Rumsfeld and his associates faced was a lack of respect for them on the part of the senior brass. And individual staffers, like Cambone, did not even understand what he was talking about, which the brass took as an insult. He was not interested in hearing what they had to say—even though they were the professionals. Rumsfeld made matters worse by interfering in the general and flag officer appointment process. Although he would make mistakes, his message seemed clear—"get me yes-men!"

Rumsfeld's problem was the lack of a meaningful "game plan." To make matters worse, the army did not have enough troops to do the jobs it had been given—and Rumsfeld wanted to disband two divisions! Rumsfeld himself could not fully explain why he wanted to do this. He would herald the use of Special Forces troops on horseback in Afghanistan as a major breakthrough, while at the same time arguing for more emphasis on information technology. Indeed, it was clear to the generals and admirals that Rumsfeld himself did not know what he wanted. Something new, something different, but what did that mean? For officers who were used to following orders, vague instructions were worse than no instructions at all. Horses and computers might go together in Rumsfeld's mind, but that was not the case for most of the senior military.

Unfortunately, Rumsfeld's worst days with the military still lay ahead. Indeed, a good part of 2002 would be spent battling the army, with particular focus on General Shinseki. It was be a very unpleasant experience, one that left a bad taste in the mouths of those who respected Shinseki's honesty and willingness to stand up and be counted when it mattered.

# 3
# Rumsfeld, Reform, and Shinseki

I play my game . . . I play hardball.
  *Donald Rumsfeld*

General Eric Shinseki was Rumsfeld's fiercest critic regarding army issues. Fortunately, Shinseki did not have the volatile temper of some other members of the top brass, like former General Norman Schwarzkopf. As it was, Rumsfeld's handling of Shinseki and one major army weapons program convinced numerous army officers that his hatred of their service knew no bounds. Although he did not know all of the details of transformation, Rumsfeld was certain that Shinseki and the army were not part of his team.

Following 9/11 President George W. Bush said he would ask for the biggest military budget increase since Ronald Reagan's first term—$43 billion in 2003. This included a permanent increase of $38 billion, which would go for pay raises, operations, and procurement, as well as money to support the transformation effort. He also asked for an additional $10 billion as a "war reserve."[1] The latter proposal would not go over very well on Capitol Hill. The idea of the executive having its own wartime "slush fund" raised serious concerns about the separation of powers in the minds of a number of members of Congress.

## Rumsfeld Preaches Reform

Rumsfeld became quite the evangelist for military reform. He never tired of proselytizing his colleagues in uniform. In February, for instance, he urged the generals and admirals to find "'new ways of thinking and new ways of fighting'—and billions of dollars in new spending—to prepare for enemies he said may attack with weapons far deadlier than hijacked airliners."[2] Indeed, he continued to focus on the need for a personal change of heart in dealing with senior officers. Like a convert at a revival, Rumsfeld seemed to expect senior officers to experience a "conversion" to his way of thinking. Indeed, the need for officers to think anew on security issues became a major theme in his discussions of transformation. He was still enamored with the idea of a "U.S. cavalry" in Afghanistan, noting "the creative use of existing weapons and personnel, like the Special Forces soldiers in Afghanistan who, riding horseback, called in precision missile strikes from Air Force, Marine and Navy jets."[3]

In April 2002 Rumsfeld made three grievous violations of military culture. First, he announced that General James Jones, the Marine commandant, would become the top military commander in Europe, a position normally occupied by an army or air force officer. The army generals heard Rumsfeld loud and clear: "I don't have to use you in key positions, I am perfectly capable of putting a Marine in that slot."[4] The appointment only served to fuel the long-standing rivalry between the army and Marine Corps. The army had been put in its place.

Second, as mentioned previously, Rumsfeld leaked his plan to tap General John Keane, Shinseki's chief of staff, to succeed him—fourteen months before Shinseki's tour ended.[5] Such an announcement from a secretary of defense was unprecedented. Essentially, Rumsfeld had told the head of a military service that he was irrelevant. Rumsfeld deliberately turned Shinseki into a "lame duck" because he considered the general to be an uncooperative, old-style thinker not prepared for the twenty-first century. Rumsfeld would later deny that he had intentionally leaked the comment about Keane succeeding Shinseki, but few in the Pentagon believed him. Most thought he did it intentionally in the hope that Shinseki would resign. However, Shinseki refused to step down and continued on as chief of staff of the army.

Then during the first week of May, Marine Lieutenant General Gregory S. Newbold, director of operations on the Joint Staff, became so upset with the way Rumsfeld was handling intelligence matters that he retired. He later became one of the generals who spoke out against Rumsfeld and his handling of the Iraq War in 2006. In the meantime, the Pentagon corridors echoed many of Newbold's complaints. As one reporter noted, "Some in the Pentagon speculated that Newbold was fatigued by Rumsfeld's management style, which has been variously described by Pentagon officials as "hands-on," "brutally honest" and even "abusive."[6] Another general commented, "I widely hear the comparison to McNamara, normally with the caveat that he's much worse than McNamara."[7] From the military's stand-point, a person's reputation could not get any lower.[8]

Rumsfeld, however, was determined to keep the military on a very short leash. This was demonstrated in a public exchange between General Myers and Rumsfeld. The event was a news briefing at the Pentagon. Reporters asked about secret surveillance footage of a missile strike in Afghanistan that had killed a suspected member of al-Qaeda. Myers and Rumsfeld huddled, and then Rumsfeld spoke, saying Myers had asked him, "How far do I go?" Rumsfeld replied "not very." As the reporter who wrote the story noted, this event, like many others, demonstrated that "this administration expects its military brass to be loyal team players and never publicly challenge the civilian leadership."[9] Granted the issue was sensitive, but Myers was the top officer in the U.S. military, yet he still had to get permission from Rumsfeld, a civilian, on what to say. Around this time rumors began circulating inside the Pentagon that officers were complaining about Myers privately (and anonymously). They griped, "He is not squarely on their side when it comes to defending such perquisites as the number of four-star jobs or championing the service's spending requests for weapons."[10] Myers was in a difficult position. Everyone knew that he had been selected because Rumsfeld believed he was "on board" with his program and that he would not stand up strongly or publicly for the military point of view. As a result, every time Rumsfeld did something officers in the Pentagon felt was anti-military, someone would ask, "Where was the Chief?" Many assumed the answer was that he was silent, or that if he objected, he would quickly acquiesce. If anything, Rumsfeld's behavior undermined Myers's ability to lead when he dealt with other generals or admirals.

Strangely, Rumsfeld seemed to take great joy in abusing people. For example, he liked to tell the story of a glass bowl in his office. He told people that if he said anything nice about someone, he had to put a coin in the bowl. And he reveled in the fact that the bowl was almost empty. This approach to management "puzzles some generals that he would take pride in such a hard-line approach."[11] It represented a clear clash of cultures—the military with its formality and politeness at that level versus the "take no prisoners" approach of the business executive. Rumsfeld was convinced that the military had become too independent, and he needed to whip it back into shape at every opportunity.

The 9/11 tragedy did not change Rumsfeld's style of dealing with the military. In fact, James Fallows recounts an incident that took place after 9/11. It demonstrated just how little attention Rumsfeld and his civilian colleagues were paying to the generals. According to Fallows, a man working in the Pentagon told of walking down a hallway and noticing General John

Abizaid, who would succeeded General Tommy Franks in Iraq, standing beside a door. There was a planning session for possible operations in Iraq taking place, but the civilians had told Abizaid he could not participate.[12]

## Cancel the Crusader

Meanwhile, the army and Rumsfeld were about to engage in one of the worst bureaucratic battles of his tenure in the Pentagon. The issue was whether or not to produce a new artillery system: the Crusader. The system was put into development in 1994 because officers believed their Vietnam-era artillery was not as effective as it should be. The Crusader was a 155 millimeter, self-propelled howitzer. It could be driven into battle, not towed, and it could fire 10–12 rounds per minute, "or three times as many as the system it would replace, known as the Paladin. The Crusader could hit targets 30 miles away, compared with Paladin's range of about 19 miles."[13] As Shinseki would point out to Congress, this new artillery piece was desperately needed because units in the field normally have to wait about 25 minutes between the time they call for air support and when it gets there.[14] With the Crusader, artillery would be on the battlefield with the troops—available at a minute's notice. As one general put it, "If you're an infantryman, and you're standing on a hilltop and you call in close air support, you can be waiting for up to an hour to get that. . . . And when you're in combat, minutes turn into hours. It becomes a like ordering a pizza from a subcontractor on a Saturday night."[15] Many in the army believed that Rumsfeld had decided that artillery was no longer critical and was intentionally downplaying its role. "To soldiers this seems unfathomable. Artillery fire is accurate, long-range, and continuous—three things indispensable on the battlefield that really aren't found together in any other land weapon."[16] Many officers found this whole discussion confusing. Rumsfeld's comments made no sense, but of course he was not going to be called upon to go to war, and sit in a fox hole watching over his soldiers as shells rained down, wondering where the air support was.

Rumsfeld claimed he was not opposed to artillery. However, he saw a number of flaws with the Crusader. First, it would have been a follow-on to the current artillery pieces in use, something that Rumsfeld opposed in principle. He also believed that the $11 billion allocated for the Crusader could be better spent on developing next-generation weapons. More important, Crusader opponents pointed out that the original model could only be transported by ships or very large cargo planes, although there had been improvements in the weapons system. For example, Shinseki had ordered the Crusader to be reconfigured and its weight cut in half. Now it could be carried by a C-17 transport plane. But Rumsfeld was still not happy.

He and his supporters pointed to the Crusader's accompanying ammunition carrier, which weighed 30 tons, arguing that both the Crusader and its ammunition carrier would be too heavy for local roads and bridges. It was designed to face the Russians in a war in Europe, and it was not the kind of highly mobile weapon Rumsfeld wanted. It could be moved, but not easily transported from one place to another. Paul Wolfowitz summed up Rumsfeld's position when he stated, "The decision is not about killing a bad system. This decision is about canceling a system originally designed for a different strategic context, to make room for more promising technologies that offer greater payoffs, and are more consistent with the army's transformation effort."[17] Rumsfeld canceled the program even though it had been recommended for full funding—$475 million in the president's 2003 budget. Indeed, he believed this was a test of his bureaucratic strength and credibility. He had to prove that he could take on the army, Congress, and the defense lobby and win.

Rumsfeld and Wolfowitz handled cancellation of the Crusader in a very crude way. For example, on May 2 the deputy secretary told army leaders that they had thirty days to defend the Crusader—or to propose alternatives. Reportedly, the conversation went as follows:

> Wolfowitz summoned Army Secretary Thomas White and told him point blank, "We're canceling Crusader."
>
> "Please give me thirty days to make one more study," countered White.
>
> "OK," said Wolfowitz.
>
> After White left, one of Wolfowitz's aides, who had been listening to the conversation, pointed out, "Now, you're going to have to go and tell Rumsfeld that you've changed your mind and given him thirty days." An unhappy Wolfowitz trudged off to break the news.[18]

Given Wolfowitz's comment, the army mistakenly believed that the issue was still in play. Meanwhile, the army's Office of Congressional Liaison had prepared talking points in response to a congressional request. The talking points argued the merits of the Crusader, while making the point that the Paladin was obsolete. It maintained, "Soldiers would die in combat if the system were cancelled." The talking points soon leaked, which infuriated Rumsfeld. He warned the army that the Pentagon was looking into reports that army officers had personally lobbied their friends on the Hill. A secretary of defense, as he put it, should "be able to expect the leadership and overwhelming majority [of the army] will in fact be supportive."[19]

The question then focused on Army Secretary White. He was clearly on the army's side in this debate, and rumors began to circulate that his job could be on the line.[20] White, however, stated that he had no intention of resigning. But on May 7, while Rumsfeld blasted those army officers who had lobbied Congress, he exempted White. Instead, he expressed confidence in him. However, Rumsfeld made it clear that he felt, "Some individuals in the army were way in the dickens out of line."[21]

The House took up the issue on May 10, approving a massive increase in military spending, including funds for the Crusader. The spending bill was approved 359–58. The White House Budget Office said it would call for a veto if funds for the Crusader were included.[22]

On May 16, Shinseki and Rumsfeld went before the Senate Armed Services Committee to discuss the Crusader. They were once again at loggerheads. Rumsfeld said the $9 billion left over from canceling the Crusader would be utilized to develop two alternative artillery systems that were lighter and were capable of firing precision-guided munitions, such as the Excalibur, which has a shell that is guided to its target by satellites and can be easily transported. The other was a multiple-launch rocket system, also easily transportable.[23] In his words, "Skipping Crusader to emphasize precision munitions and rocket systems does not put U.S. forces at risk, as some have suggested. . . . Rather, it will reduce future risk and speed the introduction of other systems."[24] And then bringing in his own heavy artillery, he added, "The president . . . is solidly behind this decision; there is no ambiguity."[25]

When he had his turn, Shinseki defiantly stated, "Abrupt program termination would expose U.S. ground troops to more risk while a new generation of weaponry is being developed. That window of risk is extended now until we find a replacement version."[26] Despite Shinseki's courageous comments, the army had been muzzled. At this point an alliance of industrial firms that stood to lose a lot of money in the $11 billion deal created a "Crusader Industrial Alliance." It lobbied the Hill while also running ads pointing out that defense officials believed the system was crucial. Then Rumsfeld decided to finally cancel it, far short of the thirty days he had promised and without warning the army in advance.[27]

### Get New Army Secretary

White's problems went beyond the Pentagon. Most important, he was being challenged by consumer advocate Ralph Nader, who accused him of having a conflict of interest because he was conducting business with his old company, Enron. While he recused himself from dealing with army contracts, he was involved in the privatization of energy sources at army installations, which involved millions of dollars.[28]

Meanwhile, the secretary was getting tired of White's constant support for the army. White not only clashed with Rumsfeld over the Crusader, they also locked horns over the Stryker brigades, primarily made up of Stryker combat vehicles, which were fast, quiet, and could carry fourteen soldiers. They also disagreed about General Shinseki, as White refused to discipline the general for his comments on the number of troops needed for an invasion of Iraq.[29] Although service secretaries had disagreed with the secretary of defense in the past, Rumsfeld would have none of it. "He expected the secretaries, who are civilians appointed by the defense secretary, to be agents of change, serving to push the somewhat recalcitrant military branches into shedding old ways of fighting and obsolete weapons systems."[30] From White's perspective, the problem was that Rumsfeld was convinced that he and Shinseki were opposed to transformation, which was not the case. The problem was that they strongly opposed Rumsfeld's version of military transformation. They believed that he did not recognize the importance of having an army that could fight against large land forces, nor did he understand the problems the army faced in occupying and pacifying a country like Iraq in the postwar period. Coming up with new high-tech weapons was fine, provided that, in the meantime, the United States maintained sufficient military strength to protect its interests. Convinced that he had lost his war with Rumsfeld, White resigned on April 25. Rumsfeld then announced that Secretary of the Air Force James G. Roche would succeed White. This too was seen by many as a slap at Shinseki and the army, because Roche was a retired naval officer. "His selection appeared to signal that Rumsfeld is determined to impose sweeping changes on the army, which he has come to see as the most resistant of the services to his agenda."[31]

## Reject the Stryker Brigades

When he took over as the army chief of staff, General Shinseki began to search for a new weapon, one that would be small enough to be transported by air (22 tons), yet fast enough (65 mph) to provide the mobility and speed needed on the modern battlefield. He wanted a weapon that would serve as a bridge between legacy and objectives forces. It would fill the gap between the heavy-weapons systems, which were powerful yet difficult to move, and the light ones that were highly mobile but too lightly armored to be of use on the battlefield. The answer was the eight-wheeled Stryker, which was based on one of the Marine's light armored vehicles used in Operation Desert Storm. It could be used to transport troops (fourteen at a time) from one position to another before the enemy could react. It would be useful both for peacekeeping as well as urban warfare. The first 300 Strykers were sent to Fort Lewis, Washington, where the army set up two interim brigade combat teams. Each unit would have 3,500 soldiers. Shinseki specified that the army must be able to deploy them anywhere in the world in ninety-six hours.

Shinseki also had critics within the army, who maintained that, by placing emphasis on these lightly armored vehicles, the general was endangering the average soldier. The weapon that protected the soldier was tanks. How would Shinseki's plan enable them to counter the threat posed by the enemy's tanks on the battlefield? The answer was speed. They would be able to move into—and out of—a combat area very quickly before a tank could respond. In any case, in November 2000 the Pentagon signed a contract with a consortium led by General Motors and General Dynamics, calling for the production of 2,131 Strykers.[32]

At first the Rumsfeld regime did not seem to support the Strykers. This reaction puzzled the army brass, as the Stryker was the first building block in Shinseki's effort to transform the army from a Cold War focus to one more suited for the twenty-first century. It filled the gap while the army was developing objective weapons systems, plus it was fast, deployable, and the troops liked it. The whole idea of eliminating the Stryker was absurd, because the army was following Rumsfeld's order by developing deployable, fast weapons systems that were not just modifications of existing weapons.

However, Rumsfeld was determined to gain control over the army's efforts to modernize itself. So he ordered Stephen Cambone to convince the generals to back down and cancel the Strykers. Cambone faced a difficult situation; most of the generals despised him—and they did not like Rumsfeld, either. According to one report, "A lot of generals and admirals in the Pentagon don't think much of Donald Rumsfeld." In their opinion, neither the secretary nor Cambone knew much about military transformation. Cambone, who had never even served in uniform, was telling senior officers what kind of weapons the army needed, with the invasion of Iraq looming. Cambone's ignorance combined with Rumsfeld's own ignorance and personality—reports continued to come in calling him "abusive and indecisive"[33]—did not make for a positive relationship. Personality, however, was only one part of the war between Rumsfeld and the army. The generals had learned how to put up with such individuals a long time ago. This time, however, the concern was substantive. For example, *Defense News* reported that army generals were "fuming." They had realized that the war over the Stryker was part of a bigger plot by Department of Defense officials to raid their budget to pay for other projects. According to this report, Cambone's goal was to save "$10 billion" a year by taking the following steps:

- eliminate funds for the Fourth, Fifth, and Sixth Stryker Brigades,
- delay fielding the Future Combat Systems (FCS) program—the center-piece of the army objective force—by two years, from 2008 to 2010,
- reduce the number of RAH-66 Comanche helicopters the army buys, and
- slash funding for the non-line-of-sight cannon system.[34]

Faced with Cambone's attempt to cut the number of Strykers, the army set up a demonstration of the Stryker's mobility in front of Cambone and former House Speaker Newt Gingrich (R-GA) at Andrews Air Force Base. A C-130 transport plane "pulled up in front of a large hanger in the rain, dropped its ramp and off-loaded a Stryker and all its gear, plus two crew members and nine infantrymen. All in eight minutes."[35] A few minutes later a C-17 arrived and three Strykers sped out of the plane toward the officers and congressional staffers.

Shinseki also reportedly met with Rumsfeld. To his credit, the quiet, diplomatic Shinseki stood up to Rumsfeld using what one source called "uncharacterically strong public language."[36] Shinseki also defended the Stryker Brigades in a speech to the Association of the United States Army. As he explained, "We must see the Stryker fielded to provide soldiers the capabilities that they've needed for the last 12 years. It's time and the right number is six."[37] The airport demonstration, together with Shinseki's actions (and presumably calls from the Hill), were enough to get Rumsfeld to back down. The next month it was reported that "the army finally won one." Rumsfeld decided to spare the other three brigades.[38]

The Stryker decision was a symbolic victory for the army, because it demonstrated that it was possible to reach common ground with Rumsfeld. Shinseki had won this battle. Had he lost, the message to the army would have been—you are totally incapable of producing a weapons system that is relevant in the era of military transformation. That was not a message Rumsfeld wanted to send.

The average soldier was happy with the Stryker. One reporter, who said he had carried out more than a dozen interviews, stated, "Commanders, soldiers, and mechanics who use the Stryker fleet daily in one of Iraq's most dangerous areas unanimously praised the vehicle."[39] In another report soldiers compared its ride to a cross-town bus because of its rubber tires. Its speed also drew attention, because it gave the soldiers an advantage in hit-and-run battles with insurgents.[40] It is far better armored and stronger than the Humvees. Strykers are also relatively quiet, which gives them a stealth advantage. Insurgents often do not know they are there until the vehicles have already arrived and left. Shinseki's Stryker paid off handsomely in terms of saving soldiers' lives.

## Afghanistan Opportunities

Rumsfeld was very upbeat about the Afghan War's implications for the future of military transformation.[41] His key point was not that he thought the future of the army lay in the use of horses to fight such a war. Rather, he was pleased that the army had come up with new ways of thinking. Although few of the troops had been trained to use horses, they did what was necessary.[42] Rumsfeld hoped that such creative thinking and adaptability would lead the generals to be more accommodating regarding transformation.

Rumsfeld also used the Afghan War to emphasize the importance and value of moving away from the old "threat-based" approach. Instead of asking who threatens us, he maintained, it was time to begin asking how we might be threatened and what the United States must do to deal with those threats. He wanted the military to examine vulnerabililties, anticipate enemy actions, and look beyond traditional conventional warfare. Rumsfeld believed that transformation was not an event, "It is an ongoing process. There will be no point at which we can declare that U.S. forces have been 'transformed.'"[43]

Specifically, Rumsfeld emphasized the importance of shifting the balance between manned and unmanned capabilities. The same was true of short- and long-range systems, stealth systems, and hardened and vulnerable systems. Rumsfeld continued to harp on the need for the United States to rethink how to fight a war. He wanted the military to borrow the "entrepreneurial" approach from business, because it pushes people toward being proactive rather than reactive. Despite the war on terrorism, Rumsfeld also would not accept the idea that the United States should stop trying to transform its military. "Some believe that, with the United States in the midst of a dangerous war on terrorism, now is not the time to transform the U.S. armed forces," he said. "I believe the opposite is true: Now is precisely the time to make major changes."[44]

Rumsfeld's call for transformation to take place during one war—even a limited one—and during preparations for another, put the military in a very difficult position. As Kagan observed, "These ongoing operations and threats have combined to stretch the U.S. armed forces beyond the breaking point. The army has been compelled to deploy tens of thousands of soldiers for a full year at a time rather than the normal six months, to forgo important training for those soldiers, and sometimes to send soldiers returning from one such deployment immediately to another."[45]

Unfortunately, developing new weapons and the procedures for using them is a slow and tedious process. It involves repeated testing in addition to training soldiers how to use the new weapons and equipment. To try to do that while conducting military operations in Afghanistan, and training the next rotation for that war, puts the armed forces under considerable pressure. The army brass were not only expected to move and deploy troops and weapons systems over great distances while planning for a new war, they were also trying to convince the secretary of defense that the military was transiting from legacy weapons to objective weapons. And to make matters even more interesting, in his June 10, 2002, speech to the graduates of West Point, the president announced the United States was moving away from its old Cold War doctrine of deterrence and containment toward one that permitted preemptive action against states or terrorist groups if they were developing chemical, biological, or nuclear weapons.[46] Bush was arguing that the United States had the right to preempt; that is, to use force if it had good reason to believe that the other side (whether a state or a terrorist organization) was planning to attack it.

## Test Future Combat Systems

In addition to the Stryker, General Shinseki had an important role in the development of the future combat systems (FCS) program. At Shinseki's insistence, the army devoted considerable time and effort to creating a battlefield combat system that would meet Rumsfeld's demands. A specific definition of FCS is difficult because the program is still in development and because the army itself has not thoroughly considered the issue. Nevertheless, one source defined it as follows: "The Future Combat Systems will develop the capacity to rapidly project a dominant ground force everywhere in the world within days."[47] Another source tied it to network-centric warfare: "It changes the way commanders look at their armies. Instead of a contest of numbers (my 3,000 troops can beat your 1,000 troops), the U.S. Army becomes one entity with many parts that can shift and adapt to quickly changing situations. Information is shared across the entire network."[48]

FCS is based on a family of vehicles and consists of four distinct components:

1. System of systems/common operating environment
2. Battle command
3. Software, communications, and computers
4. Intelligence, reconnaissance, and surveillance

These four components are all linked and interact synergistically to enable the U.S. force to see the other side, while concealed, and to act first with devastating results.

To be effective, however, the FCS concept must satisfy three requirements. It must be able to

1. Balance sustained lethality, survivability, and deployability
2. Reduce strategic lift requirements to move and sustain the force and
3. Provide battlefield awareness at all levels of command through secure, digitized communications.[49]

One of the key problems is networking. FCS uses a combination of remote sensors, unmanned aerial vehicles, and ground vehicles to help troops see the battlefield. For example, as an enemy approaches an area where FCS is deployed, unmanned aircraft could provide information on the enemy to carefully hidden U.S. forces. In theory, the enemy force would be wiped out before U.S. forces even came into range of the enemy's weapons. Essentially, they would not know what hit them.

But there are tremendous problems with this model. For example, to be as effective as an armored M1 tank, the FCS deployment would have to have almost perfect intelligence and disseminate it accurately and instantaneously. No one is quite sure that this is really possible.

The airpower enthusiasts would need such intelligence to target the enemy systems effectively, but army units would require it merely to survive on the battlefield. Even if they did survive, moreover, they would contribute few capabilities that airpower did not already provide, considering that they could not get close to the enemy or even safely occupy positions within range of the enemy's weapons systems.[50]

This strategy also assumes that it is possible to make the battlefield completely predictable and to have intelligence and weapons systems that operate perfectly. However, is it reckless to create an army that is no longer capable of engaging in close combat? In any case, much of the material needed to make the FCS a success has not been developed, let alone weaponized. To be successful, a number of scientific breakthroughs are required. "It is to be the army's major research, development and acquisition program [and] to consist of 18 manned and unmanned systems tied together by an extensive communications network. FCS is intended to replace such current systems as M-1 Abrams tanks and M-2 Bradley infantry fighting vehicles."[51] This is a very ambitious undertaking.

## Push to Increase Budget

As the war in Iraq approached, military transformation tended to recede to the background, despite Rumsfeld's constant effort to keep it in the public eye. He was not about to give up, although in some ways the battle became even more difficult. Rumsfeld's budget proposals are a good indicator of the progress toward transformation. They certainly show what Rumsfeld and his associates thought they could get away with.

The Pentagon's proposed budget for 2002, dubbed "the first true 'transformation defense budget'" by its proponents, called for funding two new, expensive items. The first line item was satellites, including one that carried communications via laser beams. The second item was radar ground surveillance.[52] Rumsfeld's influence was clear, but, at the same time, "Rumsfeld has lowered his sights, and the military has generally accelerated its efforts to change."[53]

Nevertheless, Rumsfeld and the military would battle over three different weapons systems in the coming years. The first flashpoint was the air force's F/A-22 fighter plane, even though the Pentagon had made it clear that it would cancel a number of them. This aircraft had been in development for twenty-three years, a considerable investment of time, effort, and money that could not be cancelled without careful consideration. The other two systems were the navy's next-generation aircraft carrier and the long-troubled V-22 Osprey troop transport, used primarily by the Marines.

## Use Special Operations Forces

Rumsfeld strongly supported special operations forces. As noted previously, he liked their performance in Afghanistan and he liked their non-traditional, non-conventional way of fighting. He also favored them because he was so frustrated with the intelligence agencies—especially the CIA—and what he saw as their inability to do their job. Rumsfeld believed that the military must assume a larger role in the so-called black world of covert operations. He was convinced that a number of political leaders, starting with Saddam Hussein, were up to no good; yet the CIA seemed either unable or incapable of finding out what was happening in the world.

As a consequence, the special operations community was expanded and given broader authority. For example, Rumsfeld approved giving the Special Operations Command (SOCOM) expanded authority to plan and fight the global war on terrorism. In addition, "The Pentagon will give the command $7 billion to buy equipment and aircraft, and to accommodate 4,000 more personnel."[54] Bureaucratically, this meant that SOCOM would have more independence in planning and carrying out operations. Traditionally SOCOM personnel were sent in when requested by combatant commanders. Now they were permitted to act independently. Thus, if intelligence sources spot terrorists in Yemen or Somalia, SOCOM did not have to clear the operation with CENTCOM. It could independently carry out an operation to neutralize the threat. There was one exception—a regional war. In that case the SOCOM forces would be subordinated to the combatant commander. Regional and SOCOM forces would continue to work closely together regardless of the situation. For example, each of these commanders had his own special operations forces, which worked closely with SOCOM on specific joint covert operations. Then Rumsfeld announced that he had given the power to the nation's covert forces to kill and capture al-Qaeda operatives and other terrorists. He was deadly serious about the increased importance of special operations forces. He was out to prove that warfare was no longer the kind of large-scale linear warfare conducted by traditional conventional forces such as tanks and armored personnel carriers. These units would be small, but with highly trained personnel, men able to exist and fight in very difficult conditions around the world.

## Iraq and Military Transformation

Rumsfeld and his supporters were euphoric over the invasion of Iraq. They maintained that it demonstrated the efficacy of their strategy of military transformation.[55] Indeed, the day Baghdad fell, Vice President Dick Cheney declared that the victory was "proof positive of the success of our efforts to transform the military." Cambone also commented, "What you see in Iraq in its embryonic form is the kind of warfare that is animating our desire to transform the force."[56] For his part, Rumsfeld maintained that the war showed that the path to victory was not through "overwhelming force," as had been the case in the 1991 Gulf War. Mass, in the form of troops and weapons systems, was no longer the key to victory. There were only 100,000 American troops on the ground when Baghdad fell.[57] General Tommy Franks, the combatant commander, added that this campaign had validated the new type of warfare. The only task left was to improve the process.[58] Wolfowitz also proclaimed that the new strategy had won the war. He claimed that networking and communication technologies had provided soldiers and Marines with instantaneous access to air power, allowing U.S. troops to advance so fast.[59]

Studies done by the army raise serous questions about the claims by Rumsfeld and his colleagues regarding the value of military transformation in the Iraq War. One of these, headed by Stephen Biddle, then at the U.S. Army War College, was so critical that the army refused to release it, even though there was nothing classified in it. It was later leaked and is now available. The army was concerned that Rumsfeld would get upset over the study, because it stressed the continuing importance of legacy systems in any combat situation. The study points out that one of the reasons why the high-tech military did so well in Iraq was the lack of skill on the part of the opponent. "The Iraqis' shortcomings created a permissive environment for coalition technology that a more skilled opponent elsewhere might not." It then blasted Rumsfeld's approach noting, "This explanation holds some very different implications for transformation than the 'speed, precision, and situational awareness' view now commonplace in accounts of the war."[60] Translation: legacy systems played a critical role in the Iraq War.

Biddle's study was followed by the official army history of the campaign, which found major problems with interoperability, which in turn undercut the effectiveness of network-centric warfare. "The efficacy of net-enabled means to clear artillery fires did not apply to clearing CAS [close air support]. CAS was available, responsive, and effective during OIF [Operation Iraqi Freedom]; but generally speaking, clearing CAS was not enabled."[61] As far as interoperability was concerned, the authors noted,

> Major General [James] "Spider" Marks recalled that at one point, he and Major General [Jim] "Tamer" Amos, commanding the third Marine Air Wing, became action officers, passing images that Amos and the Marines required, because Marks could not do so digitally. Similarly, at one point the Marines generated great data from one of their unmanned aerial vehicles, which V Corps needed but could not access since it had no means to link up to the data stream.[62]

These criticisms are not intended to demean the accomplishment of the soldiers, sailors, airmen, and Marines on the ground. Their dash to Baghdad was impressive and let the rest of the world know that the U.S. military was not a force to trifle with. Rather, the point is that the claim by General Franks and civilian authorities that transformation was the key to victory in Operation Iraqi Freedom is simply not justified by the facts. There are numerous problems with this argument. First, often one or more of the systems did not work. Second, the Iraqi army was no match for the U.S. military in terms of morale, equipment, training, or any other dimension. Kagan got it right: "The wars in Iraq and Afghanistan do not prove that network-centric warfare does not work any more than they prove that it does. Since neither one was really fought by a military that actually had the full range of promised NCW techniques, neither one really tested the concept at all."[63] Indeed, Rumsfeld's determination to show off his high-tech weapons was a major reason for many of the problems the United States encountered after it defeated the Iraqi army and occupied the country.

Despite all of the problems noted above in Operation Iraqi Freedom, Rumsfeld was determined to push ahead with his transformation plans. His primary focus was on the size of army units, in particular the divisions. Rumsfeld and his colleagues saw these as one of the major reasons for the army's problems. The divisions, which normally contained 15,000–20,000 troops, were slow moving. They were structured to fight one enemy—the Soviet Union, but now the Cold War was history. The new goal was to set up "battle groups," replacing the army's ten divisions with some thirty battle groups. Rumsfeld believed battle groups would be better able to fight jointly with the air force, Marines, and navy.[64]

*Get New Army Chief of Staff*

Shinseki further alienated Rumsfeld with his outspoken opposition to the secretary's efforts to keep the invasion force in Iraq small. He twice testified on the Hill that the United States and its allies would need "several hundred thousand" troops.[65] Then, in another unprecedented move, Shinseki refused to invite either Rumsfeld or Wolfowitz to his retirement ceremony. Furthermore, Shinseki did not mention Rumsfeld by name in his retirement remarks, although he clearly had him in mind when he said, "We understand that leadership is not an exclusive function of uniformed service. . . . So when some suggest that we in the army don't understand the importance of civilian control of the military, well, that's just not helpful and it isn't true."[66]

Rumsfeld managed to ruffle many feathers when it came time to name Shinseki's replacement. He first offered the position to three army generals: Tommy Franks, John Abizaid, and John Keane. They all declined. Franks wanted to retire, Abizaid wanted to become CENTCOM, and Keane supposedly declined for personal reasons.[67] Then instead of looking elsewhere among army generals, he recalled a former special operations officer, General Peter J. Schoomaker, from retirement to active duty. Such an action was almost unheard of in the army. However, Rumsfeld's action was consistent with his desire to "break china" by doing things differently. The *Washington Post* quoted one unidentified senior officer who said, "Rumsfeld is essentially rejecting all three- and four-star generals in the army . . . undermining them by saying, in effect, they aren't good enough to lead the service."[68]

One of Schoomaker's first acts was to change the army's transformation plan. First, he redesignated the objective force initiative as the "future force." Then he placed emphasis on "the fielding of useful FCS program capabilities as soon as they became available. This meant that, instead of waiting a decade or more before they could be integrated into other FCS platforms and technologies under development,"[69] they would be used as they became available. Furthermore, Schoomaker shifted emphasis in the FCS program from the FCS platforms themselves to emphasizing the various networks linking army units together, a problem identified during the invasion of Iraq.

From the standpoint of Rumsfeld's efforts to transform the military, the 2003 budgetary process looked good. For example, the budget passed by the House on July 9, 2003, included $1.7 billion for the FCS; $35 billion for the Stryker Brigade Combat Teams; $4.2 billion for the Joint Strike Fighter; $158 million for the navy's Littoral Combat Ship; and $100 million to "accelerate the development and procurement of the [Air Force's] next generation bomber."[70] It also included $4.6 billion for Special Operations Forces, a major increase in its budget.

Despite Congress's willingness to purchase the kind of weapons systems favored by Rumsfeld, the active duty army's ability to fight the real, not imaginary, war was suffering. In December 2003, for example, 40 percent of the active duty force was declared not fully combat ready. It would take up to six months to get them to that point, thereby leaving the "nation with relatively few ready troops in the event of a major conflict in North Korea or elsewhere. . . . Once these divisions return from Iraq, army readiness will be at its lowest point since the end of the 1991 Persian Gulf War."[71] New weapons were a good thing, but in the meantime, the Iraq War was wearing out the army's personnel and equipment.

Despite problems with the Iraq War, the Hill continued to support Rumsfeld's efforts to transform the military. The FY 2004 budget, presented to the Hill by the executive branch, called for major increases. Thus, money for the air force increased by 5.3 percent; the navy/Marine Corps budget increased by 3.1 percent; while the army's budget went up by 3.3 percent. Significantly, Rumsfeld's favorite—the Special Operations Forces—again saw their budget increased, this time by more than 57 percent.[72] In May the House and Senate endorsed the Bush administration's budget. "Lawmakers said the advanced hardware and military staffing that the bills will provide were justified, as the nation prepared for an extended campaign against terrorists."[73]

## Cancel the Comanche

Rumsfeld did not force the army to cancel the Comanche reconnaissance helicopter. The program had been in trouble for a long time, taking twenty-one years and $6.9 billion to produce. Another problem was that this helicopter was designed for use against the Soviet Union. "When the Comanche was conceived in 1983, the army faced a far different threat. Army officials were eager for a lightweight, stealthy helicopter that would be able to move ahead of large tank formations in a conventional war to gather and distribute intelligence and attack the enemy."[74] Unlike with the Crusader, there was no bitterness toward Rumsfeld and his associates regarding the cancellation of this weapons system. The army itself realized that the concept—a helicopter that could deal with high-tech anti-aircraft missiles and artillery—was no longer needed, and continuing to pour money into it made no sense. The army promised that $14 billion allocated to the project between 2004 and 2011 would be reprogrammed to other army aviation programs.[75]

*Redesign the Army*

Schoomaker agreed with Rumsfeld's argument that the army needed to be broken up into smaller units, dubbed "units of action." As Schoomaker put it, "We will not be effective and relevant in the twenty-first century unless we become much more agile, but with the capacity for a long-term, sustained level of conflicts."[76] Toward this end, he decided that the total number of soldiers would remain the same in the army. However, instead of being organized by divisions, they would be placed in smaller brigades. These maneuver units would be assigned support units, an important change. In the past, support units, such as military police, had to be added at the last minute to a division to enable it to go to war. Now they would be an integral part of the unit of action so that they could be immediately deployed. This meant breaking up the army's ten divisions into 33–48 combat brigades.[77] Instead of divisions with nearly 20,000 soldiers, the army's main combat units would have only 3,500.

During the summer of 2004, Schoomaker published an article with Les Brownlee, then acting secretary of the army. In it, he laid down his primary concerns: "The foundations of Army Transformation must be diversity and adaptability. The Army must retain a wide range of capabilities while significantly improving its agility and versatility. Building a joint and expeditionary Army with campaign qualities will require versatile forces that can mount smaller, shorter duration operations routinely—without penalty to the Army's capacity for larger, more protracted campaigns."[78]

Overall, Schoomaker's actions meant that heavy-armor units, like heavy artillery units, would become less important—a major change from the Cold War era. Instead, the Special Operations Forces and the army's smaller brigades would become increasingly important. Instead of linear conflict, the military now had to prepare for non-linear conflict, including political conflicts, insurgencies, and peacekeeping operations. Indeed, Larry Sequist was right when he observed that in Iraq the military learned that "the nature of conflict has changed and that our military doesn't perform very well in these circumstances."[79]

Experts were divided about how much the military had really transformed by late 2004. Some, like James Carafano, thought very little had changed. Carafano, a retired military officer at the Heritage Foundation, in reference to the Pentagon's Office of Force Transformation, argued, "Its hard to pin down anything concrete that has come out of this office," while retired colonel Douglas Macgregor commented, "Apart from better linking of military data networks, the armed forces have largely ignored [Transition Director Admiral Arthur] Cebrowski's efforts."[80] At the same time, there were reports that civilian officials in the Pentagon were considering ways to continue the shift in spending away from programs dedicated to larger-scale conflict in favor of more agile, specialized units able to fight guerrilla wars, confront terrorism, and handle less conventional threats.

## Anticipate Review Problems

By late 2004 many in the Pentagon had come to realize that the costs of the wars in Iraq and Afghanistan were getting in the way of Rumsfeld's transformation efforts. To jump start the process, Rumsfeld set up six panels. He had learned his lesson from his experience with the first set of panels he created. This time he included both senior civilians and senior military officers. The panels concentrated on Washington's ability to respond to threats in four areas: Islamic extremism, the proliferation of weapons of mass destruction, the military's role in homeland security, and its ability to deal with the disruptive threats and conventional military of an emerging power.[81] In other words, primary focus should be on dealing with unconventional threats. The QDR also mentioned Rumsfeld's efforts to transform the military and called for changes across the board, not only improving technology but enhancing the way the Pentagon did business. The focus was on increasing efficiency.

At the same time, the Pentagon issued Department of Defense Directive 3000.05, which was based on the Iraqi experience. Its focus was on the significance of "stability operations" (the combination of Phases III and IV, a decision taken after the Iraq War). In addition, the QDR put creating stability on the same level as war fighting.[82] On the negative side, from Rumsfeld's standpoint, it did not suggest eliminating any existing weapons systems. One of the shortcomings of the 2005 QDR was that while it defined the kinds of threats the services must deal with, and endorsed elements such as Special Operations Forces and troops trained in psychological warfare and civil affairs, it said little about how the United States was to go about achieving victory, or what weapons systems would be best able to do the job. One reason Rumsfeld had less influence on the document than he had in 2001 was the war in Iraq. To quote a former Pentagon official, "In

2001, you couldn't make a major decision without Secretary Rumsfeld in the room. . . . This time, he didn't take the hands-on role that he did in 2001."[83] The disorganized way in which the QDR included—and excluded—items led one critic to call it a "hodgepodge." Some from category A, some from B, and a bit more from C.[84] Not only was it unsystematic in its approach to what to include and exclude, there were few major changes in it.[85]

## Sticky Systems

By 2006 a few things were becoming clear. First, no matter how hard he tried, Rumsfeld was unable to get rid of some weapons systems he believed did not fit into his idea of a twenty-first century military. One of the best examples is the air force's F-22 Raptor. For five years Rumsfeld had done everything in his power to eliminate the F-22 program. He believed the program's budgeted $65 billion could be spent better on his new transformational systems. In 2004 the administration told Congress it planned to cut the program in order to stanch the deficit and the costs of the war in Iraq. The plan failed, and the F-22 was saved somehow. Another policy channel dealt with the C-130J—the workhorse of the air force. It had so many flaws "that it cannot fly its intended combat missions."[86] But Congress put that line item back in the defense budget. Again in May 2006, the Pentagon could not convince the Hill and its supporters at Boeing to stop with the 180th plane, fulfilling the current contract, because there were too many jobs at stake. The same was true of the F-22 Raptor. It was still in the 2006 budget thanks to lobbying by the air force, Lockheed Martin, and their allies in Congress. The point is not the utility of these weapons, only that they demonstrated the limits on Rumsfeld's ability to reshape the budget.

## Technology and Realism—The FCS

The future of transformational weapons systems such as the army's FCS remain very much in doubt because they are heavily dependent on the size of the defense budget and the speed of technological innovations. A careful examination of the period between 2002 and 2007 shows just how difficult it was to develop and deploy such weapons. For example, the original plan called for the first unit to be equipped with the FCS Unit of Action in 2012. The army expected to have thirty-two fully equipped brigades by fiscal 2014.[87] The five areas where work was to be accelerated were: "the non-line-of-sight cannon, the non-line-of-sight launch system, the unattended ground sensors, two classes of unmanned aerial vehicles, and armed robotic vehicles."[88] But no one could predict when there would be a technological breakthrough in something like sensors, cannons, and robotic vehicles, or how much it will cost. One source pointed out that whereas the estimated cost of FCS was $175 billion in May 2003, by 2006 the cost would be up to $307.2 billion over its entire lifetime.[89]

In 2007—after Rumsfeld had left the Pentagon—reports emerged that the FCS had once again been redesigned. Four of the original eighteen systems were being deferred (i.e., the heavy armed robotic vehicle system, the intelligent munitions system, and two types of unmanned aerial vehicles). In addition, the timeframe for the army to field the fifteen FCS brigade combat teams had been stretched from ten to fifteen years, starting in 2015.[90]

## Control the Budget Process

The budget process controls military assets, and Rumsfeld realized he needed to control the purse strings. Normally, each service submits a Program Objective Memorandum (POM) to the secretary's office, outlining how much money it needs to meet its obligations for the next fiscal year. The secretary and his staff review the forms, and then the Department of Defense submits a final budget request to the White House and Congress.

However, in September 2006, the army was told that its share of the defense budget would be $113.8 billion. The army strongly objected and put forth a budget request of $138.8 billion. The army's argument was that it was already short $50 billion when 9/11 occurred, and it needed at least $17.1 billion just to repair and replace equipment worn out in Iraq.[91] Instead of pressing for the additional funds, Rumsfeld told Schoomaker to try to get the money himself from the White House and Congress—in essence giving up the budgetary battle by delegating budgetary authority to the army's chief of staff.

## Conclusion

Unlike General Shinseki, Rumsfeld's impact on military transformation when he left office in November 2006 was more negative than positive. Rumsfeld made several important contributions to the U.S. armed forces. First, he pushed the army to become more deployable by promoting the FCS approach. Full realization of the concept is far off, but the idea of having units better linked to each other is first-rate. Better communications can improve warfare. Second, his idea of having modular brigades will make it easier to send the right mix of weapons for a given situation. Being forced to send an entire division of 20,000 troops in the past often created a situation in which the United States arrived too late with too much. This was especially true with the Afghan war, when only a few, well-trained special operations forces were available for Phase III. Third, the greater emphasis he placed on special operations forces was long overdue. Armor, artillery, and infantry officers often saw little or no need for large numbers of such troops, yet there were many cases in fighting unconventional wars where special forces were much more useful than conventionally trained troops. Not only did Rumsfeld improve their status, he also gave them greater autonomy. Fourth, under Rumsfeld's leadership the U.S. military became better at reconnaissance operations. "Its ability to use multiple platforms to find targets and then to get information on their locations to the proper shooters has radically progressed."[92]

He also did considerable damage. While any group would have resisted Rumsfeld's cavalier treatment of its professionals, his constant violation of military culture when dealing with force transformation acerbated the situation. First, it is true that generals and admirals often resist change. However, the art of leadership at any level is to get the people you lead to willingly follow you. Rumsfeld apparently was convinced that the generals would oppose him regardless of how he treated them, so he often excluded them from discussions on force transformation, discussions that would have a major impact on their services. He made it clear that he was not interested in their opinions. Needless to say, they were unhappy—if not furious. Such a situation was guaranteed to intensify conflict.

Second, military officers are professionals. Some, such as submarine or missile officers, may have advanced degrees and have worked on extremely complex weapons and equipment. All have commanded personnel in difficult situations. However, Rumsfeld treated the generals and admirals like they were school children. While an officer always tries to treat others with respect, that was clearly not one of Rumsfeld's concerns. As a result, it is likely that more than one senior officer did only what was absolutely necessary to carry out his orders.

Third, Rumsfeld came up with ideas that, from a military standpoint, made no sense. For example, his plan to jump a whole generation of weapons not only assumes the continuance of a benign external environment, it also assumes that the technocrats will be able to invent the necessary weapons and equipment in a short period of time. The leader is also assuming that Congress will continue to fund such weapons until they can be deployed. But as the experience with FCS demonstrates, those assumptions often prove misguided.

Such wishful policy also costs lives. After Rumsfeld resigned, it was revealed that the Pentagon knew that Mine Resistant Ambush Protected

Vehicles (MRAP) would do a far better job of protecting solders than armored Humvees. Their high ground clearance and V-shaped underbodies help deflect bomb blasts. But since Rumsfeld did not think the war would last very long, and because he wanted to jump a generation in vehicles, he thought it made little sense to propose using such a relatively low-tech weapon. As a result, the military did not have MRAPs in Iraq. Thousands of lives could possibly have been saved if the secretary had permitted the army and Marine Corps to purchase the MRAPs.[93]

Fourth, Rumsfeld openly violated the military promotion system. While the system has its problems, traditionally it is left to the armed forces to manage, except at the most senior levels. Peer groups decide who should be promoted, not a civilian who knows little about the military. Thus, Rumsfeld selected Generals Myers and Pace not because of their military records or willingness to stand up to him when military interests were involved, but because he was convinced he could control them.

Fifth, by focusing so heavily on high tech, and by doing his best to cut thousands of troops, Rumsfeld took attention away from post-combat operations. If he had focused on that period of combat, he would have realized that the army needed large numbers of troops. But raising troop levels would take considerable sums of money away from Rumsfeld's efforts to develop high-tech weapons.

The irony is that, in the beginning, it appeared that Shinseki and Rumsfeld could work together. Both understood the need for transformation; indeed, Shinseki had been pushing it in the army since 1999. However, it soon became clear that Rumsfeld was not interested. He wanted money from the army's budget to pay for projects he believed would better facilitate transformation—even if it were in another service. The only surprising factor is that the relationship did not become even worse. But the damage Rumsfeld did related to the problems of transformation pale in comparison with the bitterness that ensued from the invasion of Iraq.

# Rumsfeld's War in Afghanistan and Preparations for Iraq

> I am reasonably certain that [the Iraqi people] will greet us as liberators; and that will help us to keep requirements down.
> *Paul Wolfowitz, U.S. Deputy Secretary of Defense*

Concern over Saddam Hussein and developments in Iraq predated the George W. Bush administration. In 1991 the United States and its coalition partners threw Saddam's invading troops out of Kuwait and seized small sections of the southern part of Iraq. The United States, however, went no further and stood by while Saddam's forces slaughtered segments of the predominately Shia south that rose up in rebellion. Indeed, some U.S. officials, Paul Wolfowitz in particular, were so bitter that they vowed to remove Saddam Hussein from power and set the Iraqi populace free if they ever got the chance. To these future officials, U.S. inaction was more than an embarrassment, it was a moral outrage. However, Washington did respond, at least in part, to Hussein's attack on the Kurds in northern Iraq with operation Provide Comfort, which forced Saddam's troops out of the north, leaving it for the Kurds.

For the rest of the 1990s, U.S. policy in Iraq primarily focused on containing Saddam. No-fly zones were created in the north and the south, meaning Iraqi planes could not enter either area. U.S. and U.K. aircraft patrolled both zones. Any Iraqi planes operating in these areas were fair game and could be shot down. In 1995 the UN Security Council created the Oil for Food program, which was intended to permit Iraq to sell oil on the world market in exchange for food, medicine, and other humanitarian goods. Many policymakers believed that Saddam had been contained. His army was weak following the Gulf War, and while he remained a despot, there was little he could do to threaten the United States.

Not everyone shared the view that Saddam was contained, however. Paul Wolfowitz, Douglas Feith, and other "Iraq Hawks" believed he was a threat to the region and to Israel. To these observers the battle with Saddam and terrorism was nothing less than a fight of good against evil. They believed that democracy was the preferred form of government throughout the world, and that all people, regardless of their specific political culture, would adopt it if given the chance. By getting rid of Saddam, the Iraq Hawks were convinced, they would open a new chapter in the Middle East. Democracy in Iraq would have a domino effect. Other countries in the region would also become democratic, just like the United States, which they believed could serve as a role model for the rest of the world. Even better, they were convinced that democratic countries in the Middle East would be more pro-American than their autocratic predecessors.

Wolfowitz and Feith had focused on foreign policy throughout their careers, and they were politically active during the Clinton administration. In 1996, for example, Feith, Richard Perle, and David Wurmser were part of a group that produced a paper for a conservative Israeli think tank, in which they concluded that "removing Saddam Hussein from power" was "an important Israeli strategic objective."[1] They also began to call for the United States to take action against Iraq. By December 1997, Wolfowitz was "explicitly calling for the use of the military to remove Saddam from power."[2] The following January Perle and Wolfowitz made use of the conservative Project for the New American Century think tank to send an open letter to President Bill Clinton calling for a ground campaign to oust Saddam. From their perspective, the best option would be one involving Washington's allies and friends, but if that turned out to be impossible, then the United States should be prepared to bring about regime change unilaterally.

Under pressure from the Iraq Hawks, in the fall of 1998 Congress passed the Iraq Liberation Act, which declared, "It should be the policy of the United States to seek to remove the Saddam Hussein regime from power in Iraq and replace it with a democratic government."[3] With those words, regime change in Iraq became official U.S. policy. Congress allocated $100 million dollars to the State Department with the expressed purpose of ending the Saddam regime.[4] This was followed in December by a four-day bombing campaign by U.S. and U.K. aircraft in response to Saddam's failure to comply with UN Security Council resolutions on top of Iraqi interference with UN inspectors on the ground in Iraq. The United States fired a total of 417 cruise missiles, more than in the Gulf War.[5] Although

Clinton authorized the use of force against Saddam and was willing to sign an executive order authorizing the CIA to go after Osama bin Laden and his terrorist operations (as a response to the bombings of U.S. embassies in Nairobi and Dar es Salaam in August 1998), the supporters of regime change were far from satisfied. Bombing was fine, but it did little to bring about their desired end—the fall of Saddam Hussein. However, Clinton saw the situation differently. From his perspective, the purpose of the air strikes was to degrade Saddam's power, and that had been accomplished. In fact, the Saddam regime was reportedly so badly damaged by these air strikes that it nearly collapsed, causing concern on the part of a number of Middle Eastern governments.[6] While the administration had other problems to worry about—like China and missile defense—the Iraq Hawks remained undeterred. They believed they would carry their message with them when they became a part of George W. Bush's administration in 2001: the only answer to Saddam was regime change in favor of a democratic regime. In fact, during the transition period, Vice President-elect Dick Cheney, who would side with Wolfowitz and Feith on almost all issues related to Iraq, sent a note to outgoing Secretary of Defense William Cohen, commenting, "We really need to get the president-elect briefed up on some things," adding that he wanted a serious "discussion about Iraq and different options . . . . Topic A should be Iraq."[7]

The Iraq Hawks considered General Colin Powell, who would become secretary of state, to be an anomaly in the new administration, because he did not believe in the absolute necessity of regime change in Iraq. The always pragmatic Powell thought they were naive at best when it came to the Middle East, a point Woodward emphasized: "Powell thought that Wolfowitz was talking as if 25 million Iraqis would rush to the side of a U.S.-supported opposition. In his [Powell's] opinion, it was one of the most absurd, strategically unsound proposals he had ever heard."[8]

The general was not convinced that an invasion of Iraq would lead almost immediately to the adoption of Western democratic values and that U.S. troops would be welcomed by the Iraqi people as liberators. His long military career had taught him the importance of being realistic when drawing up plans. It would be nice to believe that the Iraqis would welcome the Americans as liberators, but what if they greeted the troops with gunfire instead? Good military planners always consider a "worst case" option. A planner always assumes the worst and hopes for the best. That way the military is prepared, regardless of what happens. Powell was this kind of leader. He always assumed the worst in war so that the United States would be ready for any contingency. Conflict between Powell and the confident Wolfowitz, Feith, and Rumsfeld was inevitable.

The Iraq Hawks also resented Powell for another reason. The general had written the so-called Powell Doctrine, which assumed that before the United States went to war, a number of preliminary actions had to be taken. Of the eight principles that Powell laid down several were of particular importance for a potential war with Iraq. For example, is there a clear, attainable objective? Have the risks and costs been fully and frankly analyzed? What about an exit strategy? How will success be measured? Finally, and perhaps most important, the United States and its partners should use overwhelming force against the enemy. This would minimize U.S. casualties, force the other side to capitulate quickly, and enable U.S. forces to pacify the country after combat stopped.

Powell's approach was anathema to Rumsfeld. He was not interested in a war involving large numbers of troops. Instead, Iraq represented an opportunity for him to prove his military transformation theory by defeating and subduing Iraq with as few troops as possible. The United States certainly did not need the overwhelming force that Powell recommended. To Rumsfeld, the Powell Doctrine was out of date. Besides, Perle considered Powell to be a "soft-liner," not the kind of individual who should be in a top-level position.[9] As a result, Rumsfeld and his colleagues would do everything possible to marginalize Powell and to steal the action from him at every opportunity. There was too much at stake with the impending war in Iraq to allow someone like a former four-star general to mess things up.

National Security Adviser Condoleezza Rice's primary concern was the president. Her job was to coordinate foreign and security policy, a brutally difficult task, especially when the administration is composed of intense competitors, each of whom were out to control policy. For many of these men, there was no such thing as a division of labor in formulating and implementing policy; whatever he could seize belonged to him—period. Unfortunately, Rice's forte was her ability to explain highly complex issues in a way that the nonspecialist could understand. This ability was invaluable to a president who made no claim of being an expert on foreign policy. The problem, however, was that she was not a Henry Kissinger when it came to directing traffic between such political heavyweights as Rumsfeld and Powell. As former State Department analyst David L. Phillips noted critically,

Responsibility for the interagency breakdown rests with Condoleezza Rice. The job of national security advisor is to maintain a level playing field and force consensus between the president's national security team. When it came to policy, Rice was a manager, not a deep thinker. She had few opinions of her own; indeed, her primary concern was to preserve her relationship with the president. Inconsistency created the impression of an administration in disarray. . . . Though Rice is "like a daughter" to Powell, she did little to prevent Cheney and Rumsfeld from marginalizing the secretary of state.[10]

Rice's refusal to crack the whip in dealing with Cheney and Rumsfeld would have very serious, negative implications for the administration, as the two men fought Powell for turf.

The Iraq Hawks were especially suspicious of the State Department's Foreign Service. To them, too many Foreign Service officers (FSOs) had spent a good part of their careers working in or on the Arab Middle East. They were biased against Israel, and they believed that the FSOs' view of the world was "pie in the sky." From the FSO standpoint, introducing democracy into a country like Iraq would not be easy, because the country had never experienced it. Democracy assumes a certain set of attitudes and beliefs that take years, if not centuries, to develop, so it seems unreasonable to assume that the Iraqis would instantly become democrats just because the U.S. military showed up and got rid of a brutal dictator. The West suffered hundreds of years of war over issues such as ethnicity and religion, but the hawks expected the Iraqis to ignore tribal and religious differences and immediately be willing to negotiate and compromise with each other. Traditionally in Iraq one ethnic or religious group has exploited the others, making politics a zero-sum game. Under Saddam, the minority Sunnis had ruled over the majority Shiites. As Iyad Allawi, an Iraqi politician, explained, "Iraq is one of those countries that lack a key requirement of a social polity, namely a unity of thought and ideals, and a sense of community. The country is fragmented and divided against itself, and its political leadership needs to be both wise, practical, and morally and materially strong."[11]

## Launching a Military Operation

Military officers are trained to plan for all identifiable or potential eventualities. If nothing happens, then the plan can be updated from time to time. However, if conflict is the order of the day, the Pentagon must have a plan ready to implement. That is why planners spend so much of their time working and reworking existing plans or drawing up new ones. For example, soon after he took over as chief of staff of the army, General Shinseki ordered his subordinates to carry out war games to get a feel for what kind of military assets would be required if the United States went to war with Iraq. Reportedly, Shinseki was more concerned about a potential conflict in the Caspian Sea than Iraq, but he believed it only prudent to look at all possible scenarios.[12]

Marine General Tony Zinni was the master of war games involving Iraq. As CENTCOM during the Clinton years, Zinni believed that the possibility of conflict with Iraq was real, and he put together an Iraq war game, Desert Crossing, which involved seventy military, diplomatic, intelligence, and governmental officials. The games were conducted in Washington, DC, in late 1999 and they were very comprehensive.

> The scenarios looked closely at humanitarian, security, political, economic, and other reconstruction issues. We looked at food, clean water, electricity, refugees. Shia versus Sunni, Kurds versus the other Iraqis, Turks versus Kurds and the power vacuum that would surely follow the collapse of the regime. . . . We looked at all the problems the United States faces in 2003 trying to rebuild Iraq. And when it was over, I was starting to get a good sense of their enormous scope and to recognize how massive the reconstruction job would be.[13]

According to one source, Zinni estimated that it would take about 400,000 troops to take and occupy Iraq.[14] Furthermore, his conclusions "drew pessimistic outcomes of such action."[15] Conquering the Iraqi military might not present a major problem, but Zinni was concerned about the many problems the United States would face in occupying and rebuilding a country the size of California, one that had been plundered by Saddam and badly hurt by sanctions. He tried to interest official Washington into looking at these issues, but as he put it, "'Well, who's going to take the next step,' I asked? The answer. Nobody. There was no interest in Washington in pursuing it. . . . Post-Saddam Iraq was simply too far down the priority list of any agency with a reason to be interested in the problems."[16]

## Bush and Iraq

On January 10, 2001, ten days before his inauguration, Bush went to the Pentagon for a briefing from the Joint Chiefs of Staff. About seventy-five minutes was devoted to a discussion about Iraq and the Persian Gulf. As one participant put it, "Iraq was the first topic briefed because 'it is the most visible and risky area' Mr. Bush will confront after he takes office."[17] For his part, Bush apparently did not show his hand, limiting himself to asking some probing questions.

On January 30, 2001, the National Security Council met with Bush in attendance. According to Karen DeYoung, Rice commented, "We have a regime change policy that isn't really regime change." Secretary Powell agreed, but he thought the sanctions could be salvaged, "at least temporarily by shifting 'from a list of what is allowed to a list of what is prohibited'—specifically, weapons and their components."[18] Rumsfeld dismissed Powell's suggestion out of hand, arguing that his primary concern was weapons of mass destruction.

When the NSC met on February 5, 2001, it was revealed that the White House had already decided to fund Iraqi exile groups and to support anti-regime groups inside the country. Meanwhile, Rumsfeld noted that pilots patrolling the no-fly zone had been given a number of new options. They were now permitted to attack radar, antiaircraft, and command-and-control centers—even if they were outside of the no-fly zone. "The military response would escalate if a pilot was shot down, or if Saddam's forces launched a direct attack against northern Iraqi Kurds or the southern Shiites."[19] This was followed on February 7 by a principals meeting that focused on Iraq. According to CIA Director George Tenet, it was primarily to gather information.[20] A little over a week later, while Bush was visiting Mexico, U.S. and British aircraft flying in the no-fly zone hit twenty military communication targets—including some on the outskirts of Baghdad.[21] It was clear that Iraq was one of the administration's primary concerns. Terrorism was not.

## Fighting Terrorism

Meanwhile, the battle against terrorism continued. Richard Clarke, who headed the Clinton administration's fight against terrorism and continued in that capacity during the early days of the Bush administration, pushed hard for action against al-Qaeda and for support for rebel groups in Afghanistan who were fighting the Taliban. Deputy Secretary of State Richard Armitage agreed that the United States should expand support to the Northern Alliance in Afghanistan. Wolfowitz, on the other hand, downplayed any threat from al-Qaeda and instead continued to argue that Iraq was the primary danger. He pushed for Washington to create a protectorate in Southern Iraq around the city of Basra. Wolfowitz's fixation on Iraq eventually began to draw the ire of the other participants.

The CIA was worried that al-Qaeda had something in the works. For example, on May 30, 2001, Tenet and some of his assistants met with Rice and noted the increased warning signs of a possible attack on the United States. Then on July 10 Tenet received a briefing from the chief of his counterterrorism unit, Cofer Black, who "laid out the case, comprised of communications intercepts and other TOP SECRET intelligence, showing the increasing likelihood that al-Qaeda would soon attack the U.S."[22] As soon as Black finished, Tenet picked up his secure phone, called Rice, and said he had to see her immediately.

Tenet described Black's briefing as follows: "The attack will be 'spectacular'. . . . and it will be designed to inflict mass casualties against U.S. facilities and interests. 'Attack preparations have been made.' Condi then looked at Black and said, 'What should we do?' Cofer responded, 'this country needs to go on a war footing now.'"[23] The problem facing Rice and the CIA was that no one knew when or where such an attack would take place. Putting the country on a war footing without knowing the target or the timetable could create chaos. Next, the briefing was given to Rumsfeld and Attorney General John Ashcroft. Rumsfeld dismissed the threat, sarcastically suggesting that the CIA was falling victim to "vast doses of al-Qaeda disinformation," and "mortal doses of gullibility."[24] He constantly questioned the validity of Tenet's information, suggesting that it could be part of a big deception. Furthermore, while Rice listened politely, it was clear to both men that she and the president had other priorities, such as ballistic missile defense.

In early August Rumsfeld called in General Shelton, the operations directors, and the section chiefs. He wanted to focus on war plans for Iraq and North Korea. In typical Rumsfeldian fashion he grilled those present. He wanted to know their assumptions and, in the process, he discovered that most of the plans were four or five years old and called for a massive use of force—as in the Gulf War. In almost every case, the Pentagon's plan was to move large amounts of military equipment to the area—regardless of whether it was Asia or the Middle East—over the course of several months. Given his dedication to flexibility and small-unit warfare, Rumsfeld was nonplused by the army's plans.

## September 11, 2001

Despite Tenet's warning, the administration was only partially focused on a possible terrorist attack. In a meeting on September 4, for example, the focus was on the unarmed Predator plane and whether the president should approve the CIA's request to fly it in a weaponized form. Further, there was the question of who should operate it; if it was firing missiles, perhaps it should be the military. Then on September 10, Tenet reported that a source in a foreign country had told his handler that something big was about to go down. Unfortunately, "the handler dismissed him."[25]

The events of Tuesday, September 11, changed everything. According to General Myers, "The 9/11 attacks galvanized all our thinking."[26] Those working around the president noticed that he had become a different person. "It transformed him in ways I don't think any of us could have fully predicted," said Tenet.[27] Bush's first response was to order Powell and the State Department to issue an ultimatum to the Taliban, ordering them to turn over Osama bin Laden or "We'll attack them."[28] He was serious and wanted to know what the Pentagon was prepared to do to punish the Taliban if military force were necessary.

While Afghanistan would turn out to be a sideshow to the Iraq War, it was the main focus of the Bush administration for the last few months of 2001. To say that the attacks on the World Trade Center and the Pentagon were a shock to official Washington would be an understatement. True, everyone knew that the terrorists were out there, and Tenet and his colleagues had been warning Rice, Rumsfeld, and others that an attack was imminent, but the idea that terrorists would hijack commercial aircrafts with hundreds of civilians and then slam the planes into buildings, killing thousands of innocent Americans, seemed beyond belief. Bush wanted an immediate response by U.S. military forces—a response that would make the terrorists pay a very heavy price for what they had done to the United States.

## Keeping Iraq Alive

Rumsfeld and his colleagues assumed Saddam was behind the 9/11 attacks, and used the tragedy to argue even more strongly in favor of taking out Saddam. Tenet recounted a September 12, 2001, conversation between a senior military officer and Feith that is repeated here because it points to the tremendous gap in the way the Iraq Hawks and the uniformed military saw 9/11.

> They caught a ride aboard an Air Force tanker, one of the few planes permitted to transit the closed airspace of the United States. Onboard the flight, the military officer told Feith that al-Qa'ida was responsible for the previous day's attacks and a theater-wide campaign would need to be launched against them starting in Afghanistan. To his amazement, Feith said words to the effect that the campaign should immediately lead to Baghdad. The senior military officer strongly disagreed.[29]

On September 12, there was an NSC meeting to discuss the U.S. response to the attacks of 9/11. Not surprisingly, Rumsfeld raised the issue of Iraq, suggesting that the United States should attack Iraq as well as al-Qaeda in Afghanistan. It would be an opportunity to kill two birds with one stone.

Powell strongly disagreed, maintaining that there was public support for going after al-Qaeda but not for an invasion of Iraq. According to his biographer, Cheney agreed with Powell. As he reportedly put it, "'Iraq needs to be part of our discussion eventually,' he said, 'but right now it is a distraction.'"[30] Bush also made it clear that he did not think that now was the time to resolve the Iraq issue. He had spoken with Clarke about the matter, who had assured him that "al-Qaeda did this."[31] The president's primary concern now was to see a military plan that would inflict "real pain and destruction on the terrorists."[32] Rumsfeld, however, was not about to let the opportunity slip away. According to a military planner inside the Pentagon, at that time his group was told to draw up "scenarios for an assault on Iraq, not just Afghanistan."[33]

## Afghanistan and Command Relationships

Before discussing military operations in Afghanistan, it is important to understand the relationships among the key players. The president, of course, had the final word before any actions were taken. However, in accordance with his CEO leadership style, Bush relied primarily on his secretary of defense to run military matters. He expected to be consulted, but it was up to Rumsfeld and the military to decide what forces to use and how they were to be employed.

Rumsfeld was in an ideal situation. He had already selected a very amiable chairman of the Joint Chiefs, a man who was not prepared to go public in defense of the military, and who would never use his authority to go directly to the president without the secretary's permission. He now also had a direct, one-on-one relationship with the combatant commanders. Rumsfeld could expect the chairman to facilitate the implementation of whatever operations he and the combatant commander selected and to not openly disagree with him the way Shelton had in the past.

This one-on-one relationship was also welcomed by General Tommy Franks, who was CENTCOM. Franks knew the region well. He had served as General Zinni's deputy, and Zinni had recommended him as his successor. Franks was also the type of individual who resented and resisted outside involvement in the conduct of operations in his area of operations. With only Rumsfeld to deal with, he felt he could more rationally design and conduct policy. The problem, however, was that while one could sympathize with Franks and his desire to keep other hands out of his operation, he appears to have overestimated his intellectual prowess as well as his negotiating skills when dealing with Rumsfeld. He was clearly impressed by the secretary—that much is obvious from his memoirs. Shortly after meeting him Franks commented that Rumsfeld was "a leader who wanted to use his own ideas to bring about change."[34] He also seemed impressed by Rumsfeld's intention to push through his military transformation policy. Franks would soon learn, however, that when Rumsfeld had made up his mind on something, it did not matter what the military—or Franks—thought. It would be Rumsfeld's way or the highway. Unfortunately, if Franks had been willing to stand up to Rumsfeld as the combatant commander, Rumsfeld's leverage over him and his planning would have been limited. No secretary of defense wants to be seen overruling a combatant commander on something as important as a military campaign.

## The Assault on Afghanistan

Because the Pentagon did not have an actionable plan to move ground forces into Afghanistan, the CIA took the lead role in setting up a war plan at the September 12 meeting of what Tenet called the "War Cabinet." The CIA's plan for action called for deploying "a CIA paramilitary team inside Afghanistan to work with opposition forces, most notably the Northern Alliance, and prepare the way for the introduction of U.S. Special Forces."[35] The CIA had been operating in Afghanistan for a long time—at least since the Soviets were there in the 1980s. They knew the tribes, the ethnic groups, the leaders, the culture, and to some degree the languages, not to mention who would and would not cooperate with the United States and coalition forces in getting rid of the Taliban.

Meanwhile, although the Pentagon did not have contingency plans to deal with Afghanistan, the military was hardly idle. General Franks had spoken with General Shelton shortly after the attack. Shelton told Franks, "'The President is determined to act.'. . . 'And Secretary Rumsfeld wants military options for Afghanistan.'"[36] This meant starting from scratch. As Tommy Franks put it, "But CENTCOM had *not* developed a plan for conventional ground operations in Afghanistan. Nor had diplomatic arrangements for basing, staging, overflight and access been made with Afghanistan's neighbors."[37] In response, CENTCOM began to work around the clock on drawing up plans while starting to move ships, planes, and troops so they would be in a position to attack al-Qaeda and remove the Taliban regime in Afghanistan when the order was given. The problem was not just a lack of planning. The military also needed time to implement any plan. As Franks's deputy, General Mike DeLong, observed in discussing the option Rumsfeld favored, it takes time to move forces from one point to another: "The third option, which we favored, packaged cruise missiles and bombers with 'boots on the ground,' using Special Forces and possibly other Army and Marine units. We would need at least ten to twelve days to get our forces in-country. If the administration wanted an instant retaliation, this was not the way to go."[38]

Senior decision makers gathered at Camp David on September 15. The president was there and he wanted to act, and to act decisively. While the meeting's primary focus was on Afghanistan, Wolfowitz tried again to interject Iraq into the equation. He argued against tying up 100,000 American troops in the very difficult Afghan terrain, pointing out that it would be much easier to invade Iraq. The place was run by a dictator who most of the populace hated, and the regime would probably fall apart of its own weight. He maintained that all it needed was a good shove. He also argued that there was a "10–50" percent chance that Saddam was involved in the attacks on the Pentagon and Twin Towers. Besides, "The U.S. would have to go after Saddam at some time if the war on terrorism was to be taken seriously."[39] In the end, four of those present, Vice President Cheney, Secretary Powell, Director Tenet, and Presidential Chief of Staff Andrew Card, all voted against taking on Iraq. Rumsfeld abstained. Bush spoke privately with General Shelton, asking him if he was making a mistake by first going after al-Qaeda. Shelton said his action was correct and noted that an attack on Iraq would upset the balance of power in the Middle East. More important, he told Bush that he knew of no information linking Saddam to the events of 9/11. "That's what I think," Bush told Shelton. "'We will get this guy but at a time and place of our choosing,' Bush added, referring to Saddam."[40] While Iraq would not disappear from the agenda, it was now put on the back burner. The leadership's attention was focused on Afghanistan. Tenet noted the change in outlook by CIA operatives. Where in past meetings held at headquarters those present had focused on "what if we go to war," now they were discussing what we should do "when we go to war."[41]

Tenet updated the president on the CIA's plan, which would provide immediate assistance to the Northern Alliance and speed up contacts with southern leaders. The CIA also told the president that Uzbekistan would play a critical part in any action the United States took against Kabul. And then Tenet said something that must have irritated Rumsfeld to no end. "*We were ready to carry out these actions immediately, because we had been preparing for this moment for years. We were ready because our plan allowed us to be.*"[42] Thus the CIA would take the lead in responding to al-Qaeda's attack on the United States—not the Pentagon.

When the group reconvened on September 17, Bush announced that the government would move ahead with Tenet's plan. "Start now," he said.[43]

From the CIA's standpoint, "'the gloves came off' that day."[44] The CIA could use its own paramilitary teams, its case officers, and the Predator in Afghanistan. Tenet told Bush that the CIA teams would be in Afghanistan in eight days.[45] The agency was prepared to hit back, to make the Taliban pay for what they had permitted al-Qaeda to do. Bush then ordered the Pentagon to prepare a set of military options, ones that included the use of cruise missiles, bombers, and troops, to use against the Taliban. The president wanted to know what kind of targets the Pentagon proposed to hit, how soon it planned to hit them, and what allies would support the United States. Meanwhile, with Iraq still very much in mind, Bush told Rice that he wanted contingency plans drawn up in case it turned out that Iraq was implicated in the 9/11 attacks after all. He reaffirmed this position on Iraq in a War Council meeting on September 18.

Despite the move toward war with Afghanistan, senior civilians in the Pentagon still pushed for an attack on Iraq. Wolfowitz, for example, sent a memorandum to Rumsfeld arguing that the odds were far better than one in ten that Baghdad was involved in the attack on 9/11. When the advisory Defense Policy Board met in the Pentagon on September 19–20, with Rumsfeld in attendance, it discussed the importance of ousting Hussein.[46]

To be fair to the military, there was a logic to having the CIA focus on the conflict in Afghanistan. After all, it was fighting the war on terrorism. Prior to 9/11 it would have sounded ridiculous to urge the military to prepare plans for an attack on Afghanistan. Rumsfeld had previously asked General Myers about contingency plans for a war with Afghanistan and when he was told the Pentagon did not have any, he responded, "When I've asked to see various plans, I've not been happy with what I've seen. They are neither imaginative nor creative."[47] Even if the military had the plans, it is doubtful that Rumsfeld would have approved them unless they embraced his high-tech, low-manpower ideas.

Meanwhile, the military was still planning for a ground operation to insert Special Forces units into Afghanistan, a situation that did not please Rumsfeld. He was growing increasingly frustrated. For weeks he had heard that the United States was not in a position to respond on the ground immediately. For Rumsfeld, the slow military response confirmed the importance of pushing military transformation harder. Washington needed forces that were flexible, capable, and lethal—and it did not have them.[48]

Rumsfeld wanted to be directly involved in military planning. In the aftermath of the 9/11 attacks, he, General Peter Pace, General Myers,[49] Wolfowitz, and Feith would spend extended hours going over intelligence reports. While he trusted Myers and Pace, Rumsfeld was not about to leave the planning process to other members of the military. The staffs could plan, but he would be the one who would consult with General Franks in planning the U.S. response. In fact, Franks reported that he spoke daily with Rumsfeld and Wolfowitz by secure telephone or video telephone conference.[50] Rumsfeld decided early on that he would have to push Franks and the military hard if he hoped to get U.S. troops in Afghanistan. For example, when he spoke with Franks, who had told him it would take months to plan a response, Rumsfeld responded, "You don't have months."[51] Franks's efforts to explain the difficulties of an operation halfway around the world were to no avail. The president weighed in as well. As he stated in an NSC meeting, "General Shelton should go back to the generals for new targets. Start the clock. This is an opportunity. I want a plan—costs, time. I need options on the table. I want Afghan options at Camp David. I want decisions quick."[52] The message from both Rumsfeld and the president was clear: Stop giving us excuses and come up with a plan. Even Powell was taken aback by the long lead time the Pentagon needed to deploy troops in Afghanistan.[53] The danger of this kind of pressure is that military culture is imbued with a "can do" attitude. Consequently, in an effort to carry out the mission, the military may go into combat mode before it is ready to do so.

## Deciding on a Military Plan

Rumsfeld himself admitted that dealing with him to come up with a plan would not be easy. The secretary told General Franks that his first draft for invading Afghanistan was "unimaginative." In response to a question about his approach for dealing with others, he said, "I am very blunt, I am very outspoken. . . . It is entirely possible that I may have said something at one point or another that could lead some observer to think that way."[54] The one aspect that both men agreed upon was that any U.S. ground force should remain small—they desperately wanted to avoid a repetition of the Soviet experience, which involved large numbers of troops finding themselves trapped for years in a hostile Afghanistan.

As noted above, the Joint Chiefs were not directly involved in military operations. That was the purview of Franks as the combatant commander. However, the Joint Chiefs controlled resources that the combatant commander would need to carry out his mission. Furthermore, they were four-star generals and admirals—the most senior officers in their services—and they believed they should be at least peripherally involved in all military operations, especially Iraq—the biggest operation in years.

As a result, on September 20 Shelton called Franks and said that the service chiefs had asked to be present with the secretary to hear his plan before it was presented to the president. Franks's immediate response was "Damn it." He did not want to go through a session with the chiefs, but Shelton asked him to do it. In the end, it was a total disaster.

At the meeting the army argued the efficacy of land power and described the difficulties of sustaining army forces. The Marine view suggested "from the sea" as the most effective approach to war-fighting—even in a land-locked country. The air force chief of staff offered airpower as the most powerful approach.[55]

The briefing soon became very adversarial. According to Lieutenant General Mike DeLong, one part of the discussion went as follows:

> One of the chiefs said: "No one's ever fought a war using an indigenous rebel force, reinforced only with Special Ops, agency people, and fire support. What you're proposing is completely unprecedented."
>
> "I'm fighting this war—you're not," Franks said.
>
> "We don't think it will work."
>
> "Bullshit," Franks answered, standing up. "It's my plan. And I am responsible for its execution."
>
> And with that, he walked out.[56]

The next day the general met with Rumsfeld prior to briefing the president, and gave the other officers hope that he would be willing to stand up to Rumsfeld—at least on this issue. As Franks tells it, Rumsfeld asked him, "Would you please explain what *that* was all about yesterday?"[57] Franks told him that the one thing he could not live with was split-command authority. Either he was in charge or he wasn't. And if he wasn't in charge, it was time to put someone else in the job. Rumsfeld assured him that he was in charge.

This event clearly demonstrated Franks's antipathy toward dealing with the service chiefs and his willingness to stand up to Rumsfeld—at least on this issue. He intended to work closely with Rumsfeld in creating plans for the invasion not only of Afghanistan but any other military action. He was not prepared to put up with a bunch of Monday-morning quarterbacks who knew little or nothing about how to run an operation as complex as Afghanistan. Franks was determined to do everything possible in the future to avoid the service chiefs. The long-term problem was that, by cutting himself off from the chiefs, he also cut himself off from the Joint Staff and the Army War College, both of which would have very useful ideas as the war plan was finalized.

While the Pentagon was having problems figuring out how to get ground troops to Afghanistan, it prepared its air power assets to send a message to the Taliban. On September 15 Franks briefed Bush on the upcoming air war. He went through the different phases, outlining the kinds of targets the U.S. aircraft would go after. In reply, Bush emphasized the importance of avoiding collateral damage.

Responding to a question from Bush about whether or not the military would be ready to start the air war during the first week of October, General Shelton said that the problem was combat search and rescue (CSAR). The military could not send in planes unless it had helicopters present in the area in case a pilot was shot down. Uzbekistan eventually agreed on October 3 to permit Washington to station CSAR forces on its soil. The Pentagon was ready to go, but it would take sixty-seven deliveries from C-17s before the necessary equipment would be on the ground in Uzbekistan. Consequently, the senior officers decided to rely in the first instance on B-2 bombers stationed in Missouri. They began military action on October 7, and quickly ran out of targets to hit in this fifteenth-century country.

Meanwhile, the CIA's covert teams were inserted into Afghanistan in late September. These teams, together with the Special Forces groups and the local insurgents, would combine to defeat the Taliban. The U.S. teams linked up with the Northern Alliance on October 20, and by November 5 they were attacking Mazar-e-Sharif, the most important city in the north. They had close air support from U.S. planes. Mazar-e-Sharif quickly fell—a major victory for coalition forces. According to General DeLong, it also had a major impact on Franks's relationship with Rumsfeld. "Franks had validated Rumsfeld's trust in him. From that moment, their relationship went straight uphill and never wavered."[58] The real question was whether or not Franks would be prepared to use the respect Rumsfeld had for him to stand up to the secretary in the future. And if he did, would he lose Rumsfeld's favor?

## The Goal of the Operation?

One of the major policy problems with the administration's approach to the war in Afghanistan—a difficulty that would haunt it during the Iraq invasion as well—was its primary emphasis on military force. All it could think of was how to defeat the Taliban and al-Qaeda. But then what? The policy seemed to assume that once the bad guys were defeated everything would be fine. As a result, it never thought through the Phase IV period—post-hostilities reconstruction. No one had decided what kind of a government would be put in place after the Taliban was defeated. "Part of the problem was that the Bush administration was not clear about its objectives. . . . The failure to establish clear objectives caused serious problems for the military operation and, especially, the postwar reconstruction and stabilization effort."[59] Indeed, according to Woodward, on October 12, the president commented that he opposed "using the military for nation building. Once the job is done, our forces are not peacekeepers."[60] It would be up to the CIA and its suitcases of money to put the country back together again.

## Who Is in Charge?

One of the most confusing aspects of the Afghan War was trying to figure out who was in charge of U.S. forces, a situation that frustrated Rumsfeld to no end. At a meeting with the president and General Franks on September 15, Rumsfeld brought up the question of command relationships, noting, "I recommend that operational command of the CIA be given to the Department of Defense." He was assured by Vice President Cheney that the chain of command would be clarified before the operation began.[61] For its part, the CIA was not concerned about bureaucratic turf fights over Afghanistan. Tenet had made it very clear that, while the CIA was the only agency with ground forces in the country at that time, they felt they were working for CENTCOM—General Tommy Franks.

Rice drove this point home to Rumsfeld after an especially chaotic meeting. She reportedly said to him, "Don, this is now a military operation and you really have to be in charge." "Got it," he answered.[62] Unfortunately, the Pentagon still did not have boots on the ground. While the CIA paramilitary groups claimed to be working with the military, the bottom line was that they were not working for the Department of Defense. Their chain of command ran through CIA headquarters at Langley, Virginia—something that irritated Rumsfeld.

Finally, on October 19, five weeks after 9/11, Special Forces were on the ground in Afghanistan. Now, instead of just bombing the Taliban, the Pentagon could make an important contribution on the ground.

Despite assurances from the CIA, Rumsfeld was perturbed by the fact that the agency was dictating strategy on the ground. In essence, the CIA's "new approach" meant that CIA operatives were dropped into Afghanistan with suitcases full of money in an effort to reinforce the Northern Alliance while trying to buy the assistance of Afghans willing to fight against the Taliban. Tenet admitted that there was considerable bureaucratic tension over this issue. He maintained, however, that the only way CIA units could operate effectively was if they were permitted as much autonomy as possible. They would take their directions from General Franks, but when it came to on-the-ground knowledge, the CIA teams knew a lot more than the army units. In fact, at one point General Franks visited Tenet and said, "I want you to subordinate your officers in Afghanistan to me." Tenet responded, "It ain't gonna happen." As Tenet explained, "I knew that if we fell under Pentagon control, the big bureaucracy would stifle our initiative and prevent us from doing the job we were best equipped to do."[63] Rumsfeld was not happy about the operational autonomy enjoyed by the CIA's forces in Afghanistan, but all indications are that the troops on the ground worked well together, leaving egos stateside.[64]

According to Tenet, on October 25 he received a paper from Rumsfeld that had been written by the Defense Intelligence Agency and that demonstrated how little the Pentagon understood about Afghanistan. The document made a number of points, among them the assertion that "Northern Alliance forces are incapable of overcoming Taliban resistance in northern Afghanistan, particularly the strategic city of Mazar-i-Sharif." The paper went on to argue, "The Northern Alliance will not capture the capital of Kabul before winter arrives, nor does it possess sufficient forces to encircle and isolate the city."[65] In fact, by early November Mazar-i-Sharif had fallen and shortly thereafter, Kabul fell. The Taliban and al-Qaeda were in full retreat. All of the complex plans, discussions, and concerns about how to take Kabul were now irrelevant. Kandahar fell on December 7. The Northern Alliance, its Pashtun allies, and the United States now ran the country. The irony of the debate on how many troops would be needed to take Afghanistan was that, in the end, 110 CIA officers and 316 Special Forces troops toppled the Taliban regime.

## Tora Bora

Osama bin Laden, members of al-Qaeda, as well as some of their Taliban allies retreated to the eastern mountains that border Pakistan. The region was not only rugged and high (up to 13,000 feet), it was also an area where the central governments—in both Pakistan and Afghanistan—had only limited control. It also included a large cave complex built by the mujahideen in the 1980s. The caves were equipped with food, water, weapons, electricity, and a ventilation system. Afghans hid in them during their war against the Soviet Army. Many of these caves stretch for miles, including some that reached into Pakistan.

The generals had to decide whether or not the United States should send its own forces to pursue al-Qaeda and the Taliban. General Franks and Lieutenant General DeLong argued that sending a massive number of troops into that area would have resulted in the deaths of Afghan civilians as these forces clashed with local tribesmen. Franks decided to send in Special Forces units that carried special communications equipment that permitted them to call in air power as needed. They were supported by Afghan tribal militiamen.

There are people who believe that if Washington had committed large numbers of ground troops, bin Laden and his followers would have been either killed or captured. Franks has continued to maintain that bin Laden was never within the U.S. grasp. That debate is now moot, and it does not appear to have had a direct bearing on how Rumsfeld conducted the war. The decision appears to have been made by Franks. His former deputy, Mike DeLong, supported this decision:

> The reality was, if we put our troops in there, we would inevitably end up fighting Afghan villagers—creating bad will at a sensitive time—which was the last thing we wanted to do. So, instead, using the CIA, our Special Forces, and friendly Pushtun [sic] generals, we created "Eastern Alliance" forces. The plan was to force al-Qaeda and the Taliban from the high ground of the mountains and into the caves, and then bomb the hell out of the caves.[66]

According to DeLong, moving up in those mountains was slow going and everyone—including Rumsfeld—complained. But DeLong stood his ground and Rumsfeld backed down. The Special Forces troops and their allies finally took the high ground and forced al-Qaeda into the caves, which were then bombed with powerful penetrating bombs. Unfortunately, Osama bin Laden slipped away into Pakistan.

## Was it Military Transformation?

Speaking at the Citadel on December 11, 2001, Bush argued that the war in Afghanistan proved the validity of the administration's new approach to war. "We are fighting shadowy, entrenched enemies, . . . enemies using the tool of terror and guerilla war—yet we are finding new tactics and new weapons to attack and defeat them. This revolution in our military is only beginning, and it promises to change the face of battle."[67] For his part, Rumsfeld would maintain that the United States had come up with "a new defense strategy." According to him, "It is a strategy that is more appropriate for the twenty-first century than what we had believed."[68]

Several writers have taken both the president and Rumsfeld to task for letting bin Laden escape. Stephen Biddle, for example, maintains that the

"Afghan campaign was actually far less different or unusual than most now suppose: it was a surprisingly orthodox air-guided theater campaign in which heavy fire support decided a contest between two land forces."[69] Meanwhile, Kagan maintained that, by the end of November 2001, the military's only accomplishment was that it had removed the Taliban from power. It had not destroyed enough of al-Qaeda to make a difference nor had it laid down the preconditions for the establishment of a new regime. He went on to argue that claims like Rumsfeld's that the war was won by precision-bombing and U.S. Special Operations Forces were wrong. "The Northern Alliance forces and the indigenous troops raised in southern Afghanistan by [future Afghan president] Hamid Karzai and Gul Agha Sherzai won the war, supported by U.S. airpower."[70] The problem for both Bush and Rumsfeld was that they seemed to be equating the U.S. military victory in Afghanistan with the word "innovation." There was no doubt that innovation contributed significantly to the military outcome. But by using a term as broad as innovation and never defining it, the phrase became meaningless. Riding horses while calling in air strikes became the defining characteristics of "innovation." From the material presented in the first part of this book, it would seem that both the president and Rumsfeld had something very different in mind when they used the term.

## Conclusion

Before and after 9/11 Iraq seemed to be in the back of the mind of almost everyone in the Bush administration. It certainly was true for Rumsfeld, Wolfowitz, Feith, and to some degree the president as well. Bush, with considerable support, insisted that Afghanistan be the first target, but with the notable exception of Powell and perhaps Rice, there appeared to be a general consensus that it was just a matter of time before the United States took on Iraq. It was considered the source of evil in the Middle East, and, until it was destroyed, the United States would never be safe. In many respects a war with Iraq seemed to be just a matter of time—at least in the eyes of the Iraq Hawks.

Another interesting aspect of the Afghan experience was the relationship that developed between Franks and Rumsfeld. By the end of the war, Franks had impressed Rumsfeld with his malleability. He was flexible and seemed to know what he was doing. He appeared ready to stand up to Rumsfeld, more so than many others. What he did not know was how far Franks would go in making the military's case to the secretary. Would he threaten to resign if pushed too far or would he become captivated by the secretary's ideas on transformation and Iraq? Time would tell, but given the secretary's overbearing personality, and his pliable chairman, there was reason to believe that if Franks were to stay around, he would have to make further compromises with Rumsfeld. The big question, however, was how much? Would he agree to an arrangement that would put U.S. troops in harm's way just to keep his job? Would he allow Rumsfeld to beat him down as time for the invasion drew near?

# Finding a Reason to Overthrow Saddam: The Die Is Cast

By caving to Rumsfeld, high-ranking officers of the U.S. armed forces failed to fulfill their responsibilities to their own brave fighting men and women—and to Congress, to which they are also entrusted by law with providing advice.

*Michael O'Hanlon, Brookings Institution*

In the weeks following 9/11, the U.S. government began preparations for two separate wars. The CIA proceeded with plans to invade Afghanistan to root out al-Qaeda, while the Pentagon continued to focus on Iraq, despite the lack of evidence proving an Iraqi connection to the terrorist attacks. On September 17, 2001, President George W. Bush issued a secret directive calling on the military to review its plans for an invasion of Iraq. This led to the meetings on September 19 and 20 of the Defense Policy Board, the advisory group chaired by Richard Perle. Rumsfeld attended the meetings, which focused on the importance of ousting Hussein.[1] Rumsfeld purportedly argued that it was time for the United States to demonstrate U.S. power. The search for a plan to invade Iraq was underway.

## Taming Franks

On November 21, 2001, Bush asked Rumsfeld to talk to General Tommy Franks and confirm that the Iraq invasion plan was being updated. He stressed that he wanted the plan to remain secret, because at this point he was still speaking in the conditional sense. Nevertheless, he told the secretary, "Get Tommy Franks looking at what it would take to protect America by removing Saddam Hussein if we have to."[2]

On November 26, Rumsfeld flew to see General Franks at CENTCOM's headquarters in Tampa, Florida. As soon as they were together privately, Rumsfeld noted that while the president had not yet decided to use force against Iraq, he wanted to see his options. As Franks recounted, Rumsfeld told him, "General Franks, the President wants us to look at options for Iraq. What is the status of your planning?"[3] Rumsfeld then made it clear that he had little regard for the current invasion plan, known as OPLAN 1003-98. This is the plan that had last been updated in 1998 by General Tony Zinni when he was CENTCOM and approved by then-secretary of defense William Cohen. When asked by Rumsfeld what he thought of the plan, Franks, aware of the secretary's opposition to massive invasion plans, described the old plan as "Desert Storm II. It's out of date, and under revision because conditions have changed. We have different force levels in the region than we had when the plan was written. And we obviously have learned some valuable lessons about precision weapons and special operations from our experience in Afghanistan."[4]

*Plan for War—in Iraq*

In fact, General Franks was shocked by Rumsfeld's announcement that the president wanted to see plans for invading Iraq. According to Woodward, Franks commented to his staff, "Goddamn, . . . What the fuck are they talking about?"[5] It is also worth noting that, according to one source, Franks found Rumsfeld "so overbearing" during the Afghanistan campaign "that he hinted he might resign."[6] Regardless of whether that account is correct, the request to plan for a second war while they were still fighting the first one clearly came as a bit of a shock.

Rumsfeld was particularly upset about the numbers involved in the old plan—it called for a force of some 500,000. Rumsfeld also knew that, just like Desert Storm I, it would necessitate a long, extended period of force buildup. It was a classic example of the Powell Doctrine—when the military is needed, use overwhelming force to achieve the objective. Such a military behemoth would raise serious questions about the validity and utility of military transformation, and Franks himself thought there was some merit to Rumsfeld's argument. He thought the old plan was "the classic kind of plodding, tank-heavy, big-bomb massing of military might from another era."[7] In the broadest sense, Franks agreed with Rumsfeld: CENTCOM needed a new battle plan. The real question was how far Franks would go in accommodating the secretary. He did not believe he could count on

General Richard Myers, the chairman of the Joint Chiefs, to back him if the two could not agree. It would be up to him to act alone.

Many senior figures in the military did not share Rumsfeld's desire to invade Iraq. For example, General Jack Keane, the army's number two officer, "Told colleagues that he thought the United States should put aside the Iraq question and keep its eye on the ball."[8] He believed it made more sense for the United States to put troops on the Pakistan border and focus on getting Osama bin Laden. Furthermore, unlike the happy picture of headquarters that Franks paints in his memoirs, there were numerous reports that he ran a very unhappy command, characterized by General Franks "berating subordinates and shouting and cursing at them."[9] The issue in the minds of fellow military officers was: Would Franks ensure that any plan that came out of his meetings with Rumsfeld would protect the troops? Would it be structured in such a way that the Iraqi Army would not only be defeated, but that a viable, stable government would be created so U.S. troops could leave and go home?

## Talking Points

Rumsfeld was well aware of the danger that a freelancing Franks would present. In fact, Rumsfeld went out of his way to ensure that the general did exactly what he wanted him to do. He took several approaches to the problem: first, he provided Franks with "talking points" that had been drawn up by Paul Wolfowitz and Doug Feith. They made clear how the secretary expected the war in Iraq to be fought: "The campaign, the talking points note, should be marked by surprise, speed, shock, and risk, as well as actions that. . . . would add to the momentum for regime change."[10] Franks could work out the details himself, but in a military sense, Rumsfeld was interfering all the way down to tactical level—telling Franks how to deploy and maneuver his troops. Rumsfeld was going to be in overall charge; he believed that was the secretary's job.

## Outlast the General

Rumsfeld's second approach was simply to wear Franks down. For example, on November 26, he did not ask the general for a full-blown plan, but instead requested a "concept" and gave him three weeks to complete work on it. There was logic behind Rumsfeld's actions. He wanted the world to think that Franks had drawn up the war plan against Iraq—that it was a military plan, not his. True, he would meet often with Franks, but he would try to portray such meetings as opportunities for him to be "brought up to speed." Franks was focused on long-term goals, such as assuring that the military got the credit for a successful military action against Iraq. Rumsfeld was more focused on the outcome of the invasion, a result that would confirm the validity of his movement toward military transformation. Rumsfeld ultimately decided that the most effective way to deal with Franks was to treat him like a piece of salami, wearing him down one slice at a time.

Finally, according to one account, Rumsfeld and his colleagues told General Franks that he was not to consult with General Zinni, the man who knew more about Middle Eastern history, culture, and leaders than any other senior officer in the U.S. military.[11] That was unfortunate, because one of the points Zinni emphasized in both his plan and in subsequent conversations was the extreme importance of planning for the post-hostilities phase. Furthermore, all indications were that the invasion plan had been updated and refined—even after Franks took over.[12] No general likes to have another one looking over his shoulder, but Rumsfeld probably realized that Zinni would not go along with his small and fast approach to invading Iraq. Zinni thought the situation was far too complex to allow for minimal forces.

Franks and several of his planners met with Rumsfeld on December 4 via the secure video teleconference system at the Pentagon. Interestingly, Franks commented that, prior to providing his brief, he noticed that in addition to Secretary Rumsfeld and Chairman Myers, General Peter Pace and Doug Feith were present. He wrote that while he had no problem with Pace, he did with Feith. In his own words, "Feith was a theorist whose ideas were often impractical; among some uniformed officers in the building, he had a reputation for confusing abstract memoranda with results in the field."[13] Unfortunately, Feith would be a constant source of concern for the uniformed officers, most of whom would repeat variations on Franks's comment.

Most of Franks's discussions with Rumsfeld focused on the issue of numbers. Rumsfeld was intent on using as few troops as possible, while Franks would argue for larger numbers. As a result, no one paid much attention to an overall strategic plan. It was all about operations and tactics. In a certain sense, for Rumsfeld and Franks, strategy was the same as tactics. This neglect would have very a negative impact on the outcome of the invasion when it took place.

Cognizant of the secretary's penchant for a small number of troops, Franks and his staff claimed they had recalculated the original number. Now, he suggested, the number of troops could be reduced from 500,000 in the current plan to only 385,000. According to Zinni, this was the actual number that he planned to use. As Zinni told me, "The plan was for 380,000–400,000. In the OPLAN, you run your worst-case scenarios so the Joint Staff can program forces. I felt 380,000 was a minimum to secure the border, control internal problems, and reorient the military (which we did not plan to disband.)"[14] Franks was familiar with Zinni's thinking on the topic, so he was presumably just putting forth Zinni's number, knowing that it had been worked out and updated by the staff. However, it is remarkable that he was willing to cut more than 100,000 troops out of the original plan without even being asked. Presumably, he hoped that Rumsfeld would be pleased, but that was a mistake.

Franks provided three options: the "robust option," involving all of the countries in the region, the "reduced option," involving fewer countries, and the "unilateral option," consisting of only U.S. forces. Rumsfeld suggested that, as a result of the way U.S. troops had performed in Afghanistan and the availability of new weapons like the Predators, the United States would not need even 400,000 troops to invade Iraq. Franks responded, "You'll get no argument out of me," effectively ignoring the work CENTCOM had done.[15] Satisfied that Franks was moving in the right direction in terms of numbers, Rumsfeld then called on him and his staff to come up with some "out of the box" ideas to be presented at a follow-up meeting on December 12.

At this meeting, Rumsfeld wanted to know if the force buildup could be done in secret and even expanded. Franks responded that they would have to be careful when it came to large units or components.

According to Gordon and Trainor, Franks presented a matrix that indicated he was prepared to "reexamine the very foundations of CENTCOM strategy for Iraq."[16] He had also decided to cut ground forces to 300,000. He was clearly going overboard in an effort to satisfy the secretary of defense. Franks focused on the military's ability to efficiently produce a small force in a shorter amount of time and whether or not this preparation for a possible invasion of Iraq could be kept secret.

To make things even more complex, Franks noted that invading Iraq would be much more difficult than taking Afghanistan. Iraq was a relatively modern country, with an educated population and a military, even though its fighting ability had deteriorated since Operation Desert Storm. Numbers had also come down. Rumsfeld reportedly expressed support for the new iteration, but, as might be expected, he sent Franks back with a request that the invasion force be even smaller and faster. Then Rumsfeld dropped another bombshell when he added that Franks should consider actions the military could take as early as April or May of 2002—only four months away. That request left Franks and his staff breathless. Rumsfeld obviously had no idea of the complex planning required for such an operation. Just the complexity of the logistics boggled the mind.

By the time of the December 19 meeting, Franks had cut the size of the initial invasion force down from 500,000 to 145,000, which could be deployed in ninety days. He proposed that reinforcements then be sent until the total number of troops reached 275,000.[17] Rumsfeld saw that as an improvement, but again ordered Franks to make it smaller still and even faster.

Rumsfeld then informed the general that he, Franks, would be flying to the president's ranch in Crawford, Texas, on December 28 to brief him on the plan. Meeting with Bush, Franks focused on the existing CENTCOM OPLAN 1003, noting that he and Rumsfeld had discussed it and considered it to be "outdated. It called for troop levels of at least four hundred thousand, which would require a very visible six-month force build-up."[18] The difficulty was that an existing plan could not simply be tossed away without a new plan to replace it. Franks then explained that the war would be divided into four phases. His major point, which impressed the president, was the idea that "force could be applied selectively and carefully across the different points."[19] Significantly, Franks also acknowledged that internal security could be a problem during Phase IV, as could creating a new and stable government. Finally, the general emphasized the importance of international support in the form of troop contributions from other countries.

Franks was not working alone in briefing the president. Rumsfeld also weighed in by teleconference. When Franks mentioned 275,000 as the number of troops that might be needed for the invasion, Rumsfeld interrupted to say, "We are still working through the numbers. The number Tom is giving you is soft."[20] In any case, the president seemed pleased by the briefing and suggested that the government needed to start doing some of the things Franks had mentioned. Then, in a display of political machismo, Rumsfeld commented, "Tom and I will talk about these things."[21] The point was that while Franks was giving the briefing, it was Rumsfeld who would make the decision on what actions the Defense Department would take regarding Iraq.

General Franks had his own take on post-hostilities operations. He realized that this would be the longest phase, lasting years, not months.

> So Gene Renuart's graphics people had split that phase's wide arrow into segments, and marked its duration UNKNOWN rather than x-days. The endstate of Phase IV included the establishment of a representative form of government in a country capable of defending its territorial borders and maintaining internal security, without any weapons of mass destruction.[22]

There are two important aspects of this quotation. First, while Franks, like every U.S. officer, understood the importance of Phase IV, it was clear that he had no idea how the matter would be handled. Apparently, he believed it was someone else's problem. Furthermore, it was also clear that the military was primarily concerned about WMDs.

Once the question of the number of troops had been decided, and Rumsfeld and Wolfowitz had the outlines of the operation, they left Franks to his own devices. It was up to the general to decide when and how an operation was to be carried out—as long as it fit within the parameters of Rumsfeld's understanding of "small and quick." Unfortunately, Feith wanted to be hands-on. He often tried to get involved in operational matters and drove General Franks and his staff crazy. In one case, for example, Franks told his staff that Feith was "getting a reputation around here as the dumbest fucking guy on the planet."[23] Feith had what the military would call operational control over the Pentagon. He could and did make decisions that had a major—often negative—impact on the military's ability to carry out its mission.

By the end of 2001, it was clear that the United States was taking the possibility of employing the U.S. military against Saddam Hussein very seriously. However, it would be wrong to suggest that a decision had been taken to invade. That was certainly the option that Rumsfeld, Wolfowitz, Feith, and Vice President Cheney wanted, but the president was still considering it. The real question was whether the Iraq Hawks could justify the need to send troops into combat.

One innovative aspect of Franks's planning was the idea of a "running start." Traditionally, the U.S. military has operated a "generated start" for combat operations. That meant that, prior to the start of ground operations, a week or so of air operations would be undertaken—to soften up the enemy. Ground forces would not move into action until that operation was done. Franks's idea was "to compress the air campaign to the point that air and ground operations—preceded by extensive Special Forces work—would be virtually simultaneous. And we could launch the operation while follow-on forces were still deploying."[24] Rumsfeld loved it. Meanwhile, there was the question of what to do about captured al-Qaeda members.

## Afghan Prisoners in Guantanamo

These prisoners could not simply be turned loose because the government assumed—correctly, in most cases—that they would rejoin their friends and begin war against the United States all over again. Furthermore, they were not prisoners of war in a formal sense. They did not wear uniforms and they were not subject to the laws of any state; in fact, many did not recognize state sovereignty.

The Bush administration feared that if these individuals were brought to the United States, U.S. courts would rule that they had to be given the protections enumerated in the U.S. constitution.

Instead, Bush decided on January 18, 2002, that they were not subject to the Geneva Convention and instead would be declared "unlawful combatants." It was also decided to house them outside the United States, at the U.S. naval base at Guantanamo, Cuba. That way they would not be subject to U.S. laws. General Myers opposed the decision, as did Secretary Powell, because "It would open the door for mistreatment of U.S. personnel taken as POWs."[25] Myers argued with Rumsfeld about the issue and, to his credit, at a subsequent NSC meeting, Myers made his position crystal clear.

> Mr. President, . . . you may notice that I'm the only guy here without any backup. I don't have a lawyer . . . I don't think this is a legal issue. And I understand technically why the Geneva Conventions do not apply to these combatants. . . . I got that. But I think there is another issue we need to think about that maybe hasn't gotten enough light.[26]

Myers said he worried about the impact on U.S. POWs.

The president eventually compromised; Taliban members would be subject to the Geneva Convention, while al-Qaeda would not. The upsetting aspect of this meeting was that it took place while Powell was out of the country, and the attorney general had not tendered a legal opinion on the issue. Politics, not the law, reigned supreme.

When he returned from abroad, Powell went to see the president, where he made his dissatisfaction known—both types of prisoners should be subject to the Geneva Convention. Bush agreed to discuss the issue again at an NSC meeting on January 28. General Myers stated that military lawyers at the Pentagon had argued persuasively that rejecting the Geneva Convention posed serious risks for U.S. troops. Meanwhile, a memo by Cheney's legal adviser had leaked. It blasted the State Department's point of view and claimed that State had not made its objections known. "Powell was beside himself with rage . . . less at the substance of the memo than 'the way the process was being pushed. It was not being put in the *Washington Times* in order to have a balanced view of the issues.'. . . It was in the *Washington Times* in order to try to screw me."[27] For his part, Rumsfeld argued that he thought it would be OK if the president said that the prisoners were treated "consistent" with the conventions. The issue was never fully resolved, but what it did point out was that with Cheney siding with Rumsfeld, Powell was at a decided disadvantage. Meanwhile, Bush's upcoming State of the Union Speech would refocus the White House's concern with terror.

## The "Axis of Evil" Speech

The president planned to use his speech as a vehicle to outline how he planned to proceed in the future. He was convinced that 9/11 was not an isolated event. "The president was not just talking about opposing threats, he was talking about a reorientation of American foreign and defense policy."[28] It is fair to say that he succeeded. He took the terrorists on directly. He noted, "States like these and their terrorist allies constitute an axis of evil, arming to threaten the peace of the world." He said that the United States would "deliberate," but he made it clear that time was not on America's side. "I will not wait on events while dangers gather. I will not stand by as peril draws closer and closer. The United States of America will not permit the world's most dangerous regimes to threaten us with the world's most destructive weapon."[29] Powell was reportedly "turned off" by the president's rhetoric. He saw phrases such as "axis of evil" as unnecessarily provocative. It was meaningless, and while it would make some on the right happy, it would do little to advance U.S. foreign policy goals.[30]

## Blindly Marching toward Iraq

Phase III was the primary focus of a January 30, 2002, meeting at the White House. Bush wanted to hear what the chiefs had to say about the plan. Myers said he was happy with it. Vern Clark, the chief of naval operations, and John Jumper, the air force chief of staff, praised it. Shinseki's endorsement was more qualified. He specifically said that he would feel better if the United States had Turkey's agreement to open a northern front and more forces in place before combat action began.

Also in January, at an NSC meeting, Bush had asked Franks about post-invasion plans—who would be in charge, and how it would be implemented. Franks acted as if everything was in hand. "Don't worry, he said, according to a senior NSC official present for the exchange. We've got that covered. The U.S. military would keep the peace. Each major Iraqi town and village, Franks explained, would have a 'lord mayor'—an appointed U.S. military officer—who would be in charge of maintaining civic order and administering basic services."[31] This answer was complete nonsense. In fact, almost nothing had been done (or would be done) to deal with Phase IV and Franks should have known it. There would be a retired military officer who would oversee—or at least try to oversee—the distribution of humanitarian relief and who would do his best to get the Iraqi government back on its feet, but to suggest that such a detailed procedure had already been worked out was wrong.

On February 1, 2002, Franks was at the Pentagon for the fifth iteration of the plan to invade Iraq. The new strategy was now called the "Generated Start Plan" (i.e., the U.S. would quickly generate the necessary air and ground forces to get rid of Saddam). Franks expected that it would take about ninety days to bring 160,000 troops to the region. Eventually, there would be some 275,000 troops in the region.[32] The assault into Iraq would begin after twenty days of air operations. Special Operations Forces would be used extensively. Franks estimated that it would take 135 days to complete the operation and move to Phase IV.[33] Rumsfeld was still not happy. He wanted the force-generation stage to be cut from sixty to thirty days. However, the problem with that approach was that it meant using far fewer numbers of troops. Rumsfeld and Franks talked daily. The secretary wanted to know everything and could be counted upon to provide his input to whatever idea Franks and his staff offered.

On February 7, 2002, General Franks presented his plan for an invasion of Iraq to the NSC, with the president in attendance. This would be the first time Bush would actually see a plan that he could order carried out. Franks's approach was more traditional than revolutionary—i.e., the way Rumsfeld wanted it. Franks said the operation would take a total of 225 days. He used the term, "90–45–90." Specifically, ninety days of preparation and force movement, then forty-five days of heavy bombing prior to using ground forces. At the end of the forty-five days, a force of 300,000 would invade, which he estimated would take another ninety days.[34] As far as timing was concerned, Franks said that December 1 through February would be the best because of the weather.

After Franks had finished, Rumsfeld told the president that they were working on another, more revolutionary approach, dubbed "shock and awe." It was based on the idea of forcing the collapse of the Iraqi government. There would be so much force applied by bombing and other special operations forces that the regime might collapse on its own. Franks, however, was not fully on board. He suggested that it would take a lot more work, particularly during Phase IV. Clearly, Rumsfeld had more work to do before Franks was won over to his view of warfare.

In May 2002 the CIA set up and carried out a war game to determine what kinds of problems and outcomes the United States could expect from an invasion of Iraq. For example, how would the U.S. military deal with weapons of mass destruction and civil disorder, an issue that kept coming to the fore during the game. Interestingly, representatives from the Defense Department were included in the game at the beginning, but as soon their superiors at the Office of the Secretary of Defense learned about it—e.g., Feith—they were ordered not to participate any further. Fallows maintains that the primary reason for pulling them back was a concern on the part of top Pentagon officials that postwar planning would emerge as a major problem and, even more important, "an impediment to war."[35] In other words, there was concern that if too much time were devoted to Phase IV and security issues, the rest of the government might decide invading Iraq was too hard and too complicated, a conclusion that Rumsfeld and his colleagues wanted to avoid.

On June 1, 2002, Bush used a speech to the graduating class at West Point to introduce the concept of preemption. The United States, he told the cadets, will not be able to win the war on terror by being on the defensive. "We must take the battle to the enemy, disrupt his plans, and confront the worst threats before they emerge."[36] The logic of that statement meant that the United States must be prepared to take preemptive action if it was convinced that another state or organization such as al-Qaeda was preparing an attack. If the United States had taken such action prior to 9/11, Washington might have been able to avoid the bloodbath that marked that fatal day. In discussing this speech, Fallows added a very interesting comment: "As a rule, the strongest advocates of preemptive attack, within the government and in the press, had neither served in the military nor lived in Arab societies."[37] More than one serving officer or FSO would likely agree.

By June the United States was working with two invasion plans. The first one, preferred by Rumsfeld, was the Running Start, and the second was the more traditional Generated Start. When Franks met with Bush on June 19, 2002, the president did not come down in favor of either option. Instead, he seemed to be more concerned about the question of weapons of mass destruction, and what the United States should do if Saddam used them on his neighbors or U.S. forces. By the end of June, Franks told his planners to put primary emphasis on Rumsfeld's Running Start as they prepared for an attack on Iraq.

The military as a group still had doubts. They still did not understand the necessity of an invasion of Iraq. As far as the military was concerned, their primary target was al-Qaeda, which was located in and around Afghanistan. It made no sense to put scarce resources into Iraq when the other job was not finished. In addition, analysts who had access to sensitive intelligence knew that there were major questions about almost everything, particularly Iraq's ties to al-Qaeda and the presence of WMD. Finally, none of the civilians seemed to understand the difficulties and dangers associated with urban warfare. One officer who managed to get a look at the intelligence section of the war plan came away "puzzled" by the way weapons of mass destruction—which would become one of the major justifications for the war—were treated. That section was full of qualifications that made it clear that the U.S. war planners knew very little about the topic.[38] Military leaders were also skeptical about Rumsfeld's insistence on capping the number of troops that could be used in the Afghan war. It violated one of the basic laws of any military—you fight as you train. But there were holes in units. As Ricks noted, in the battle of Shahikot Valley the army did not have the artillery necessary to hit al-Qaeda heavy machine guns, because Rumsfeld's minimalization policy had forced the army to leave its artillery behind.[39]

These differences of opinion came to the surface in an article in the *Washington Post* in late July. According to this article, senior military officers still did not understand the logic of getting rid of a containment policy in favor of an invasion of the country. After all, many senior officers argued, the current policy was working. Saddam had not threatened his neighbors and, as far as they could tell, he had not supported terrorist organizations. Not only were there the normal military concerns, but senior military officers were also worried about the possibility of an attack leading to chaos in the country. It would, at a minimum, intensify anti-Americanism in the region. Several officers also questioned Bush's motivation. As one general involved in the war in Afghanistan put it, "I'm not aware of any linkage to al-Qaeda or terrorism, . . . so I have to wonder if this has something to do with his father being targeted by Saddam."[40] Typically, Rumsfeld dismissed this criticism, noting that there were lots of different points of view in the Pentagon. What to do about the U.S. military was such an issue that the Defense Policy Board included it on its agenda for its meeting on July 20. It was clearly a matter of considerable concern to civilians in the Pentagon. In fact, one person at the board meeting reportedly called for action, noting, "You have to have a few heads roll, especially in the Army."[41]

The military was not the only institution that was concerned about military intervention in Iraq. The Department of State and the CIA were both worried that civilians in the Pentagon and the Vice President's Office were leading the country into an unnecessary war.[42] Karen DeYoung, author of a biography of Powell, recounts a comment made by State officials dealing with the Pentagon. They came back from meetings with civilians at Defense and the Vice President's Office saying, "Our counterparts at the Pentagon and the vice president's office are too cocky. It's like they know something we don't."[43] To make matters worse, the time for dialogue was over. The Vice President's Office and the civilians in the Department of Defense were so bent on invading Iraq that any questioning of their position was seen as an act of disloyalty. A second unfortunate result was that Franks was increasingly being put in a position where questioning civilian (i.e., Rumsfeld's) advice would also be seen as an act of disloyalty.

## The British Become Alarmed

In July 2002 the British government sent Sir Richard Dearlove, head of MI6, to Washington for talks. When he returned, he observed that, based on his talks with U.S. counterparts, there was no longer a question of *if* there will be a war, it was now only a question of *when*. He did not mean that the Americans had set a date for the invasion, only that it appeared to him that Bush had decided that an invasion would be necessary. He was also convinced that U.S. authorities were determined to use the issue of weapons of mass destruction and Saddam's alleged ties to al-Qaeda as justification for the conflict. He felt that intelligence material was being manipulated to justify policy.

Dearlove was also alarmed to learn that no one seemed focused on the post-conflict period in Iraq.[44] In that regard, British officials were much less sanguine that coalition troops would be welcomed with open arms. This is why they were pushing strongly to involve the United Nations, an organization that Rumsfeld and Cheney, especially, distrusted. What most upset British officials was when they learned "that in the postwar period the Defense Department would still be running the show."[45] According to one source, "British cabinet ministers, Foreign Office diplomats, senior generals, and intelligence service officials all weighed in with concerns and reservations. Yet they could not dissuade their counterparts in the Bush administration—nor, indeed, their own leader—from going forward."[46] Alastair Campbell concurred, noting that by July 23, Prime Minister Tony Blair and his advisers had "a strong feeling that the U.S. had pretty well made up their minds."[47]

## Get the Right Intelligence

Wolfowitz, Feith, and other Iraq Hawks were convinced that their view of the threat presented by Saddam was accurate. They were also very frustrated at what they considered to be the incompetence of the CIA. If it was a proficient organization, they argued, it would have provided them with the material needed to prove Saddam's involvement with al-Qaeda and his possession of WMD. "The level of competence on past performance of the Central Intelligence Agency, in this area," said Richard Perle, "is appalling."[48] More to the point, not only did the Iraq Hawks show disdain for the CIA, there are reports from CIA analysts "that senior Defense Department officials and other Bush administration officials sought to press them to produce reports that supported the administration's positions on Iraq."[49] The real problem was that no one in the intelligence community—and that included the Defense Intelligence Agency—was prepared to tell Feith, Wolfowitz, Perle, Cheney, and Rumsfeld what they did not want to hear. This was particularly true of the argument that somehow, Saddam Hussein was responsible for 9/11 by giving aid and comfort to al-Qaeda. The administration desperately wanted to find information that would confirm this tie. However, the professional intelligence community simply could not find any. The civilians in the Pentagon decided to take matters into their own hands. They set up a shop that would provide them with more "accurate" data.

In August Feith created a nondescript entity, called the Office of Special Plans, to verify CIA analysis while at the same time carrying out extensive research on its own—to find the "linkages" and "associations" among terror groups that the CIA and Defense Intelligence Agency (DIA) had either ignored or dismissed. Feith placed two of his subordinates in the office, including Bill Luti, a retired navy officer who had been an aide to former House speaker Newt Gingrich (R-GA). These individuals went through all of the intelligence information they could find, including raw data, and then tried to tie them together. They had others, including reservists, to help them.

They were certain these linkages were there; it would only be a matter of putting things together. Several people who visited the windowless office commented on the extensive charts on the walls, showing purported ties between one group of individuals and others. This office would not only read and reread CIA analysis, Feith demanded that they be provided with raw data so they would better be able to find the connections that the intelligence analysts had missed. This approach runs counter to that of professional intelligence analysts. Either there is a connection or there isn't, no matter how many leads are followed. In fact, unless a professional intelligence analyst, who has been working on the issue for several years, is doing the work and tying it into other classified and unclassified information, the connection may never be found. The diligent amateur may succeed in figuring out such ties, but the reliability of work done by a professional is considerably higher.

When asked about the linkage between al-Qaeda and Saddam Hussein, General Myers responded, "I never saw compelling evidence that there was a strong link between the Iraqi leadership and al-Qaeda leadership before major combat." He went on to note that he saw nothing wrong with questioning intelligence, but emphasized that he "was not involved with the OSD policy shop with regard to their intelligence analysis activities."[50] However, it seems odd that the chairman of the Joint Chiefs did not want to be involved, if only to express his opinion. After all, it was one of the key justifications the administration was using to send U.S. troops to fight a war.

## Stop the Leaks

By the beginning of August, Rumsfeld's dissatisfaction with the military on Iraq was leaking out. For example, on August 1 CNN reported, "Rumsfeld is very unhappy with the various military plans and options," and told the generals to "rework military options for Iraq." He wants "lightning-quick attacks."[51] Based on all the available information, it is clear that there was a split, despite General Franks's special relationship with Rumsfeld. Indeed, it is interesting that Franks does not even mention such problems in his memoirs. He covers the period from mid-May to late July by noting that he made three trips to his area of responsibility (AOR) and that he briefed the NSC, including the president, on an undisclosed date in which he discussed the steps he had taken in planning a possible invasion. Rumsfeld seemed in total agreement with him.[52] I mention this because it was clear from newspaper reports that officers inside the Pentagon were unhappy, to the point that there were rumors that the uniformed military had formed an alliance with Colin Powell and the State Department.[53] General Franks was not representing the views of the military. For him, it had become a "Tom-and-Don" affair. Unlike Shinseki, Franks appears to have believed that his primary task was to please Rumsfeld, not to make sure the secretary was cognizant of military unease by his colleagues as well as experienced leaders such as Powell. The concern was not only over how many troops the United States would need to invade Iraq—ranging from 68,000 on the part of some civilians or around the 120,000 minimum that Franks considered critical—it was also over what to do to prepare for Phase IV. Some believed that the Iraqis would welcome the United States enthusiastically. But what if they did not? What if there was widespread instability in the aftermath of an invasion? "All the experts agreed that what came after the fall of Baghdad would be harder for the United States than what came before."[54]

On August 5, 2002, Franks briefed the NSC and the president, presenting his new "hybrid" start of military operations. Like all other military operations, the hybrid approach had four phases. During the first phase, the United States would use "five days to establish the air bridge, which included enlisting all necessary U.S. commercial aircraft to augment the military aircraft to the combat region." Then eleven days would be needed to transport the initial forces. During Phase II there would be sixteen days of air attacks and Special Operations. Phase III would run 125 days of "decisive" combat operations. At the beginning of the 125 days, they would try to get a division inside Iraq and within a week another division of ground forces. Finally, Phase IV would be dedicated to stability operations "of unknown duration." When he was specifically asked about the duration of Phase IV, Franks replied, "I don't know how long."[55]

Franks was aware of the problems associated with Phase IV. During the August 5 briefing he assumed that a representative Iraqi government would be in place. His plans also said that the Iraqi Army would still be intact. After hostilities, there would be a 2–3 month stabilization phase, then an 18–24 month transition phase. At the end of this stage—32–45 months after the invasion began—there would only be 5,000 U.S. soldiers left in the country. The Department of State would "promote the creation of a broad-based, credible, provisional government—prior to D-Day."[56] That assumed, of course, that the Department of State would be closely involved in Phase IV operations. However, Feith made sure that never happened.

On August 5 Secretary of State Powell had his longest conversation with Bush prior to the second inauguration. Powell used the opportunity to point out to the president (and Rice) the implications of the actions he was considering taking. He also noted that senior military officers shared his views even if the civilians at the Pentagon did not.[57] An invasion of Iraq could destabilize the entire region and could drive up the price of oil. It would also take attention away from the war on terror and become the dominant foreign policy issue. Powell told the president that while he had been getting briefings on the military plan, he was concerned about the aftermath. That would be a gigantic undertaking and Washington needed to be prepared to do it right. Furthermore, Powell emphasized that the United States needed allies not only for military forces, but to help rebuild and stabilize the region. And then he added his now famous comment,

> "When you hit this thing," Powell later recalled telling the president, "it's like a crystal glass . . . it's going to shatter. There will be no government. There will be civil disorder." . . . I said to him, "You break it, you own it. You're going to own it. You're not going to have a government . . . not a civil society. You'll have twenty-five million Iraqis standing around looking at each other."[58]

Bush looked at Powell, and asked, "What should I do?" Powell's response was that if he was intent on going ahead with the invasion, he should first take the issue to the UN. The key was to get allies—to internationalize the problem. But there were those like Feith who "did not want foreign help." He argued, "We can do it better than anybody else: leave us alone."[59] Powell discussed the question with Cheney, Rice, and Rumsfeld the next day. At first Cheney—who thought the UN was a useless organization—opposed the idea. Then he changed his mind; this would be an opportunity to go there and point out that the real problem was that the United Nations was not doing its job. Saddam Hussein had violated numerous Security Council resolutions. The United States was only proposing to do the work the UN should have done but refused to do. They agreed to use Bush's already scheduled speech to the UN to "focus on Iraq and the Security Council's failure since the end of the 1991 Persian Gulf War to deal with Hussein's defiance of disarmament resolutions."[60]

## Iraq after Saddam

An important principals' meeting was held on August 14. The issue on the table was Washington's goals regarding Iraq. It couldn't be to simply get rid of Saddam. The United States had to go further—to build a democratic polity. Washington would keep the bureaucracies that ran the country, but it would reform them.

The "Top Secret" document they were working on called for the elimination of weapons of mass destruction and everything that went with them, including ending Iraqi threats to its neighbors. Further, it called on the United States to end Iraq's support of terrorism. Washington would employ "all instruments of national power to free Iraq." It was important that the U.S. action be seen by Iraqis and others as an action to "free" Iraq, not to invade it. This distinction made clear that the U.S. would help with the reconstruction of the country.[61]

Meanwhile, Brent Scowcroft, the retired air force general and former national security adviser, published an op-ed entitled "Don't Attack Saddam" in the *Wall Street Journal*.[62] In this article he argued that there was no evidence to indicate that Saddam's Iraq intended to attack the United States. Furthermore, as Powell had said, invading Iraq would take attention and resources away from the war on terrorism. According to Tenet, Scowcroft's advice was not well received in the White House.[63]

This act gave the Pentagon complete and total control of postwar Iraq, a decision that was to have fateful consequences. UK General Jackson, for example, commented, "The difficulties were greatly exacerbated by the President's fateful misjudgement in transferring responsibility for the post-conflict period from the State Department to the Pentagon. All the planning carried out by the State Department went to waste."[64]

In an effort to convince the CIA that Feith and his subordinates knew what they were talking about, Feith asked Tenet to permit his analysts to brief the CIA on the tie between Saddam and Al Qaeda, Tenet and his people agreed to hear what Feith and his colleagues had to say. So Feith and a small group of analysts went to the CIA headquarters on August 15, 2002. The CIA discovered that Feith's people had been going through raw intelligence data trying to tie it together, and they were interested in what the CIA thought of their conclusions. "Trouble was, while they seemed to like playing the role of analysts, they showed none of the professional skills or discipline required."[65] What they were doing was collecting data that supported their preconceived ideas, while ignoring information that questioned their assumptions. "Feith and company would find little nuggets that supported their beliefs and seize upon them, never understanding that there might be a larger picture they were missing. Isolated data points became so important to them that they would never look at the thousands of other data points that might convey an opposite story." To make matters worse, the briefer stated that there should be "no more debate" on Saddam's relationship to al-Qaeda. The briefer said "its an open and shut case." Tenet's response was "I knew we had trouble on our hands." While he said he tried to be polite, Tenet said he considered the briefing "crap."[66] Unfortunately, this briefing was being given all over Washington, and it was presented as if it was 100 percent correct.

## State Expertise Ignored

Foreign Service officers in the State Department were well aware of the pitfalls involved in trying to put Iraq back together after the end of combat operations. In the fall of 2001 there had been a conference at Columbia University where a number of former Iraqi military officers met to talk about what to do to reform the Iraqi armed forces. This led to suggestions for a larger study, one that would look at all aspects of Iraq's reconstruction. Subsequently Congress authorized $5 million to fund the studies that would make up the project. It would be run by the Department of State and headed by Thomas Warrick, who had worked in the State Department for many years. It was split into seventeen working groups, each of which would have 10–20 members. The State Department spokesman commented on October 4, 2002:

> The U.S. Government has been working with Iraqi academics, opposition figures, [and] independent Iraqis outside the country, since about April on planning for the Future of Iraq project. We're convening one of the five . . . working groups . . . today, and through the weekend, more than a dozen Iraqi engineers, scientists and technical experts convened in Washington for the first meeting of the Future of Iraq project's working group on water, agriculture and the environment. It's the fifth such working group that we've held since April 2002 planning committee meeting.[67]

One group was devoted to the military, attempting to come up with ideas for how the armed forces could be demobilized and reconstituted, while another dealt with post-Saddam stability and argued, "The removal of Saddam's regime will provide a power vacuum and create popular anxieties about the validity of all Iraqi institutions."[68] The groups maintained that whatever happened, one thing was clear: the United States would be forced to spend considerable time rebuilding and stabilizing Iraq.

The tragedy was that despite all the work done by the Future of Iraq Project, it had little impact, primarily because the civilian leadership in the Pentagon wanted no part of it.[69] If it became official U.S. policy and people on the Hill and elsewhere began to focus on the extent of the problems involved in a post-invasion Iraq, they might decide not to invade. Consequently, when control over the group working on post-invasion Iraq was transferred from State to the Pentagon in January 2003, the project sank into oblivion. Almost nothing from it was used. Indeed, Warrick, the man who probably knew the most about post-invasion reconstruction, would be barred from playing any role in post-invasion Iraq. Even General Zinni, the former CENTCOM commander, weighed in, noting a whole list of problems including "the need to 'maintain law and order, provide for force projection, do peacekeeping, protect threatened groups and deal with civil unrest and acts of retribution, counter external threats, and develop local security capabilities."[70] Phase IV would be beset with all kinds of problems.

Cheney, however, would have none of this equivocating. Speaking to the Veterans of Foreign Wars in Nashville, Tennessee, on August 26, 2002, Cheney stated, "There is no doubt" that Baghdad had weapons of mass destruction. He called for war. Having the inspectors return would accomplish nothing, because Saddam had no intention of complying with the UN Security Council resolutions. "The risks of inaction are far greater and than the risks of action," Cheney argued. "We *know* that Saddam has resumed his efforts to acquire nuclear weapons fairly soon."[71] The simple fact was that Washington did not know whether or not Saddam was producing or in the final stages of research on nuclear, chemical, or biological weapons. However, the impact of Cheney's speech was to box Powell in a corner. No loyal official wanted to openly contradict the vice president. In hindsight, Tenet observed, "Policy-makers have a right to their own opinions, but not their own set of facts. . . . I should have told the vice president privately that, in my view, his VFW speech had gone too far."[72]

As Cheney was detonating his bomb, army commanders were meeting at the Army War College to take a critical look at the Afghan operation. Two key points emerged. First, they recognized the failure to take a careful look at the long-term implications of short-term actions. Franks was apparently criticized by one observer for failing to learn one lesson from Afghanistan: "taking the enemy's capital wasn't the same as winning the war, a conceptual error he would repeat in Iraq."[73] The second criticism was for "not using established deployment plans for units, and instead sending them out piecemeal." "Headquarters had to utilize scores of individual Requests for Forces (RFF) to build organization in key theaters."[74]

The State–Defense feud continued. Powell's discontent was obvious by his failure to chime in with the bellicose statements being made by others. He did not want to wreck the president's upcoming UN speech. He did not want other countries to believe that the United States had already decided to invade. Meanwhile, the Pentagon was taking a look at post-invasion Iraq. But because of opposition on the part of civilians in the Pentagon, their work was not shared with State. Feith was obsessed with secrecy and went out of his way to cut anyone who maintained ties with State out of the action. He did not want anything about the post-invasion period to leak out.

> The fear, one official said, was that such people would offer pessimistic scenarios, which would challenge Rumsfeld's aversion to using troops as peacekeepers; if leaked, these scenarios might dampen public enthusiasm for the war. . . . Thomas E. White, the Secretary of the Army during this period, told me, "With the Department of Defense the first issue was 'We've got to control this thing'—so everyone else was suspect." White was fired in April, Feith's team, he said, "had the mind-set that this would be a relatively straightforward, manageable task, because this would be a war of liberation and therefore the reconstruction would be short lived."[75]

Indeed, there are reports that Rumsfeld ordered Franks not to worry about post-invasion problems, because he feared it would distract the general's attention while he was planning for the war.[76] At one point, Rumsfeld reportedly "threatened to fire the next person who talked about the need for a post-war plan."[77] What this would mean in practice was that the United States would go into Iraq without an effective post-invasion plan or strategy. There would be an attempt to patch things up as the war drew near, but it was half-hearted, last minute, and not supported by the civilians in the Pentagon or the uniformed military.

On September 4 Bush invited senior members of the House and Senate to the Cabinet Room of the White House. The president's message was simple. He would work with them, but in return, he wanted a quick vote in Congress on a resolution giving him the authority to take on Saddam. Cheney followed Bush's meeting up with a trip to Capitol Hill where he spoke with the leadership. He shared with them what he thought was convincing evidence that Saddam was a threat and that the United States had to do something. "When the Congressional leaders departed that briefing they looked grim."[78]

On September 6, General Franks and Rumsfeld briefed the president. Franks make a statement that should have set off doubts about the "certainty" of U.S. intelligence information. Turning to the president he commented, "Mr. President, . . . we've been looking for Scud missiles and other weapons of mass destruction for ten years and still haven't found any yet, so I can't tell you that I know that there are any specific weapons anywhere. I haven't seen Scud one."[79] If the key war fighter did not know where the alleged WMD or Scuds where, then how could the civilians in the Pentagon be so certain of themselves?

## The UN Speech and the NIE

On September 12, Bush spoke at the United Nations. He began his speech by arguing that "All the world now faces a test," and then focused directly on the United Nations, arguing that the UN faced "a difficult and defining moment. Are Security Council resolutions to be honored and enforced, or cast aside without consequence? Will the United Nations serve the purpose of its founding or will it be irrelevant?"[80] Bush's key point was that he hoped the UN would act. However, it if did not, he left no doubt that the United States was prepared to act on its own. Given the military preparations the United States had undertaken, Bush was hopeful that he would be taken seriously. His efforts led to a Security Council resolution calling on Iraq to make a full statement of all of its chemical, biological, and nuclear weapons programs to the Council. The resolution also warned Iraq that it had been "repeatedly warned . . . that it will face serious consequences as a result of its continued violations of its obligations."[81]

Facing congressional pressure for an analysis of the situation in Iraq, on September 12 Tenet directed the National Intelligence Council to do a new National Intelligence Estimate (NIE) on "the status of and outlook for Iraq's weapons of mass destruction programs." Because of the upcoming congressional vote on the war resolution, a task that often takes eight to ten months would be due in just three weeks. To make matters more difficult, the intelligence community was on the defensive after failing to predict 9/11, which damaged the credibility of its conclusions.

In defending the NIE, Tenet pointed out that it was less conclusive than many believe. For example, the phrase "we do not know" appeared thirty times in ninety pages; the phrase "we know" was present only three times.[82] The problem, as Tenet pointed out, came in the "Key Judgments" section. The first judgment stated, "We judge that Iraq has continued its weapons of mass destruction/WMD programs in defiance of U.N. resolution and restrictions." The real problem, however, came in the second sentence: "Baghdad has chemical and biological weapons as well as missiles with ranges in excess of U.N. restrictions; if left unchecked, it probably will have a nuclear weapon during this decade." The sentence is declaratory— "Baghdad *has*"— and it leads the reader to assume it will only be a matter of time before Iraq has a nuclear bomb. The second judgment notes, "We lack specific information on many aspects of Iraq's WMD programs," but then makes the following assertion: "We judge that we are seeing only part of Iraq's WMD efforts."[83] Given the deceptive nature of the Iraqi government in dealing with WMD, as well as deep-seated suspicions on the part of U.S. congressional and civilian leaders, it is not surprising that the statement about lacking specific information was interpreted by most observers to mean that, although we did not have information on it, there was no doubt that they were there someplace. Besides, U.S. and foreign intelligence analysts had obtained information for many years that pointed in the direction of active WMD programs.

Unfortunately, senior decision makers seldom read beyond the Key Judgments section. They have neither the time nor, often, the interest. In any case, according to Tom Ricks of the *Washington Post*, it was this NIE and Tenet's comments about it that convinced the president that "[going to war] was the right thing to do."[84] Much of it would also reappear in Colin Powell's infamous February 3, 2003 UN speech.

It is important to emphasize that Tenet fully admitted that the intelligence community did not do its best work in producing this NIE. As he put it, "If you want it bad, you get it bad," and that was precisely what the U.S. government got. He further argued that while the NIE was too assertive and certain of its facts, "If we had done a better job in all our analysis and in this NIE, war critics would have had a harder time today implying that 'the intelligence community made us do it.'"[85] Too much was demanded of the intelligence community in too short a time, and mistakes—fatal mistakes, it turned out—were made. Congress—and the White House—should have insisted on taking more time, and if that had happened, Rumsfeld, Cheney, and their allies might not have had the kind of NIE they wanted—one that many would see as a justification for the war.

The NIE was a problem, but Feith's actions made things even worse. For example, on September 16, a pair of researchers from his Office of Special Plans arrived at the White House to brief the president's chief of staff, Andrew Card, and Stephen Handley, the deputy national security adviser. Their brief covered the same old theme—the close ties between Saddam

Hussein and al-Qaeda. This time they apparently added an assertion that there had been nearly two dozen "high-level contacts" between Iraqi officials and al-Qaeda operatives. They relied heavily on a supposed meeting between Mohammed Atta, one of the 9/11 hijackers, and Iraqi intelligence officials. Both the FBI and the CIA were aware of this report—and both of them had dismissed it. Unfortunately, leaders on the Hill were also being led to believe that not only did Baghdad have chemical and biological weapons and would soon acquire nuclear weapons, there was a clear tie between al-Qaeda and Saddam Hussein. The noose was tightening—unfortunately based on false, or at least ambiguous information.

A fateful meeting took place toward the end of September. It was between Franks and his operations director Major General Victor Renuart, plus Rumsfeld and Feith. This time Rumsfeld focused on Phase IV, the post-invasion period. He said that State was not in a position to handle matters and, for that reason, Defense would take over. Feith commented that he had been attending interagency meetings dealing with this problem and that members of this group had discussed the topic at length. Most important, when the two officers left, Renuart turned to Franks and commented that it appeared to him that Feith's office "has responsibility for planning post-conflict and our responsibility is security. And we don't own the reconstruction stuff."[86] From a military standpoint, such a statement carried major, long-term weight. It told the commander that he was not to concern himself with such things—and it guaranteed that he would not. Instead, Franks would focus on other things like strategy and tactics, while assuming that Feith and the Iraq hawks were taking care of Phase IV.

Bush delivered a direct verbal attack on Saddam in a speech he gave in Cincinnati on October 7. In it he presented Iraq as a clear and present danger to the United States. He reiterated the claim that there was a working relationship between Baghdad and al-Qaeda. Bush did not go so far as to advocate an invasion, but he left that option open. Most important, he "called on Congress 'to authorize the use of America's military,' noting that the House and Senate were 'nearing a historic vote.'"[87] That vote occurred on October 10. With a 77–23 margin Bush was given the power to use the military "as he determines necessary and appropriate in order to defend the national security of the United States against the continuing threat posed by Iraq" and to "enforce all relevant U.N. Security Council resolutions regarding Iraq."[88] In short, Bush was given a blank check to go to war.

At about this time, there was a claim that Iraq was obtaining uranium from Niger. Larry Wilkerson, Powell's executive assistant, called in an intelligence analyst to ask about it. The analyst pointed out the impossibility of trucking this material across the barely paved roads of Niger all the way to a port city to be transshipped to Iraq. Furthermore, he did not see how French officials, who had a direct interest in the uranium mines, would let such vital material slip by without acting. Although the CIA knew that the papers on which this claim was based were forged, it did not bring it to anyone's attention. The papers were simply filed. Nevertheless, this suspect "evidence" would be offered by the president as another justification for the invasion.

Meanwhile, the military continued to be upset over the administration's march to war. In mid-October combatant commanders were notified that an order would shortly be issued stating that a war with Iraq would be part of the war on terror. Senior officers were incensed. "How the hell did a war on Iraq become part of the war on terrorism?" demanded one officer on the Joint Staff, summarizing the "reaction of four of those commanders' staffers." Another argued, "There is no link between Saddam Hussein and 9/11. . . . Don't mix the two. This is going to work hell with the allies. What is going on?"[89]

General George Casey, at that time the chief of strategic policy and plans on the Joint Staff, laid down the law. "The discussion is over. Look, this is part of the war on terror." The time for debate was finished. All members of the military were now expected to fall into line and follow the same playbook. It did not matter that they saw little justification for such an action. They had two choices. They could either get on board or they could resign their commissions. As noted previously, at least one officer, Gregory Newbold, a three-star Marine general, quietly handed in his retirement papers. Newbold was "unwilling to accept the official mandated assumption that Saddam Hussein was a threat to the United States, despite warnings that his career would 'not be interesting' if he continued to talk that way."[90]

## Conclusion

A close working relationship like the one between Rumsfeld and General Franks can be useful, but Rumsfeld managed to isolate Franks from the rest of the military. There is no doubt that Franks found it difficult to put up with sniping from his colleagues on the Joint Staff, and to a certain degree he welcomed this isolation. However, in retrospect, it would have been better for him and for the country if he had interacted more with his military colleagues on the Joint Staff. It is not clear whether Franks became increasingly convinced that Rumsfeld was right, or if the constant pounding that he took from Rumsfeld gradually beat him down.[91] He should have known that he did not have enough troops to create stability once Baghdad fell.

However, in his defense, he felt he had enough troops for Phases I–III, and he thought that Feith was taking care of Phase IV. In any case, he should have thought matters through and demanded a copy of the "plans" Feith claimed to have, but he undoubtedly felt he had his hands full with the attack itself.

During the first ten months of 2002, key civilian defense officials manipulated intelligence data for their own devices. Rumsfeld, Cheney, and especially Feith were determined to find a way to convince the president of the urgent need to take action against Saddam Hussein. They set up a special office in the Department of Defense to analyze data, and not surprisingly, the data showed that the civilian leadership in the Pentagon was right. Saddam represented a serious, growing threat to the United States. Anything that got in the way, like meetings to discuss the post-Saddam period, were cancelled, while Feith went out of his way to argue that Phase IV was a Defense issue and that he was on top of it. Defense was also not interested in discussing the issue. Feith, Wolfowitz, and Rumsfeld had been told by a very shadowy Iraqi émigré, Ahmed Chalabi, that Iraqis would greet coalition troops with open arms, they would be liberators—exactly what the Iraq Hawks wanted to hear. Any intelligence information that questioned that conclusion was set aside.

Feith's role in the Iraqi invasion was significant. While the State Department-sponsored "Future of Iraq Project" was far from the complete blueprint needed to handle post-invasion Iraq, it was better than anything Feith produced. For example, the project did the same thing the military always does—assume the worse case, while hoping for the best. Unfortunately, Chalabi convinced Feith that everything would be wonderful when U.S. troops arrived, while the State Department study warned that there could be serious problems with instability. The United States would go into the post-invasion period blind.

Finally, it is worth noting that many military officers harbored serious doubts about the Iraqi operation. The mere fact that General Casey had to send out a warning to all of the combatant commanders and others to line up behind the directive illustrates just how much opposition there was among the professional military. And despite Casey's directive, that opposition would continue, although it would be more muted.

# The Invasion of Iraq

What went wrong is that the voices of Iraq experts, of the State Department almost in its entirety and, indeed, of important segments of the uniformed military were ignored.

*David Rieff, World Policy Institute*

By October of 2002, the drive toward a U.S. invasion of Iraq resembled a freight train going full speed downhill. The trio of Iraq Hawks in the Pentagon, backed by Vice President Dick Cheney, could not wait for the "shock and awe" of an invasion of Iraq. To Secretary of Defense Donald Rumsfeld, it would confirm the correctness of his policy of military transformation. To Paul Wolfowitz and Douglas Feith, it would bring democracy and hope to the Iraqi people along with a less antagonistic Iraq vis-à-vis Israel. To Vice President Cheney, it offered a chance for the United States to show the ineffective, corrupt, and incompetent United Nations that it could solve problems the world organization only talked about. For President George W. Bush, it was a necessity—having been convinced by his advisers that Iraq represented a "clear and present danger" to the United States. They argued that if Saddam were not removed, a repeat of 9/11 was a real possibility.

## A Warning from the Army War College

While much of official Washington was convinced that a war with Iraq was becoming increasingly likely, Lieutenant General Richard Cody, the army deputy chief of staff for operations and plans, was worried about Phase IV operations. He asked the Army War College to undertake a study of the problems the military could expect to face during Phase IV in Iraq, giving them a deadline of January 31, 2003, to complete it. The task was assigned to the War College's Strategic Studies Institute.

The Strategic Studies Institute produced a paper that listed 135 post-invasion tasks that had to be accomplished if Iraq were to become a viable, stable state. These included everything from securing the borders and establishing local governments to protecting religious, historical, and cultural sites, creating a police force, reforming the military, and setting up hospitals. In other words, they would have to start at the bottom in creating a new Iraqi state. The report also noted religious and ethnic problems that could produce a civil war, and it warned that rebuilding Iraq would require considerable U.S. resources. Essentially, the "longer the U.S. presence is maintained, the more likely violent resistance will develop." The report insisted that Feith, his colleagues, and émigré Ahmed Chalabi were in fantasy land—the Iraqi people would not be greeting the U.S. troops with open arms. Most important, the report added, "The possibility of the United States winning the war and losing the peace in Iraq is real and serious."[1] Equally significant, the paper argued against eliminating the Iraqi Army. In sum, the War College study concluded that the U.S. Army's real challenges would begin once hostilities were over.

Shinseki shared the Army War College's concern about Phase IV. According to Ricks, the general raised the question at a meeting of the Joint Chiefs noting, "The mission was huge, that you needed a lot of troops to secure all the borders and to do all the tasks you needed to do."[2] The military was not alone with its concerns. Woodward reported that on December 5, 2002, Steve Herbits, one of Rumsfeld's closest confidants, walked into his office and told the secretary, "You have to focus on the post-Iraq planning. It is so screwed up. We will not be able to win the peace."[3]

Unfortunately, the civilians in the Pentagon were not interested in such talk. They would claim they had a plan, just as Wolfowitz insisted in July 2003. But as Lieutenant General Joseph Kellogg, a senior member of the Joint Chiefs of Staff who oversaw systems for the command and control of forces put it, "I saw it all. . . . There was no real plan. . . . The thought was, you didn't need it. The assumption was that everything would be fine after the war, that they'd be happy they got rid of Saddam."[4]

Meanwhile, the Joint Staff drafted a plan that called for a three-star general to oversee and manage postwar Iraq. To ensure the viability of the new regime, the military headquarters would be staffed by experts drawn from twenty-one areas, such as security, public health, finance, transportation, oil, etc. General John Abizaid wanted postwar planning to be assigned to a three-star general who was not involved in the invasion so that he would not have to divide himself between combat operations and post-combat operations. The army, however, was pushed aside because Rumsfeld, backing Feith, argued that the Defense Department would take the lead in all postwar undertakings. In fact, Rumsfeld bifurcated the missions by decreeing that combat operations would be commanded by a general, while post-combat operations would be assigned to a civilian. Both would be subordinate to CENTCOM General Tommy Franks, and through him to Rumsfeld.

That fall the United States presented its case to the UN Security Council. On November 8, the Council voted 15–0 in favor of Resolution 1441, which threatened Iraq with "serious consequences" if it did *not* prove that it had abandoned its weapons programs. The Security Council, as noted above, was demanding that Iraq "prove" a negative—that there were no weapons and no programs to produce such weapons in Iraq. Baghdad now had its final opportunity to comply. It was a victory for Secretary of State Colin Powell, who had consistently argued the importance of taking the issue to the United Nations, and now the international organization backed the United States. The next move belonged to Saddam Hussein.

## Messing with the TPFDD

On November 26 Franks requested that Rumsfeld approve the deployment of 300,000 men and women to Kuwait and the surrounding area. The problem was that Franks had to mobilize 300,000 individuals for his hybrid plan. Rumsfeld was not amused and responded, "We cannot do it that way."[5] He was concerned that if the Pentagon informed 300,000 troops, including reservists, that they were being called to the colors, it would tip the United States' hand. He insisted that diplomacy be given more time. In reality, he was playing games. His claim that he wanted to give diplomacy more time was a subterfuge—a way of giving the Pentagon more time to move military assets into place.

Rumsfeld was not about to let the rest of the world know how many troops the United States was deploying to the Middle East. He also was determined to prevent the generals from sending over more troops than were absolutely necessary—and he was convinced that, given the chance, that was exactly what they would do. He was determined to use only the minimum required to carry out the operation in order to prove the validity of his military transformation scheme. Initially he suggested that the deployment be broken into modules. When he realized that was not the most efficient way of doing things, Rumsfeld decided to get directly involved with the Time-Phased Force and Deployment Data (TPFDD). "The TPFDD for Iraq was an unbelievably complex master plan governing which units would go where, when, and with what equipment, on which planes or ships, so that everything would be coordinated and ready at the time of attack."[6] The master plan was especially important for the army. The Marines already had material stored aboard pre-positioned ships located at Diego Garcia in the Indian Ocean. The army, however, faced a very complicated process to get troops and follow-on troops to their destination. Sequencing is key; tanks cannot arrive before their crews, nor can infantry units arrive before their tanks. It could take at least six months to assemble the forces needed to invade Iraq.

That long time horizon was exactly what Rumsfeld hated about the army. He had nothing but disdain for the TPFDD; to him it was an anachronism, just another area where the army refused to be flexible and modernize. As one army officer told me, "Rumsfeld believed that the information age had suspended the laws of physics."[7] He believed that moving units around the world was too important to be left to a giant logistics program; political considerations had to be factored in as well. Besides, Rumsfeld wanted to be in a position to cut off troops once he was satisfied that the mission had been accomplished, which would show how few troops were really needed. Soon Rumsfeld insisted on personally approving each deployment order. In fact, it could take up to two weeks for the military to get a reply from Rumsfeld—at a point when time was of the essence. All of the years spent crafting the TPFDD were abandoned, as Rumsfeld was making those decisions in his office in the Pentagon. As a result, some reservists ended up getting only 5–6 days' notice while others got the news thirty days prior to activation. At this point the chairman of the Joint Chiefs should have stepped in and stood up to Rumsfeld, noting the damage he was doing, but there is no record of that happening. A participant in the process said that Rumsfeld was "looking line-by-line at the deployments proposed in the TPFDD and saying, 'Can't we do this without some company?'" Or "shouldn't we get rid of this unit?" Making detailed, last-minute adjustments to the TPFDD was, in the army's view, like pulling cogs out of a machine at random. "The generals would protest, saying, Sir, these changes will ripple back to every railhead and every company."[8] But Rumsfeld was running the show.

By the end of December, Bush had authorized sending 200,000 troops to the Gulf. However, Rumsfeld's constant interference was becoming a major problem. Army officials would decide to activate a reserve unit, only to discover that Rumsfeld had vetoed it. This was the first time in U.S. military history that a secretary of defense had micro-managed matters to this extent. Lyndon Johnson and Robert McNamara would not let the generals activate the reserves, and they tried to micro-manage the war, but they left the call-up process to the generals. Rumsfeld's piecemeal approach to activating units left gaping holes in staffing. For example, by not activating certain reserve units, it was impossible to set up the Theater Support Command, which was to manage the logistics of the ground forces. Thus equipment began to flow into Kuwait, but the troops were not in place to use it. The same was true of the military police. Many MPs were in the reserves and, because of Rumsfeld's interference, the vast majority would not be mobilized, an action that would have a major negative impact on Phase IV.

On January 13, 2003, Bush asked Powell to remain behind after an NSC meeting for a very important discussion about Iraq. Bush sat across from Powell and said, "'I really think I'm going to have to take this guy out.' And I said, 'Okay, we'll continue to see if we can find a diplomatic way out of this.'" Then with an eye on the conversation they had in August, Powell said, "But, you realize what you're getting into? You realize the consequences of this?" Bush responded that he did.[9] It was becoming clear to Powell and those around him that the United States was moving closer to a war with Iraq. Bush asked him if he was with him on this issue, and Powell confirmed that he was. Woodward added in his book that Powell was not convinced that Bush fully understood what he was getting the United States into. Indeed, several of his friends found him semi-despondent.[10] It looked as though Rumsfeld, Cheney, Wolfowitz, and Feith had won.

## The Office of Reconstruction and Humanitarian Assistance

On January 20 the White House belatedly issued a classified National Security Presidential Directive that established the Office of Reconstruction and Humanitarian Assistance under the Department of Defense. This act gave the Pentagon compete and total control of post-war Iraq. State Department officials—to the degree they were allowed to work on Iraq-related issues—worked directly for the Pentagon. If Feith and company needed any added incentive to be arrogant, this document gave it to them. It read: "If it should become necessary for a U.S.-led military coalition to liberate Iraq, the United States will want to be in a position to help meet the humanitarian, reconstruction, and administration challenges confronting the country in the immediate aftermath of the combat operations. The immediate responsibility will fall on U.S. Central Command, overall success, however, will require a national effort."[11]

This office would be responsible for everything—for planning and implementation of all decisions related to the administration of postwar Iraq. This included not only security, but the economy and political issues. To head this office, Rumsfeld selected Jay Garner, a retired army lieutenant general who had been in charge of the 20,000 U.S. troops that provided critical assistance to the Kurds during Operation Provide Comfort in the aftermath of the 1991 Gulf War. He helped drive Saddam's troops out of the region and knew the people well. Equally important, from Rumsfeld's point of view, Garner and his colleagues had done their job in the Kurdish region quickly and left Iraq in a few months.

Rumsfeld then called Garner and asked him to put together an organization, ultimately known as the Office of Reconstruction and Humanitarian Assistance (ORHA), to deal with the situation in a post-invasion Iraq. Garner, however, was shocked when he first looked at the document defining the tasks ORHA was expected to perform. It looked like he would be going to Baghdad as Washington's representative and that he would have responsibility for the entire post-war reconstruction of Iraq. Administratively, ORHA was subordinated to Under Secretary Feith, which guaranteed that Washington's heavy hand would play a critical role in how he did his job. While this assignment might seem to be a minor bureaucratic victory for Defense, in practice, it meant that Feith could—and would—have his hand in every decision made in post-invasion Iraq, from the future of the Iraqi Army to deciding who could be part of the Iraqi government.

To make matters worse, the project was late in getting off the ground. It was already the middle of January and only eight weeks prior to the invasion. Garner desperately needed qualified individuals. He turned to a man who had played the key role in the Future of Iraq Project, Tom Warrick, a 48-year old State Department civil servant. Garner was very impressed with Warrick and almost immediately asked him to join his staff. Warrick accepted and showed up at the Pentagon ready for work. A few days after Warrick began, Garner was in Rumsfeld's office for a meeting with the secretary, Wolfowitz, General Richard Myers, and General Peter Pace. After the meeting ended, Rumsfeld asked Garner to stay for a minute. He asked Garner if State's Tom Warrick and Meghan O'Sullivan were working for him. When Garner replied that they were, Rumsfeld said, "I've got to ask you to take them both off the team."[12] Garner refused, stating that both of them were too valuable to lose. Rumsfeld replied, "Look, Jay. I've gotten this request from such a high level that I can't turn it down. So I've got to ask you to remove them from your team."[13] Since the president seldom involved himself in personnel decisions, the order likely came from Cheney's office. After further investigation, it turned out that Chalabi was behind the firing. He disliked Warrick and passed on the request to the Vice President's Office. Eventually, Garner would be able to keep O'Sullivan, but not Warrick.

The situation was no better with the military. In February, Garner met with General George Casey, the director of the Joint Staff, about getting some ninety-four military personnel attached to his group. Woodward reported the conversation between Casey, Garner, and Jared Bates, Garner's chief of staff, also a retired three-star general:

> "Look, George," Bates said. "Time's running out on us. We have to have these people. Have you requisitioned them?"
>
> "No," Casey replied. "I haven't done that because you guys are trying to convince me that this is a 24/7 operation and I don't believe it."
>
> "George," Garner said. "You're out of your mind. You don't think this is 24/7."
>
> "No," Casey replied.[14]

After Garner threatened to bring the matter to Rumsfeld, Casey relented and provided the personnel requested. However, it was clear that Garner's undertaking did not have a high priority in the Pentagon. Only the threat of a meeting with Rumsfeld convinced Casey to provide the resources Garner requested.

Rumsfeld's rejection of Warrick was a defining moment in the staffing fiasco. Following Rumsfeld's lead, Feith did not want anyone from the State Department involved, because many FSOs were Arabists, and they were "not welcome because they did not think Iraq could be democratic."[15] Others believed that the State Department had done a poor job in Afghanistan and therefore should not be permitted to wreck post-invasion Iraq. The issue was raised to Powell's level. He called Rumsfeld and asked, "What the hell is going on?" Rumsfeld told Powell that when it came time to put Iraq back together, the United States needed "people who were truly committed and who had not written or said things that were not supportive." The conversation became very heated, as Rumsfeld had accused FSOs and other State Department officers of being disloyal.[16]

In January, much to Feith's chagrin, two intelligence assessments were released that predicted that Saddam Hussein's ouster and U.S. occupation of the country could result in violence and be an impetus to Islamic terrorists in the region.[17] Both Congress and the White House saw these reports prior to the start of the war. The documents warned of ethnic conflict and instability. At least one former senior intelligence officer familiar with the studies maintained that they presented "a very sobering and, as it turned out, mostly accurate picture of the aftermath of the invasion."[18]

## The Search for Justification

*Bush, Powell, and the Yellowcake Speeches*

All eyes were focused on the president's State of the Union speech on January 28, 2003, to see what the United States was going to do. Bush noted that the country was still hoping for a UN endorsement of a military action against Iraq, but he made it clear that the United States would do it on its own if it necessary. He pointed out that Saddam was ignoring the new UN inspections. He brought up the connection between al-Qaeda and Saddam and he invoked the image of 9/11. He also maintained that Iraq had labs where biological warfare agents could be produced. The only new item in his speech was his claim that Saddam had been trying to obtain yellowcake uranium in Niger, Africa. Bush then stated that he was asking the UN Security Council to meet within a week and noted that Secretary of State Powell would provide more information, including intelligence on Iraq's weapons programs as well as Baghdad's ties to al-Qaeda.

Preparing Powell's UN speech led to further bureaucratic infighting. One of the most interesting and colorful commentators on this process was Colonel Larry Wilkerson, Powell's administrative assistant. Wilkerson made no secret of what he thought of Cheney and Rumsfeld. Indeed, he confirmed what others had thought about collusion between the two. "What I saw was a cabal between the vice president of the United States, Richard Cheney, and the secretary of defense, Donald Rumsfeld, on critical issues."[19] Powell himself reportedly made a similar comment when he observed, "Very often Mr. Rumsfeld and Vice President Cheney would take decisions in to the president that the rest of us weren't aware of. This did happen, on a number of occasions."[20]

Turning to the Powell speech, CIA Director George Tenet stated that Powell had assumed the speech he was to deliver had been coordinated with the CIA, a standard procedure for "clearing" high-level speeches.[21] In fact, it had been drafted in the Vice President's Office by pasting together whatever seemed to support the U.S. case. It made little difference whether or not U.S. intelligence backed up the assertions. The speech, which was written by Cheney's assistant I. Lewis "Scooter" Libby, was a disaster. It included all kinds of charges, none of which were substantiated. Material was not treated impartially; indeed, it appeared that part of the draft came from the exiled Iraqi National Congress—courtesy of Chalabi. Data were manipulated to support the U.S. case. Tenet reported that the CIA had discovered that John Hannah, from the Vice President's Office, was quite familiar with the WMD aspects of the speech, so he was invited to join the group at the

CIA. He arrived with a pile of raw data, the kind of material that Feith's Office of Special Plans specialized in. No respectable intelligence analyst would draw the kinds of conclusions that Hannah was arguing. State's Bureau of Intelligence and Research found numerous statements that were not accurate or appeared to have come from Feith's Office of Special Plans—data manipulated to prove the case.

Wilkerson was furious and accused the Pentagon and the Vice President's Office of trying to foist a half-cooked, inaccurate speech on a secretary of state that he respected and admired. According to Wilkerson, "It was clear the thing was put together by cherry-picking everything from the *New York Times* to DIA."[22] Wilkerson could take only so much. "I threw the paper down on the table and said, 'This isn't going to cut it, ladies and gentlemen. We're never going to get there. We're going to have to have a different method.' And that's when George said, 'Let's use the NIE.'"[23] Wilkerson was not going to permit the Vice President's Office and Department of Defense to make a fool out of his boss.

Powell's patience with the drafting of his UN speech was also wearing thin. On February 2, Richard Armitage joined him at CIA headquarters. After looking the draft over, Powell commented, "This is bullshit."[24] The group finally came up with a speech based on the National Intelligence Estimate and Powell presented it on February 5, at the United Nations. Powell's delivery of the speech was marvelous. The problem, however, was that all of the arguments later turned out to be false. Had the administration listened to the intelligence specialists, both in State and the CIA, they could have avoided a major U.S. embarrassment, not to mention spared the thousands of U.S. military personnel who were wounded or killed because of a war based on unsubstantiated intelligence information.

Back in the Pentagon, relations between the uniformed military and civilian officials continued to deteriorate, as Rumsfeld insisted on supremacy. For example, during a February meeting with the president, Bush turned to General Myers and asked "How long will the war last?" Before Myers could respond, Rumsfeld put a hand on his arm and said, "Now, Dick, you don't want to answer that."[25] Rumsfeld had just prevented the chairman of the Joint Chiefs of Staff from answering a direct question from the commander in chief. One of the problems with a leader like Rumsfeld is that he was a bully and gave the impression that he was not interested in hearing views he opposed. This meant that cowed officials who did not agree with his intended course of action sat by and said little. Over time, the Joint Staff became afraid of Rumsfeld, Wolfowitz, and Feith. Rather than commit bureaucratic suicide, they simply sat back and said little. Rumsfeld and Feith could run their own war and postwar plans and see how well they turn out.

## Feith and the Senate Foreign Relations Committee

On February 11, 2003, Under Secretary Feith appeared before the Senate Foreign Relations Committee to discuss postwar Iraq. Predictably, he assured everyone that everything was under control. "I do want to assure the committee that when we talk about all of the key functions that are going to need to be performed in post-war Iraq, we have thought about them across the range from worst case to very good case."[26] This seems a rather bold statement, considering how little work Feith had done on the topic.

Senator Joseph Biden (D-DE) suggested that the Defense Department did not have a plan despite Feith's reassuring words. He asked Feith to provide details but only got vague generalities. Probably the best comment on Feith's comments—as well as those of State's Marc Grossman—was made by Ali Allawi, Iraq's first civilian defense minister:

> The premise that underlay their testimony was that the conflict would be short-lived, and that the main issues that would arise would relate to humanitarian and reconstruction needs. Little understanding was shown about the nature of the Iraqi state, and whether the administrative mechanisms would be able or reliable enough to manage the demands of a post-conflict situation. . . . From their testimony, it was evident that . . . Feith had no idea about the functioning of the state that the USA and its allies were going to inherit inside Iraq.[27]

In other words, the United States was invading Iraq based on a rosy scenario provided by the exile Chalabi. Feith put his faith in an Iraqi welcoming party, while the U.S. military almost always assumed a worst-case scenario, such as an armed rebellion, so that it was ready to deal with the unexpected.

## Shinseki Disagrees

Rumsfeld believed that senior military officers were expected to repeat whatever line the secretary of defense and the executive branch held when they testified before Congress. But when a general puts on his stars he signs a piece of paper agreeing to tell Congress the truth. This places a lot of senior officers in a quandary. In most cases, because the secretary of defense and the White House control their future assignments, promotions, and tenure in office, the generals and admirals support the administration.

Not General Eric Shinseki. Not only did he disagree with Rumsfeld's military transformation plan, he also refused to sit idly by and permit Rumsfeld to run a military operation in a way that he believed put the soldiers he led unnecessarily at risk. He was prepared to tell Congress the truth—and bear the consequences.

On February 25, 2003, Shinseki testified before the Senate Armed Services Committee. Shinseki had served in Bosnia and, as he had told the chiefs earlier, he believed that the United States would need a robust force to maintain stability in Iraq. For example, the United States initially sent 50,000 soldiers to control 5 million people in Bosnia; the size of the force grew to more than 160,000 by December 2005.[28] The Pentagon's formula was one soldier for every fifty Bosnians. Using that ratio for Iraq would mean about 300,000 soldiers would be required. Furthermore, he had asked the army's U.S. Army Center of Military History what its experts thought the number should be based on past experience. They came up with a figure of 260,000.[29]

While he was testifying before the committee, Senator Carl Levin (D-MI) asked him specifically, "Gen. Shinseki, could you give us some idea as to the magnitude of the Army's force requirement for an occupation of Iraq following a successful completion of the war?" Shinseki answered honestly, "Something on the order of several hundred thousand soldiers, are probably, you know, a figure that would be required." Furthermore, he continued,

> We're talking about post-hostilities control over a piece of geography that's fairly significant, with the kinds of ethnic tensions that could lead to other problems. And so it takes a significant ground force present to maintain a safe and secure environment, to ensure that all people are fed, that water is distributed, all the normal responsibilities that go along with administering a situation like this.[30]

Meanwhile, Rumsfeld was trying to keep the number of troops down, to no more than 100,000.

The next day Wolfowitz complained to Thomas White, the secretary of the army, arguing that Shinseki was out of line. That judgment call, he insisted, was the prerogative of the commander of the operation, and that was Franks, not Shinseki. However, White told Wolfowitz that Shinseki had done exactly what Congress asked him to do—provide his own personal evaluation of how many troops would be required. Rumsfeld, however, was furious and commented that it was ludicrous to think that it would take more forces to secure the country that it would to defeat its army.[31]

Two days later, Wolfowitz appeared before the House Budget Committee, where he was asked about Shinseki's estimate. Wolfowitz dismissed it. He maintained that Bosnia was a poor case to compare with Iraq. He believed that the Iraqis would greet U.S. forces with open arms. He stated, "Some of the higher predictions that we have been hearing recently, such as the notion that it will take several hundred thousand U.S. troops to provide stability in post-Saddam Iraq, are wildly off the mark."[32] This was probably the worst public rebuke of a senior military leader by a civilian since President Harry Truman fired General Douglas MacArthur in 1951. Not only was Wolfowitz's total rejection of Shinseki's comment unusual, he did not provide any material to back up his rejection.

A month later, Shinseki appeared before the House Appropriations Subcommittee. He was again asked about his comment that the United States would need several thousand troops to invade Iraq. His answer was "It could be as high as several hundred thousand. . . . We all hope it is something less."[33] Shinseki was tactfully pointing out that Rumsfeld and his colleagues were refusing to consider a worst-case analysis. They were betting everything on what Chalabi and other émigrés told them. But what if they were wrong? The country could turn out to be hostile and unstable; rioting might break out, or an insurgency. The United States would have nowhere near enough troops on hand to deal with the situation. Shinseki was trying to save Rumsfeld and Wolfowitz from themselves.

The main impact of the Shinseki incident was that it sent a chill throughout the ranks of uniformed officers. As one military officer put it, "It sent a very clear signal to the military leadership about how and what kind of military judgment was going to be valued. . . . So it served to silence critics just at the point when, internal to the process, you most wanted critical judgment."[34] This secretary of defense was not about to put up with honest differences of opinion even on such critically important issues as the number of troops needed in a war. For Rumsfeld, proving the correctness of his military transformation policy took precedence.

## After Saddam, What?

### Garner Tries to Set Up Shop in Iraq

By the end of February, Garner had over 100 people signed up to work on post-invasion Iraq. His major problem was that neither Rumsfeld nor the military gave his work top priority, a problem that would haunt him throughout his efforts to create stability in Iraq. Even worse, the administration would not acknowledge his existence. The White House feared that if word got out that a new organization had been set up to administer post-invasion Iraq, it would give the impression that war was inevitable. That would put the president in an embarrassing situation.

Garner and his people faced a daunting task. He had to worry about providing food and water, helping refugees, avoiding ethnic conflict, and a hundred other things. To facilitate administration of the country, he broke Iraq into three segments, the north, center, and south. Next he had to decide what kind of individuals he should use to administer Iraq—what kind of skills were required. Unfortunately, Under Secretary Feith intervened again. His primary concern was to get people who were ideologically acceptable—i.e., individuals with conservative political views, individuals who strongly supported Feith's belief that Iraq could be quickly democratized. That often excluded the FSOs who actually knew the languages and cultures of the region. Wilkerson had little time for Feith's approach: "Seldom in my life have I met a dumber man."[35] Placing primary emphasis on ideology in a reconstruction program, especially one as complex as Iraq, was a certain recipe for failure.

Garner himself seemed to believe that he would complete the transition process in only four months. His team would go to Baghdad and would set up an interim government. Then there would be an Iraqi constitutional convention, which would write a democratic constitution. It would be ratified and there would be elections—with a sovereign Iraqi government in place by August 2003.[36] In late February Garner went to the White House to brief the president on how he planned to administer post-Saddam Iraq. He placed special importance on the Iraqi Army, telling the president that he planned to use between 200,000 and 300,000 former soldiers to help rebuild and administer the country because they had the right skill sets, and he said that he was planning to send his advance party to the area in about ten days, with the rest to follow ten days later. Unfortunately, Garner and his team would soon learn that no one really wanted to deal with them. At this late date, Garner was still trying to get money, trying to find out how to get his people to the region, learning when they were supposed to leave, and when the war would start. Garner's military background told him that this was not the right way to run an operation. As Woodward noted, "War was clearly imminent, but Garner was still in the Pentagon. He believed the nagging question of governance still had to be addressed, and he wanted to stand up the Iraqi ministries immediately. But again the question had not been answered: Who was going to be in charge?"[37] He asked Feith for copies of whatever plans had been drawn up, but was told there were none—he should develop his own. In fact, Feith was hoping that Garner would turn to Chalabi and the exiles for advice and help.[38]

Woodward recounts an incident that pointed to just how tenuous Garner's situation was. Garner held a press briefing in the Pentagon on March 11. After telling reporters of the need to pay people, and to get the military and police moving in the right direction, he was asked about the Iraqi National Congress. He responded, "We're not trying to hire any of them right now, Okay?" That evening Feith called Garner very distraught, as did Wolfowitz. They wanted to remind Garner that Chalabi carried a lot of weight, and therefore the Iraqi government should automatically be turned over to him. Garner was ordered to not speak to the press. Meanwhile, nothing had been done to ensure a smooth transition from occupation authorities to either the Iraqi National Congress or to those living in Iraq. Feith was too disorganized to put something that complex together, and he refused to listen to the people qualified to run this sort of operation.

On March 14 Garner and his senior leadership met with Rumsfeld and a number of senior military and civilian officials. Rumsfeld apologized for not having devoted enough time to Garner's area of responsibility, and then told him that he wanted everyone on the team to be from Defense. Garner refused, puzzled. Rumsfeld had just told him to sack some of the most competent people in the world, who had a lifetime of experience in dealing with unstable countries, in favor of his own civilian advisers. As they parted, Rumsfeld told him to call as soon as he got to Kuwait.

The reality was that Garner and his team had been abandoned. No one was paying attention to them, so they did not know what was expected of them. They just sat around, waiting to be transported somewhere, sometime. Indeed, one sign of just how bad the situation was with regard to Phase IV came on March 17, two days before the war began. On that day a ground commander asked the Army War College for copies of the handbook that had governed U.S. occupation of post-war Germany.[39] They needed something to help them decide what to do after the conflict.

## The Future of Iraqi Institutions

On March 10, 2003, Bush and his top aides met in the Situation Room of the White House to go over plans for post-Saddam Iraq. The meeting was led by Frank Miller, the top civilian from Defense on the NSC. One of the top priorities was de-Baathification, to rid the government of Saddam's henchmen. Baath Party members numbered about 1.5 million, but only about 25,000 were active. That meant only about 1–2 percent were in top positions.[40] In addition, the United States would detain war criminals, while relying on Department of Justice and police personnel—all of whom were *assumed* to be professional. Top priority was a return to the rule of law. "A successful establishment of the rule of law in the immediate post-conflict environment is critical to ensuring stability," writes Woodward, "allowing for relief and reconstruction, and rapidly rebuilding Iraqi society."[41] The president agreed, noting that he wanted the Iraqis to take charge as soon as possible.

Turning to the Iraqi military, Feith led the discussion. He argued that the Iraqi Army would be kept intact and would play a major role in ensuring security after the war. Feith was certain that the U.S. government intended to keep the Iraqi military. The United States, to use Feith's term, would "reshape the Iraqi military." The goal would be to build an apolitical, multi-ethnic organization.

Meanwhile, Cheney went on *Meet the Press* on March 16—three days before the war began. He reiterated the administration's optimistic line on post-conflict Iraq: "My belief is that we will, in fact, be greeted as liberators." He was asked about General Shinseki's comment that the United States would require several hundred thousand troops during the post-war period, but dismissed it, calling it an "overstatement."[42]

## Ultimatum and War

On March 17 Bush delivered his ultimatum to Saddam Hussein, telling him and his sons to leave the country. Just prior to issuing the ultimatum, Bush called together his commanders as well as Generals Franks and DeLong for a final teleconference. Each officer was asked if he was comfortable with the situation, and they all replied affirmatively. Saddam, however, did not believe that Bush would actually attack. But what Saddam and the rest of the world did not know was that Bush was planning to invade Iraq even if Saddam left. He believed such a move was critical in order to get rid of the purported WMD and to remove senior members of the Baath Party.

The Coalition, which was made up primarily of American and British forces, began the invasion of Iraq on March 19. Instead of the old approach of weeks of bombing and then launching an invasion force, the ground troops were actually underway a day before the bombing began, because there were indications that Saddam was setting oil wells afire. Franks's plan was for them to move on to Baghdad without pausing. This would not allow the enemy enough time to recover or move troops from one area to another. Moving ground forces ahead of air bombardment would be give Coalition troops an advantage, because it would be a complete surprise. The size of ground force troops was 145,000, far below what General Zinni had recommended. *Washington Post* correspondent Thomas Ricks believed Franks could have gotten more troops if he had held out for them. He was the one person who could have insisted on them, but he chose not to. According to Ricks, "Many believe that if we had kept the forces coming, we could have avoided the insurgency."[43]

Franks made other strange personnel decisions. For example, the First Cavalry Division was available for deployment to Iraq. It would have provided another 17,500 soldiers to deal with Phase IV problems, enough to potentially make a difference. Rumsfeld and Franks disagreed about who failed to order the division's deployment. Rumsfeld argued that it was Franks's decision, while Franks pointed his finger at Rumsfeld. He said not using the First Cavalry Division was Rumsfeld's idea, and in the beginning, he opposed it. But Franks claimed that, in the end, he decided not to use the First Cavalry, after consulting with his field commanders. "Rumsfeld did not beat me into submission," said Franks. "Initially, I did not want to truncate the force flow, but as it looked like we were likely to get greater international participation, I concluded that it was OK to stop the flow."[44] However, one of his former staff officers argued that he had wanted to deploy the division and was "disappointed that he had to do without the additional division."[45] The important point was that Rumsfeld pressured Franks to reduce the number of forces needed for Phase IV. But ultimately, Franks was responsible for the number of troops. Furthermore, it was his "call to stop the flow for forces after major combat was over."[46] Franks should have held his ground as Shinseki did.

By April 14, U.S. troops were in Baghdad and the war was over—or so the civilians in the Pentagon thought. The next day Bush convened the National Security Council to discuss getting other countries to send peacekeeping troops to ease the burden on the United States and United Kingdom. Many in the administration were convinced that although a number of countries opposed the war, in the end, the international community would send military units to Iraq once the war was over and a new government was established. The idea was to enlist four divisions. One would be made up of NATO states, another from the Gulf Cooperative Council, one led by Poland, and another by Britain.[47] Meanwhile, Franks told his commanders that assuming everything went as expected, they should begin to make plans to withdraw troops. He suggested that the U.S. contribution could be down to little more than a division of 32,000 troops by September.[48]

## The Sweet Smell of Success?

With the lightning dash to Baghdad and the collapse of the Iraqi Army, Rumsfeld was basking in the "success" of the operation—military transformation had triumphed. Rumsfeld gloated:

> General Franks did manage to get, we believe, tactical surprise and he got it by starting the conflict not with a long multi-week air war that destroyed the infrastructure and had the risk of killing innocent men, women and children,

but he started with a ground war. Second, he went in with a very brief air war that was very precise, had minimal collateral damage, we believe, and he preceded with the ground war with a number of special operators moving in and securing key areas.[49]

Coalition forces were victorious and U.S. forces reached Baghdad in record time. Unfortunately, the problems began once they arrived.

The situation in Baghdad was nothing short of a disaster. First, there were not enough Coalition troops to police the city. Iraqis begged the troops to help them, but there simply were too few. The following comment came from a Marine, a colonel who was there, and is typical of comments from most of the soldiers and Marines deployed to Iraq.

> Frantic locals ran up to tell us phones were out, doctors reported hospitals being looted, and that the water was off. They were desperate to know where they should dump the trash, could they use cell phones, or was it OK to drive to their father's house in Mosul. They approached us to arrest a strange man with a gun lurking in their neighborhood. We were approached by alleged sheiks who demanded to [see] "his Excellency the General" about their tribe's loyalty to Mr. Bush. . . . On and on the requests came.[50]

The limited number of troops that were in Baghdad did not have any orders to stop the widespread looting. Their orders covered little more than to secure the oil fields, remove the regime, and find weapons of mass destruction. The troops had been told that they would be greeted as liberators. No one had made any plans for the possibility of looting. That was not on Chalabi's list of possible actions.

The Coalition troops' refusal to stop the looting would have a major, long-term negative impact. Iraqis found it difficult to believe that the troops did not have orders to stop the looting. Many interpreted the refusal as evidence that the coalition did not care about Iraqis, the functioning of their institutions, or their cultural legacy. It was not the right way to begin life with the Iraqi population. "If they had shot a few of them at the beginning it would have stopped," remarked one young Iraqi doctor. "Instead, I saw American soldiers standing by, taking photographs, cheering them on."[51] James Fallows reported that "something like 10 times as much of the power grid was destroyed in the couple of weeks after the war as was destroyed by U.S. bombing during the war."[52]

Even more devastating to long-term U.S. policy was the perception that the United States was weak. People began to believe that they could stand up to the Americans. Now it would be extremely difficult to get the country's

ministries working again, because there was nothing left inside the buildings—not even chairs. The looting was so comprehensive that electrical
wires had been pulled out of the walls. Hospitals lost equipment and medi-
cations, not to mention electricity. The same was true for schools, police
stations, and other municipal buildings. Furthermore, what little thought
had been put into the Phase IV period had been to deal with basic humanitarian issues—refugees, food, and medicines—not the kind of rebuilding
efforts Iraq would need.

There were so few U.S. and Coalition troops that it took the U.S. military
two weeks to occupy strategic cities such as Fallujah and Ramadi. Even
then, the war was not really over. The military still had to move into and
stabilize many other smaller cities. The country's borders needed to be defended, but there were not enough U.S. soldiers and Marines to patrol the
country's open borders—especially its border with Iran and Syria—plus nobody knew where Saddam was at this point. Rumsfeld's cavalier response
to the looting was "Freedom's untidy, and free people are free to make mistakes
and commit crimes and do bad things. They're also free to live their lives and
do wonderful things, and that's what's going to happen here."[53] Such comments were typical Rumsfeld—instead of focusing on how to turn the situation
around, his ego would generally not permit him to admit he was wrong.

One of the biggest surprises for a number of people was General Franks's
decision to retire after the of city Baghdad had fallen. There were a number
of possible explanations. First, he may well have read the writing on the
wall—Iraq was sinking into the abyss of civil chaos and he did not want
to be blamed for it. Other authors have suggested that he wanted to write
his memoirs, and he wanted to be able to put only positive material in it.
Finally, Franks wanted to be remembered as the victorious commander who
destroyed Saddam Hussein, not the floundering occupation authority who
was unable to deal with problems of ethnicity, religion, and a failed state.
He formally retired on July 7 and was succeeded by Arabic-speaking Army
General John P. Abizaid. Meanwhile, as of April 15–16 there were a total
of 143,000 Coalition troops in Iraq, consisting of 122,000 U.S. troops and
21,000 British forces.[54]

## Garner Tries to Put Iraq Together

Jay Garner was like a rudderless ship attempting to navigate his way through
Iraqi culture and politics on one side, and the U.S. military on the other. His
one constant theme to his staff was the limited duration of their assignment.
In three or four months, he expected to be gone, with Iraq back together
with a functioning, responsive, and responsible government in place.

Predictably, Garner faced constant problems as a result of Rumsfeld's failure to make his mission a priority. On April 2 Rumsfeld sent a memo to the service secretaries, Myers, Feith, Franks, and other key people in the Pentagon. He told them to support Garner "as required."[55] Translated into military jargon, that means to take care of Garner if there are no other pressing problems. Given that military commanders are always faced with numerous problems, some of them severe, units in the field interpreted Garner's mission as being less important than other problems they had to deal with.

Garner and his staff were waiting in neighboring Kuwait. They were ready to go; in fact, they wanted to follow the troops into Iraq and set up their operations as soon as an area was liberated. General Franks, however, would not let them into Iraq until hostilities ceased. Finally on April 17, Garner flew to CENTCOM headquarters in Qatar to meet with Franks. He pushed the general to get him and his colleagues to Baghdad. Franks refused, arguing that the city was not secure enough. The two men had known each other for twenty-five years, so their negotiating went back and forth for a long time. Finally, Franks called Garner that evening and agreed to fly his team into Baghdad.

When Garner arrived in Baghdad he was shocked by "the swarms of Iraqis who dissected every government ministry building desk by desk, wire by wire, pipe by pipe."[56] To make matters worse, there was no electricity, the sewage plant was not working, and the heat was beyond belief. Garner's first goal was to get the ministries working again, because he believed that government services are critical. However, he immediately ran into the military bureaucracy. Troop commanders paid little attention to him because they were never told that guarding the ministries (other than the Oil Ministry) was a priority. And without orders, they were not about to redeploy their troops. However, current conditions in Baghdad made the military's help mandatory. ORHA's personnel could not travel without a military escort. Yet ORHA was far down the military's list of priorities. One officer noted a meeting with Ambassador Barbara Bodine, who was in charge of rebuilding Baghdad: "and none of the senior officers would show up. I can remember thinking, This isn't right, and also thinking that if it had been a commander who called the meeting, they would have shown up all right."[57] Neither Franks nor any of his colleagues had passed down the message that helping ORHA do its job was a top priority. That is something that Franks and his staff should have foreseen. The senior British representative said it best when he commented that the OHRA had "no leadership, no strategy, no coordination, no structure, and [was] inaccessible to ordinary Iraqis."[58]

The army was not in much better shape regarding how it was going to operate during Phase IV. The commander of the civil affairs unit with the third division comments:

I got to Baghdad and was told, "You've got twenty-four hours to come up with a Phase IV plan." . . . On the night of April 8, Col. [John] Sterling, the chief of staff of the 3rd ID, came to me and said, "I just got off the phone with the corps chief of staff, and I asked him for the reconstruction plan, and he said there isn't one." King was stunned. He had been asking for months for such a plan and had been told that when the time came, he would be given it.[59]

To make matters worse, the Army's high command seemed oblivious to what was happening on the streets of Baghdad. By April 16 Franks was telling his commanders that they should be prepared to start pulling troops out in sixty days if all went well.[60]

There was no excuse for such a situation from either a military or civilian standpoint. A month after the military "victory" in Baghdad the situation had not improved. There still were not enough troops on the streets to deal with crime—and Baghdad was slowly slipping into chaos. Neither Garner nor the military seemed to have any idea what to do. Lawlessness was spreading not only in Baghdad, but in other parts of the country as well. Meanwhile, the situation on the ground among U.S. commanders was quite different. They recognized that security was their primary problem, but they complained that they did not have enough troops to do the job.[61] Rumsfeld responded by denying charges that there were too few troops—something that was obvious to the lowest private in Iraq. He then claimed, "15,000 troops from the First Armored Division and hundreds of additional military police are soon to arrive in Baghdad, bringing the overall U.S. troop levels to almost 160,000."[62] But this statement is confusing. If there were enough soldiers in Iraq, why send an additional 15,000 troops?

General Myers's comments on troop numbers at the time were even more baffling. At a time when everyone except Rumsfeld and Feith seemed to think the coalition did not have enough troops, Myers claimed, "The invasion of Iraq likely would have been less successful if more ground troops had been deployed at the outset."[63] His argument seemed to be that the coalition had achieved tactical surprise by attacking while it had so few troops in Kuwait. While that is certainly true, having too few troops to secure the country once the battle was over means that while the Coalition might win the battles, it ran the risk of losing the war. This short-range strategy may have allowed insurgents sufficient time to organize, steal weapons and ammunition, and begin to take action against the "occupiers."

The looting in Baghdad focused on more than items that the public thought useful in their homes. It also included things like official records, making reconstruction more difficult. Feith had put his faith in the Iraqi police, but they quickly disappeared. As a result, religious and ethnic groups created their own militias that not only protected their religious or ethnic group, but in the case of the Shiites they began seeking revenge against Sunnis, who then formed their own militias to fight against the Shiites—which soon resulted in an ethnic civil war. A U.S. Army officer had the right idea when he commented about the post-invasion period, "The planning was ragged. . . . and the execution was worse."[64] While Garner may have been out of his league in overseeing the reconstruction of Iraq, Rumsfeld, Wolfowitz, and Feith tried to make him the "fall guy" for the failure. According to one Pentagon official,

> "It was ridiculous," he said. "Rummy and Wolfowitz and Feith did not believe the U.S. would need the U.S. around to run post-conflict Iraq. Their plan was to turn it over to these exiles very quickly and let them deal with the messes that came up. Garner was the fall guy for a bad strategy. He was doing exactly what Rummy wanted him to do. It was the strategy that failed."[65]

But none of the three men were about to admit that they had made major mistakes in planning the invasion of Iraq. In fact, on April 30, while smoke from burning buildings in Baghdad billowed across the skyline, Rumsfeld visited Baghdad and declared, "Each day that goes by, conditions in Iraq are improving."[66] The civilians, soldiers, and Marines in Iraq who heard him speak likely had a different perspective.

The problems in rebuilding Iraq were not all caused by the U.S. military or civilian bureaucracies. Indeed, the Iraqis themselves were a major part of the problem. Clerics, sheiks, and exiles were all attempting to grab the spoils of Saddam's downfall. Some individuals would pop up claiming to be mayors or influential figures while the Americans, few of whom spoke Arabic, had to rely on a very limited number of translators. Often the Americans never understood what the Iraqis were trying to communicate. Alarmed at what was happening—or not happening—in Iraq, Rumsfeld called Garner and informed him that he would soon be replaced by Paul Bremer.

On May 1, 2003, at the suggestion of General Franks, Bush traveled to the USS *Abraham Lincoln*, where, with much fanfare and many television cameras, Bush declared the end of the Iraq War. After all, armed resistance by organized military units had long since ended. Part of the reason for the trip was legal—by declaring the end of hostilities, Washington was making it easier for other countries to provide support for rebuilding Iraq. In the meantime, something had to be done about the withdrawal of U.S. soldiers. Creating stability was becoming increasingly difficult.

## Administrator Bremer Arrives

On May 11, Jay Garner was replaced by L. Paul "Jerry" Bremer, a former Foreign Service officer and one-time ambassador to the Netherlands. Bush made him the senior civil administrator of Iraq and head of the Coalition Provisional Authority. Bremer had experience dealing with terrorism and now had far more authority than his predecessor, because he was a presidential envoy. However, problems later surfaced because both Bremer and General Abizaid worked for Secretary of Defense Rumsfeld. Consequently neither was in a position to issue orders to the other, a situation made worse by Bremer's reputation as an arrogant individual who seldom listened to anyone else—save Rumsfeld.[67] Bremer knew nothing about Iraq or the Middle East, for that matter. Nevertheless, he made it clear that he was in charge of everything and everyone except for Rumsfeld. He also made it clear that he was not prepared to subject his decisions to the interagency process. This cut the State Department, the Pentagon, the CIA, and NSC out of the action. Bremer did not want a group of bureaucrats looking over his shoulder, second-guessing him.

When Bremer arrived in Baghdad, the city was on the brink of chaos. Lawlessness was rampant, yet security was a precondition for everything else. It made little sense to have currency on hand, for example, if the banks were not safe. Reconstruction and relief were equally impossible without security.

To his credit, one of the first things Bremer did was to halt the withdrawal of U.S. forces. Next, he began a comprehensive review of security needs in Iraq. Then he announced the indefinite postponement of the planned creation of the new Iraqi state, which had previously been scheduled for May. His idea was to first draft a constitution and then hold an election based on that constitution, a new sequence that upset many Iraqis. For the present, his goal was to establish his and the coalition's authority. Bremer was determined to put an end to the instability and violence in Iraq. He would move very quickly in that direction and take actions that, in his mind, would bring about law and order. Unfortunately, they would have the opposite effect.

## Conclusion

The invasion of Iraq provides a textbook case of what happens when leaders fail to plan for every contingency in a political-military scenario. Yet the Bush administration could hardly say that it was not warned. Red flags were raised not just by General Shinseki, but also by almost everyone who knew anything about rebuilding a state like Iraq.

Then to make the invasion more difficult, Rumsfeld began interfering with the deployment sequencing (TPFDD). True, President Bush was very concerned that the United States not tip its hand, and Rumsfeld worried that if the military began deploying its forces, Saddam would realize that an invasion was coming. In addition, Rumsfeld was determined to prove to the generals and everyone else that his military transformation plan would revolutionize warfare. In the process, however, he was creating anarchy. Units would be deployed without part of their personnel because Rumsfeld had not decided to mobilize them. Rumsfeld's interference was staggering. Never before had a secretary of defense demanded to sign every mobilization order.

Secretary of State Colin Powell tried to handle the Iraqi invasion in an honorable, yet loyal manner. In return, the Vice President's Office as well as the civilians in the Pentagon tried to force a UN speech on him that was full of questionable data. Mistakes were clearly made with regard to WMD and the tie between al-Qaeda and Saddam, among others. Like a good soldier, Powell did an excellent job delivering his speech. The sad part of it, however, was that it forced a person with an outstanding reputation for integrity and honesty to soil that esteem by making charges that would not stand the test of time.

The decision to give the Pentagon operational control of the invasion seemed logical at the time. Even Powell agreed. The military had done a good job in postwar Germany and Japan. However, those generals did not have amateurs like Feith and Bremer making major policy decisions. Despite Rumsfeld's constant interference, the military did an excellent job when called upon to invade Iraq. Looking at only Phases I–III, Rumsfeld's policy of military transformation would get an A. But a military operation must be seen in its entirety, and Phase IV of the Iraq war is ongoing and has needlessly cost the United States thousands of lives.

Feith would later argue that he did anticipate disorder and looting, but that the Pentagon decided that oil fields, refugee flows, and famine were more important. "'You can't do everything,' he shrugged."[68] Indeed, he told the House International Relations Committee that the Pentagon had anticipated "serious problems" in the postwar period and then stated that while there were "serious problems" with electricity, water, and other basic services, these problems actually existed before the war.[69] But if that were the case—and it was—Feith should have planned for it. After all, the State Department's study warned of just such a problem—but Feith refused to permit Defense people to be involved in the study. General Franks and his deputy assumed that the Pentagon was responsible for that sphere; indeed, they were told that was the case. The bottom line, however, was that not only were Feith's comments rather silly, but more importantly, a good military officer plans for more than a few contingencies—and Franks did not. There was no excuse for Franks to accept the word of a person whom he called "one of the dumbest fucking idiots in the world." He should have insisted on seeing Feith's "plan" or tasked his own staff with developing one. The fact that the United States landed in Baghdad without a plan mystified Americans who had been involved with peacekeeping duties during the 1990s.

Franks tried to defend himself by making the argument that the issue was not numbers. Instead, he maintained that the problem was composition—not enough civil affairs, or military police, for example. If that was true, why did he agree to lead an operation that was not balanced? While the secretary of defense is clearly the senior person in such an operation, a four-star general, the combatant commander, no less, has an obligation to speak out when he does not believe that he has been given sufficient forces. Furthermore, while Franks's desire to avoid the nit-picking of the Joint Chiefs of Staff is understandable, in retrospect, the operation, especially Phase IV might have been better handled had the Joint Staff, in particular, been involved.

Finally, it is impossible to pass over Franks's behavior without contrasting it with that of Shinseki. The latter could have openly supported Rumsfeld. If he had, no doubt he would have been rewarded with an important role in the civil-military bureaucracy in Washington. Shinseki, however, was interested in more than power. He was not prepared to live a lie, and he did the honorable thing by telling Congress exactly what he thought about the numbers issue. Ironically, it turned out that he was the one person in uniform who was telling the public the truth.

# 7
# *Winning the War, Losing the Peace*

I have seen this movie, it was called Vietnam.
  *General Tony Zinni*

Donald Rumsfeld could have made a major difference in post-invasion Iraq.[1] He could have recognized the magnitude of the mistakes he and his colleagues had made in not sending enough troops and by overlooking Phase IV, the post-conflict stage. He also could have supported the generals by ensuring that they had the proper tools to deal with the insurgency. Then General George Casey or his predecessor as commander of the Multilateral Forces in Iraq, General Ricardo Sanchez, would be responsible for creating a new strategy, while Rumsfeld provided them the necessary equipment, weapons, and troops. Instead, Sanchez and Casey had no choice but to design a strategy that followed Rumsfeld's basic approach, which was to combine two seemingly contradictory policies—provide security while extracting U.S. forces from Iraq as soon as possible. Unfortunately, Rumsfeld was part of the problem. According to Philip Zelikow, executive director of the 9/11 Commission, instead of micro-managing matters as he had done during the invasion, Rumsfeld now began to opt out of operational issues.[2] This meant that responsibility for developing a strategy and operational approach on the ground now rested with the general in charge. Unfortunately, neither General John Abizaid, as CENTCOM, nor General George Casey, as field commander, were in a position to pick up the baton and come up with a political-military strategy, because neither believed it was his job to do so. This was especially true of Casey, who repeated the Rumsfeld strategy, which, until the secretary was fired, would be to consolidate U.S. bases in Iraq and train the Iraqis to replace them.[3] In short, Casey did not—and would not—have a strategy.[4]

To Rumsfeld, the U.S. military had successfully carried out the kind of attack he advocated—a few troops with high-tech weapons had removed Saddam Hussein and his regime from power. That was the important point. As far as post-invasion developments, Rumsfeld refused to admit any mistakes. The invasion was a success, and post-invasion problems were somebody else's predicament. He either did not—or could not—understand that the United States was moving from a period of continual conflict to one of counterinsurgency. He seemed frozen and seemed confused; after all, Ahmed Chalabi and others had told him that the United States would be welcomed with flowers and hosannas, but that was far from the case.

Within a month an insurgency began to appear. According to Lieutenant Colonel Andrew Krepinevich, U.S. Army (Ret.), "Given, that there's no detailed plan for Phase IV, what you get is sort of the default American approach, which is muddling through. You sort of muddle through the situation. You try and adapt and react to circumstances rather than really shape them."[5] Unfortunately, with the exception of the unfortunate decisions Paul Bremer took, this is an apt description of how U.S. policy was implemented.

## The Bremer Plan

The burden of trying to make sense of an increasingly unruly Iraq fell to L. Paul "Jerry" Bremer. He had to find a way to stabilize the country to the point where serious efforts at reconstruction could be undertaken. Without security, there would not be stability, and without stability reconstruction would be doomed. At the same time, Bremer was under instructions to "democratize" the country. He had to get rid of the corrupt, brutal, and dishonest members of Saddam Hussein's regime. Individuals who committed crimes against humanity, like Saddam himself, would be treated as criminals and be subject to the Iraqi legal system. In the meantime, Bremer was out to get rid of Iraqis whose actions may not have been criminal, but who played an important role in helping prop up the old regime. That was the only way the United States would be able to convince the average Iraqi that the United States was not his or her enemy, but instead was only interested in getting rid of those who had oppressed them.

Bremer's first goal was to put the governmental structure on a more rational basis. Prior to his arrival, the U.S. plan to was pass authority on to a provisional Iraqi government. But given the chaotic situation in the country, Bremer was not about to pass authority on to any Iraqi government and certainly not to the exiles, many of whom had not lived in the country for years and were not popular with the local populace.

Bremer met with the Iraqi leadership council on May 16. This council, also known as the "G-7," was composed of individuals with a variety of ethnic backgrounds and included exiles, most notably Chalabi. However, it did not include women nor did it have a fair ethnic balance. Bremer wanted to demonstrate his authority by making a grand first public statement and did. Much to the dismay of the G-7, Bremer rather undiplomatically announced that he was dropping the idea of a provisional government. He made it very clear to the Iraqis that he was in charge. He then set up the U.S.-run Coalition Provisional Authority (CPA) to run the country. Not surprisingly, this infuriated members of the leadership council, because they had planned on taking control of the Iraqi government as soon as hostilities ended. "All the G-7 members were vehemently opposed to the dropping of the idea of a provisional government, and warned Bremer that the CPA would most certainly fail if there were no parallel Iraqi-led governmental authority with which it could liaise."[6]

It was not just the G-7 that opposed Bremer's action. Almost immediately, other Iraqi leaders began to warn Bremer that there would be resistance if he did not create an Iraqi government.[7] Some observers believe that it was Bremer's decision to put off creating a provisional government that fueled the insurgency. As one source commented, "Every Iraqi leader, including the most pro-American, says it was Bremer's decision to keep power that changed the United States from being seen as a liberator to being universally regarded as an occupier."[8] And it became clearer each day that Bremer had no intention of giving up power. He had his orders from Washington, and, besides, he did not think he could trust the Iraqis to establish a democratic polity so soon after the end of Saddam's reign. As far as he was concerned, they were not ready for it.

However, Bremer did acquiesce in setting up local neighborhood councils. They would select district councils, which, in turn, selected county councils, which selected a provincial council—which chose a governor. In theory, the move was great. It not only helped Iraqis learn about democracy, it gave them a hand in practicing it. They would be able to see how the process worked. The problem, however, was that individuals who ran for office had to be approved by Bremer and the CPA. To the Iraqis, the governmental sphere smacked more of occupation than liberation. When the local population tried to organize local councils on their own, the United States intervened. As a sergeant from a civil affairs unit explained, "We would like to see some kind of democratic system, but for now, Iraqis need to be satisfied with 'baby steps.'"[9] That kind of paternalistic approach inevitably irritated the Iraqis.

There were exceptions. One was in Mosul, where General David Petraeus was in command. Petraeus held elections two weeks after arriving. He realized that it was critical not to drive members of the old regime into a corner, because they would come out fighting. Instead, he wanted to co-opt them into the new system as much as possible. If the elections were not perfect, at least many Iraqis believed they were making the decisions, however bad they might be from the standpoint of a Western-style democracy. Colonel H. R. McMaster would adopt a similar approach in his successful counterinsurgency campaign in Tal Afar and the surrounding Ninawa province. But these were isolated cases.

Bremer did not set up an advisory Governing Council until July 13. The council consisted of twenty-five prominent Iraqis from a variety of different backgrounds. It included thirteen Shiites, four Arab Sunnis, six Kurds, one Turkmen, and one Assyrian Christian. It also contained three women. However, Bremer gave the Council limited powers and to many Iraqis it was merely an American puppet, not a true Iraqi institution, and it contradicted what the U.S. government had told the Iraqis about self-governance. The Bush administration had said that it was bringing democracy to their country. Instead, Washington set up a government it controlled. The Council could name and dismiss interim ministers, propose a budget, appoint chargés d'affaires to foreign capitals, and organize the drafting of Iraq's future constitution. All other powers rested in Bremer's hands, and he could veto any action taken by the Council.

## Launch Coalition Provisional Authority

The staffing of the Coalition Provisional Authority (CPA) was haphazard at best—yet this was the organization charged with rebuilding Iraq. Iraq needed Arabists who understood both the language and the culture of the Middle East; instead, they got the CPA. According to CIA Director George Tenet, "One of my officers returned from a trip to Iraq a month or two after CPA had taken over and told me, 'Boss, that place runs like a graduate school seminar, none of them speaks Arabic, almost nobody's ever been to an Arab country, and no one makes a decision but Bremer.'"[10] Most of the people the Pentagon was sending to Iraq did not know the difference between a Sunni and a Shiite. Many of those sent from the United States were idealistic, just out of college, with no special skills, but with a recommendation from the conservative Heritage Foundation think tank, which had compiled a list of ideologically approved conservatives who wanted to serve in Iraq. Many of these individuals were young university graduates who knew little or nothing about the jobs they would be assigned. Feith apparently felt comfortable relying on the Heritage Foundation to provide him with candidates for jobs in Iraq regardless of their substantive knowledge. Then, because of the violence—suicide bombings and rocket attacks—a number decided to return to the United States as soon as possible. As a consequence, "In short order, six of the new young hires found themselves managing the country's $13 billion budget, making decisions affecting millions of Iraqis."[11] The bottom line, according to Under Secretary Douglas Feith, was that these idealists were loyal supporters of the president's policies.

The military found the CPA very difficult to deal with. It was taken back by the level of incompetence of its staff and its inability to get anything done. In their frustration, "The battalion commanders referred to CPA as Cannot Provide Anything."[12] Another journalist noted a sign on a billboard that read: "COMMON SENSE." Underneath was a caption: "killed by the CPA."[13] Such a situation was not surprising. Bremer and his team fired most of the people Garner had brought with him, people who were selected for their technical competence first, and their political loyalty second.

The military had another problem with the CPA. There were two separate chains of command in Iraq—one military and one CPA, although Bremer argued that he was in charge of everything. Bremer may have been right, but cutting the military out of the action will hardly lead to efficient command. As a result, military officers at the time were doing things that did not accord with CPA policy. Besides, the CPA often tried to solve problems from the Green Zone in Baghdad—the barricaded U.S. enclave. The military was present on the ground around the country and could have been a good resource—but it was basically ignored. Part of the reason for that was Bremer's determination to control everything, a reputation he had as a Foreign Service officer. As a military officer commented, "I fault Bremer. He is a control freak. There is no joint planning."[14]

Meanwhile, there were a number of Foreign Service officers who were competent both in language and culture. They had lived in Arab countries—including Iraq. They were prepared to go to Iraq, and, as noted above, at one point Secretary of State Colin Powell had offered them to Rumsfeld, but the secretary of defense said, "No thanks." They were the ones who should have been advising or at least working closely with those who did the advising. But they were anathema to Feith. He believed they would be too soft on the remaining members of Saddam's Baath Party. Future of Iraq Project member David Phillips reported that "of the 1,147 Americans employed by the CPA in July 2003, only 34 were Foreign Service Officers."[15]

In addition to personnel problems, the CPA knew very little about the Iraqi economy, social structure, or political structures. Because Phase IV planning was generally missing, no one in a position of responsibility had done the difficult job of trying to understand the Iraqi economy, how it worked, where its problems were, and what needed to be done to get the country back on its feet. For example, no one in the CPA understood how much Saddam had neglected infrastructure and how much damage the international sanctions had done to the country. Public services, not to mention the oil sector, seemed to be *terra incognita*, and many of the experts were shocked and surprised when they saw the decrepit state of the country.

Given the lack of experienced, culturally sensitive personnel and the general ignorance of the Iraqi political and economic system, the CPA did a poor job. It did not, for example, understand the depths of the brewing dissatisfaction among the Iraqis. In fact, because of its ineptness and cultural insensitivity, over time the CPA lost the respect of the Iraqis. "As the CPA consistently failed to reach the performance standards it had set for itself, Iraqis became cynical about its promises. Quick results and quick fixes came to dominate the CPA's economic policy discussions." That led people to think that "genuine economic reform would prove unpopular and ought not to be tried."[16]

Throughout the summer and fall of 2003, the Pentagon tried to get Bremer to transfer governing authority from the CPA to the Iraqis. Deputy Secretary of Defense Paul Wolfowitz brought it up with Bremer on September 22. Feith had also floated the idea of transferring authority to the Governing Council, to be called a Provisional Council. Bremer dismissed the idea, saying, "You guys don't seem to understand how ineffective the GC is turning out to be. . . . Those people couldn't organize a parade, let alone run the country."[17] Bremer would sign a protocol on September 23, 2003, that set a timeline for transferring sovereignty, but Bremer was not about to be pushed by Wolfowitz or anyone else when it came to giving the Iraqis sovereignty.

That meeting was followed up on October 27 when Rumsfeld presented Bremer with what at that time was called the "Wolfowitz–Feith Option. The idea was to turn over sovereignty as early as April 9, 2004—exactly one year after Saddam's regime fell. Again Bremer argued against any transfer of power. That was too early. As he put it, "We'd risk Iraq falling into disorder or civil war."[18]

## De-Baathification

Bremer wanted to get rid of Saddam Hussein's Baath Party and identify its senior members. The issue had been discussed in Washington prior to the war. The State Department wanted a narrow definition of membership so the United States would focus on Saddam's closest supporters, in order to get rid of those who had committed crimes and those at the very top of the command structure. Predictably, Feith's office wanted a broader purge as well as to ban rank-and-file Baathist members from holding senior government positions.[19]

Undertaking de-Baathification was a major component of the U.S. plan to reshape post-Saddam Iraq. Although it is an issue of top importance, Tenet says that it was never discussed at an NSC principals meeting.[20] Another source claimed that while Pentagon lawyers and Wolfowitz and Rumsfeld saw the de-Baathification document, it was not shown to either National Security Adviser Condoleezza Rice or Secretary of State Powell.[21] As in so many other instances, civilians in the Pentagon refused to work with the rest of the government, being convinced that only Defense knew how to approach political problems like de-Baathification.

Bremer seized on de-Baathification as another opportunity to prove his boldness. "He wrote a memo to Pentagon officials noting that he wanted his arrival in Iraq to be 'marked by clear, public, and decisive steps to reassure Iraqis that we are determined to eradicate Saddamism.'"[22]

Rumsfeld accommodated him. Just prior to leaving Washington, Rumsfeld gave Bremer a memo ordering him to get rid of Saddam's cronies. "Among my other instructions," Bremer recalls, "Rumsfeld's memo emphasized: 'The Coalition will actively oppose Saddam's old enforcers—the Baath Party, the Fedayeen Saddam [a paramilitary group], etc.'"[23] On May 9, Bremer's last day in the Pentagon, Feith showed him a draft order for the "De-Baathification of Iraqi Society." He repeated Rumsfeld's theme, "We've got to show all the Iraqis that we're serious about building a New Iraq. And that means that Saddam's instruments of repression have no role in that new nation." Feith told Bremer that he intended to have Garner issue the order that day, but Bremer asked Feith to wait and let him deliver it.[24] It would help him establish his authority among the Iraqis. The order focused on the top four levels of party membership, which included individuals who had actively repressed the rest of society. Bremer claimed that the intelligence community had estimated that it included only 20,000 people, about 1 percent of the population. Tenet, however, denied the intelligence community knew anything about it, and claimed that Bremer did not receive that estimate until the day *after* he issued the order. Bremer tried to cover himself by noting that he was only building on the order General Tommy Franks had issued in April de-establishing the Baath party.

Almost every U.S. official in Baghdad opposed Bremer's interpretation of the de-Baathification Order—i.e., that it applied to anyone who had been a party member. Lieutenant General Mike DeLong, Franks's deputy, noted that both he and Franks recognized that Baathist Party membership was similar to membership in the now-defunct Soviet Communist Party. A lot of people had been members just to have a job. As he put it, "By outlawing it, we'd not just outlaw the fedayeen and Saddam's cabinet—we'd outlaw half the country. . . . We recommended that we 'fire' only the senior-level membership, politicians, and other Saddam loyalists, but offer selective amnesty for lower-level party members . . . so that we could keep the country moving."[25] Unfortunately, Franks's concern did little to reverse Bremer's decision. Allawi argued that while the order was well intended, Bremer and his colleagues failed to realize the "deep roots that the Baath Party developed in Iraq after nearly thirty-five years of power, or how the upper echelons of the Party had become dominated by Sunni Arabs from the town and villages of the upper reaches of the Tigris and Euphrates rivers."[26] For his part, after reading the order Garner told Bremer that the cuts were too deep. *Holy Christ,* he thought to himself. *We can't do this.*[27] He suggested to Bremer that they call Rumsfeld to see if they could get it changed. Bremer refused. The CIA station chief also argued strongly against the order. "By nightfall, you'll have driven 30,000 to 50,000 Baathists under ground. And in six months you'll really regret this."[28] Bremer was unmoved. He said he had his orders and that he was going to sign the order. That evening he met with staff, and again concern over the order was expressed. An army engineer told him, "If you send them home, . . . the CPA would have 'a major problem' running most ministries." In fact the day after de-Baathification was announced, "senior Baathists in the Health Ministry stopped coming to work. Eight of the ministry's top posts were now empty. A third of the staff was gone."[29]

The real test of an order of this kind is its implementation. Part of the problem here was that it was very difficult, especially for foreigners, to tell who was a committed party member and who was not. However, using Iraqis to make such a determination opened the door to individuals seeking revenge for a past wrong—a major problem in post-Saddam Iraq. For the most part, U.S. advisers were the ones who decided who should be in a job and who should not. It took a tremendous amount of their time, and it put the Americans in a very difficult and awkward position. The vast majority had little or no language skills, and, in many cases knew next to nothing about the country, its history, culture, or even the philosophy and structure of the Baathist Party. They had their jobs thanks to the conservative Heritage Foundation. There were cases, however, where the decision-making process was turned over to the Iraqis. Another problem was that individuals who were not Baathist Party members were afraid to take the jobs previously held by Baathists, because they worried about retribution. So not only did firms and organizations lose employees who had been active party members, they could not fill their empty positions.

DeLong had predicted the problem; Bremer's de-Baathification process affected half of the population. It also hit extremely hard on the people who ran the country. It would have been one thing to go after senior Baathists who had committed crimes against their own people. But the average party member was not necessarily a "true believer," a person who embraced only the evil side of party membership. It also hit people who had joined the party in order to get a decent job. Bremer's order hit "civil servants who had valuable skills, historical knowledge, and experience. It failed to consider that not all party members were guilty of crimes against humanity. It did not address Iraqis who had attained senior positions in the party but did not have positions of power in the government."[30]

Despite the strong opposition from most of his colleagues, on May 16, 2003, Bremer signed the de-Baathification order. Its impact was immediate. Ricks suggested that it purged "tens of thousands of members of the Baath Party—perhaps as many as 85,000."[31] And the process was not handled smoothly, either. In fact, de-Baathification probably did more to disrupt efforts to get the country running smoothly again than anything al-Qaeda could have done. The purge hit people at all levels, not just the senior people it targeted. For example, Tenet reported that the CIA heard rumors that many children could not go to school because too many teachers had lost their jobs because of their Baathist Party membership.

If the kids and teachers were not in school, they were on the streets. I went to see Condi Rice and complained that the indiscriminate nature of the de-Ba'athification order had swept away not just Saddam's thugs, but also, for example, something like forty thousand school teachers, who had joined the Baath Party simply to keep their jobs. This order wasn't protecting Iraqis; it was destroying what little institutional foundations were left in the country. The net-effect was to persuade many ex-Baathists to join the insurgency. Condi said she was very frustrated by the situation, but nothing ever happened.[32]

Bremer's response was to setup an Iraqi-led commission to hear appeals from the teachers. In a disastrous move, he put Chalabi in charge of it. Chalabi was determined to keep anyone who had been a member of the Baath Party from a position of authority. Instead of deliberating, Chalabi sat on the appeals. Lieutenant General DeLong also recalled the problems it created for the military's efforts to keep the city and country functioning.

As we predicted, it had a ripple effect throughout the country. Everything stopped. Iraqi workers walked away from oil wells, electricity plants, and gas stations. . . . We had to start from scratch, building a new Iraqi civil infrastructure—from an Iraqi police force to an Iraqi workforce capable of running the electricity, gas, water, and other industries and necessary services—and building it rapidly. In a time of chaos and confusion, this set back our efforts in Iraq.[33]

By keeping the de-Baathification order as rigorous as possible, Bremer was able to make a bigger splash in Iraq. However, Bremer's second order would be even more disastrous for the recovery process.

## Disband Iraqi Army

Just prior to the start of the war, Feith had asked his predecessor at the Pentagon, Walter B. Slocombe, a moderate Democrat and a recognized expert on military issues, if he would like to take on the job of dealing with the Iraqi military. Slocombe agreed, and the two men drew up a plan. Their idea was to disband the elite Republican Guard, the regular Republican Guard, and the paramilitary Fedayeen. The 400,000-man regular army would be vetted. If they passed muster, mid-level officers and below would be allowed to stay. There was no way the United States could demobilize 200,000–300,000 soldiers all at once. Putting that many trained soldiers on the street with nothing to do was an invitation to disaster. Besides, Feith "told the president that the army would be used as 'a national reconstruction force' during the transitional phase."[34]

The problem, according to Feith and Slocombe, was that the Iraqi Army had vanished soon after the end of the war. For example, a month after the end of hostilities, General Abizaid reported that there was not a single Iraqi military unit still intact. The soldiers and officers appeared to have simply taken off their uniforms and gone home. Slocombe, however, was concerned about calling them back. He worried that could cause even more problems, and now at least they were not a problem. Furthermore, their bases had been looted—where would they live? According to Feith and Slocombe, the army had dissolved, so, in another "bold decision," Bremer issued his second order, which formally dissolved the Iraqi Army.

Interestingly, Feith and Slocombe did not consult State, the CIA, Rice, or Rice's deputy, Stephen J. Hadley. According to Tenet, Hadley tried to get language in the order noting that everyone below the rank of lieutenant colonel could apply for reinstatement. "After all, the majority of army members were conscripts just trying to feed their families."[35] When the order was issued, that sentence was omitted. Jay Garner and the CIA had had their fingers on the pulse of Iraq when Bremer arrived, but they were also not consulted, because Bremer had little respect for Garner. What was really incomprehensible from a civil-military standpoint was that he did not even consult with General Myers, who—at least in theory—was the principal military adviser to Bush, Rumsfeld, and the NSC on the dissolution issue. Bremer also ignored the Joint Chiefs of Staff as well as the Joint Staff.

One of the most surprising criticisms of Bremer's actions was made in *Dead Certain: The Presidency of George W Bush*.[36] In the book, Robert Draper claims that President Bush was never told of Bremer's intention to disband the military and was quite surprised when he learned of it. In response, Bremer released copies of a letter he had sent to the president and the latter's response. In his letter to the president, Bremer noted—at the end of the fourth paragraph—"I will parallel this step with an even more robust measure dissolving Saddam's military and intelligence structures to emphasize that we mean business." In the State Department there is a long and hallowed tradition of burying something controversial in the body of a memorandum or cable so that a very busy supervisor does not notice it. This is clearly what Bremer did. Furthermore, the letter sent by Bush regarding his work is typical of the kind of letter the president sends to all of his senior subordinates—the equivalent of what the Navy calls a "Bravo–Zulu" commendation.[37]

Bremer recalls sending a memo to Secretary Rumsfeld on May 19, 2003, announcing that he planned to dissolve the Iraqi Defense Ministry as well as the intelligence, security, and propaganda services. He also told Rumsfeld that the United States would pay severance payments to hundreds of thousands of former soldiers. On May 22, back at the Pentagon, Feith carefully looked over the draft dissolution order. He then reportedly received approval from Rumsfeld.

There seems to be a general consensus that Feith and Slocombe's decision to dissolve the army was a major mistake for a number of reasons. First, calling the troops back would have given the U.S. military a chance to identify new leaders. Second, almost every U.S. commander in Baghdad had been approached by Iraqi officers and soldiers asking to get their jobs back. The vast majority of them, especially the officers, had no other livelihood. They were professional soldiers and wanted to remain as such. As one officer who dealt with some of them explained, "It was a case of proud men being unnecessarily humiliated."[38] Garner also warned Bremer, "Jerry, you can get rid of an army in a day, but it takes years to build one."[39]

Perhaps Bremer's comments about the army disappearing made him feel good, but there were other indications that there were thousands who wanted to come back. Garner, for example, commented, "We sent out feelers, and by the first week in May we were getting a lot of responses back. We had a couple of Iraqi officers come to me and say, 'We could bring this division back, that division.' We began to have dialogues and negotiations."[40] According to Gordon and Trainer, former Iraqi officers told the Americans that they had a list of some 50,000 to 70,000 names of potential recruits, including military police.[41] Former Iraqi soldiers were desperate and demonstrating. They were pleading for the Americans to help them get back on their feet. Equally important, they were warning that they could not wait forever, and if the Americans did not help them, they might become insurgents. At one point the Iraqis circulated a flier stating that they would gather at the Air Force Officers' Club and then march to the "U.S. military headquarters, to solve the problem of our salaries and our rights and also to discuss the future of the Iraqi Army."[42] The point is that the army, or large parts of it, could easily have been recalled, but Bremer and his supporters in Washington were set on disbanding it.

When Slocombe went to Iraq one of his first priorities was to try to convince the Coalition Provisional Authority to forget about the Iraq Army. It was gone. He argued, "There was no practical way to reconstitute an Iraqi force based on the old army any more rapidly than has happened. The facilities were destroyed, and the conscripts [were] gone and not coming back."[43] Slocombe also worried that bringing the old army back would mean a force once again dominated by Sunni officers, not the kind of integrated, diverse armed forces Washington wanted.

Almost all American officials serving in Iraq at the time believed that this decision was wrong and counterproductive. Barak Salmoni, who worked with the Marine Corps Training and Education Command, commented, "I don't buy the argument that there was no army to cashier. . . . It may have not been showing up for work, but I can assure you that they would have if there had been dollars on the table. And even if the Iraqi army did disband, we didn't have to alienate them—mainly by stopping their pay."[44] Phillips called it "one of the greatest errors in the history of U.S. warfare. It unnecessarily increased the ranks of its enemies."[45] If Bremer had asked the U.S. military—which he did not—he would have heard a warning from Lieutenant General David McKiernan, the first commander of ground troops in Iraq: "There are a large number of Iraqi soldiers now unemployed. That is a huge concern."[46] Even the current commander of Multinational Forces in Iraq, General Petraeus, told one of Bremer's aides that the decision to leave

Iraqi soldiers without a way to make a living "was prompting angry protests and putting the lives of American soldiers at risk."[47] Almost everyone, with the exception of Bremer, saw his action as a critical turning point in U.S. policy toward Iraq. Colonel Alan King, the head of civil affairs for the Third Infantry Division, commented that May was the critical month. "When they disbanded the military, and announced we were occupiers—that was it. Every moderate, every person that had leaned toward us, was furious. One Iraqi who had saved my life in an ambush said to me. 'I can't be your friend anymore.'"[48] Another former Iraqi officer commented, "I used to have more than a thousand men under my command. Now, I sit here with nothing to do. Of course, I'm angry at the Americans who took away everything I had."[49] Many Iraqis believed the United States had lied to them and let them down.

There was even shock in Washington. Frank Miller, Rice's senior assistant on defense affairs, found the decision upsetting. He and the Pentagon had been telling the president that they would be using 300,000 former Iraqi soldiers on public works and reconstruction. Now, all of a sudden, Slocombe and Bremer could not find them. No wonder they were upset. "That's what we told them to do, he thought—the CIA had dropped leaflets over Iraqi positions saying, 'Go home. Put down your weapons and go home.'"[50] But nobody bothered to see if they were there. There was no attempt to recall the Iraqi Army. If they had recalled the troops and no one came, then it would make sense to dissolve the army, but at least then the CPA could cite their refusal to return.

From an organizational standpoint, keeping the Iraqi Army together had a number of advantages. It had a hierarchical structure and that meant—organization. They knew how to give and take orders. They knew how to operate the complex machinery needed to help rebuild the country. They could be used to do public works-style projects. Furthermore, as Allawi pointed out, in contrast with the intelligence and security services, the army enjoyed considerable popular sympathy.[51] Even Iraqis who were not connected with the military found its dissolution humiliating. Chandrasekaran relates the following exchange:

> Months later I did see another former soldier who had been at the protest.
> "What happened to everyone there?" I asked "Did they join the new army?"
> He laughed.
> "They're all insurgents now," he said. "Bremer lost his chance.[52]

The Iraqi military could also have been used on security patrols. Putting several Iraqi soldiers together with American GIs—eventually done several years later—might have helped the United States avoid numerous problems, especially those arising from cultural and language differences. Most important, despite its ethnic problems, the army was one of the few forces for unity in the country, and its presence could have gone a long way toward limiting the militia problem.

Slocombe was aware of the trouble and did make an effort to help the unemployed troops. He tried to find public works jobs for demobilized soldiers, and he announced a plan to create a new army. U.S. leaders hoped to have a division of about 12,000 soldiers trained and operational in a year. They hoped to have three divisions a year after that.[53] They intended to recruit from the old army as well as from Kurdish and Shiite areas. The problem from an Iraqi standpoint was that the United States was constructing the new army along Western or American lines. To many Iraqis, it would be an American Army wearing Iraqi uniforms. For this reason, Bremer's order came as a shock to most of the population. Years of indoctrination had convinced most Iraqis that the army was an integral part of the state. Paul Hughes, an army colonel attached to Garner, was very upset. He had been talking with Iraqi military representatives about the conditions of the resumption of their service. "On the eve of the order to disband, he says, more than 100,000 Iraqi soldiers had submitted forms to receive a one-time $20 emergency payment."[54] The United States clearly knew who and where they were. Indeed, Iraqi officers were continuing to inundate U.S. military personnel and every one else with requests to bring back the army. As one journalist noted, "In the weeks before Bremer issued his decree, Iraqi officers were telling anyone who would listen—from visiting exiles to foreign journalists to U.S. military officials—that they were simply waiting for the Americans to order them back to their barracks."[55]

Although there was ongoing communication between the Americans and former Iraqi soldiers about returning to active duty, Bremer and Feith simply were not interested. Major General John Batiste, who commanded the First Infantry division, said, "There are a number of Sunnis who are very good, courageous, and determined people, which if given a chance, would be part of the solution in Iraq. These are proud officers with enormous energy and capability. . . . Brigadier General Carter Ham agreed, saying 'I'd like to see a policy that deals with the individual cases rather than a blanket policy.'"[56] A variety of other senior officers had the same opinion.[57] That included the British officer who had served as head of the British Army during the invasion. He called it "very shortsighted," arguing that the local military should have been maintained and put under command of the coalition.[58] However, Feith and Bremer believed they knew the Iraqi Army best, and for them, ideological purity was primary. It was hard to find anyone— military or civilian—other than Bremer, Feith, and Rumsfeld, who believed that the decision to dissolve the Iraqi military made much, if any, sense. In the meantime, hostility on the part of former Iraqi army officers grew. Cockburn reported that a month after the dissolution of the army he saw several thousand men marching on the east bank of the Tigris.

> They were ex-officers demonstrating against the break-up of the army and demanding compensation. . . . It was an angry but by no means vengeful demonstration . . . But as I walked away I heard the sound of shots. A U.S. military police convoy had driven up and demonstrators banged on the side of the vehicles. A U.S. spokesman claimed that stones were thrown and the military police had reacted by shooting two officers dead and wounding two others.[59]

There were probably other views of the incident. Perhaps the military police did feel their lives were threatened. What is most upsetting, however, is that U.S. policy toward the former Iraqi military took individuals, most of whom probably felt mildly antagonistic or neutral toward the United States, and made them into insurgents—men who not only knew how to fight, but knew where the weapons and other military supplies were hidden. For his part, Rumsfeld knew what was going on, but made no effort to intervene.

## Rumsfeld Defends Policies

The instability and chaos in Iraq quickly caught the attention of the U.S. Senate, where Republicans and Democrats alike criticized the U.S. military for failing to stabilize Iraq. Most important, they blasted Rumsfeld for not having "a coherent plan" to stabilize Baghdad. "The lack of stability concerns me," said Senator Peter Domenici (R-NM).[60] Senator Robert Byrd (D-WV) blasted Rumsfeld for the same reason.

Rumsfeld was undaunted by the questions and concerns he was hearing from all over the United States. On May 27 he gave what became his standard answer to such questions. "Just as it took time and patience, trial and error, and years of hard work before the founders got it right, so too it will take time, and patience, and trial and error, and hard work for the Iraqi people to overcome the challenges they face."[61] Rumsfeld's response makes sense from a political standpoint—deflect the criticism, make their process just like ours. The problem, however, was that the process in Iraq was fundamentally different, because they had a totally different political culture—something that Rumsfeld never understood.

On July 1, 2003, Rumsfeld again argued that the situation in Iraq was not a quagmire or a guerilla warfare campaign. Instead, he took a new approach, claiming that the United States was fighting a war against terrorism. Repeating one of his common themes, Rumsfeld noted that all new countries go through these kinds of growing pains, including our own country. He bristled when reporters suggested that the United States was caught off-guard by the violence in Iraq—two months after major fighting ended. He did admit, however, that "fighting will not be over anytime soon."[62]

In contrast to Rumsfeld's optimism, in a July 14 teleconference with the secretary, General Abizaid and Bremer both expressed concern over events in Iraq. The bottom line was simple: Coalition forces were taking growing numbers of casualties in places like Fallujah and Ramadi, as well as Baghdad. The idea of drawing down troops, at a time when they were coming under increasing attack, was not acceptable. Bremer was concerned that the Pentagon did not understand the size of the insurgency.[63] Meanwhile, Bremer was getting frustrated in dealing with Rumsfeld. In one instance, the secretary sent back cables that Bremer expected would go through Rumsfeld and then on to others—but Rumsfeld had not sent them on. He was acting like he was a king in charge of anything related to Iraq. Or, as Bremer reportedly stated during a visit he made to Washington in late July, "'Rumsfeld's impossible to deal with,' Bremer told a colleague. He was really steamed. . . . Rumsfeld was throwing his weight around, and the rest of the NSC was just too weak to do anything about it."[64]

The Pentagon finally decided it would keep U.S. forces at about 144,000 through March 2004, in hopes the country would be more secure by that time, and the United States could begin its withdrawal. However, it was also clear that reserves and National Guard troops would have to be called up and that the tours of units currently in the country would have to be extended to a full year—a situation that raised serious questions about Rumsfeld's efforts to downsize the military.[65]

The reality was that the United States was facing problems it had never anticipated. It had planned for the postwar period, but only for dealing with major disasters, none of which occurred. Now they were dealing with a collapsed state and an insurgency they never expected. After all, Chalabi had assured everyone that they would be welcomed with open arms. But in the first four months after the fall of Baghdad there were 200 serious incidents of armed resistance—according to Allawi, primarily by Sunnis who rejected the loss of their power and the presence of foreign forces in their country.[66]

## Create New Iraqi Army from Scratch

Major General Paul Eaton was placed in charge of the recruitment and training of the new Iraqi military. Given the limited number of U.S. troops and the increasingly important role they played in battling the insurgency, contractors were employed to do the actual training. The training was not making progress, however, so Lieutenant General Karl Eikenberry, who had trained Afghan forces, was sent to Iraq. He noted a number of problems, beginning with the fact that few of the instructors could speak Arabic. As far as career soldiers were concerned, training Iraqis was not considered career enhancing, so the best officers and NCOs avoided it. Then there were the shortages of equipment, a situation that was even worse among the police. For example, "In the spring of 2004 investigators from the GAO [U.S. General Accounting Office] found that the Iraqi police had only 41 percent of the patrol vehicles they needed, 21 percent of the hand-held radios, and nine percent of the protective vests."[67] The biggest problem, however, was the kind of war the Iraqi Army and police would have to fight—counterinsurgency. In this case, the primary focus is not so much on killing the enemy as it is on securing and winning the hearts and minds of the populace—not an easy undertaking. It is the hardest kind of warfare, and the Americans were trying to train a brand new army how to fight it. The problem was compounded by civilian authorities in Iraq who insisted on keeping control of the police training and equipping process until late 2004.

Unfortunately, problems continued to plague the training process.

> Through the second year of occupation most of the indications were dark. An internal Pentagon report found, "The first Iraqi Army infantry battalions finished basic training in early 2004 and were immediately required in combat without complete equipment . . . Absent without leave rates among regular army units were in double digits and remained so for the rest of the year. . . . A GAO report showed the extent of the collapse. Fifty percent of the Iraqi Civil Defense Corps in the area around Baghdad deserted in the first half of April. So did 30 percent of those in the northeastern area around Tikrit and the southeast near al-Kut.[68]

It was becoming increasingly obvious that the road to a new, combat-ready Iraqi Army would be a long and difficult one.

In the autumn of 2004, Petraeus arrived with orders to get the training program going. He began by getting rid of the often ridiculed way of measuring progress. Instead of counting the number of soldiers "on duty," Petraeus introduced the concept of "unit readiness." He also changed the training program. Given his long interest in counterinsurgency, the general immediately pushed to have U.S. advisers embedded in Iraqi units. He also introduced live-fire exercises—a major change in the way Iraqi troops traditionally trained. More money was also put into the program, enabling units to train longer and providing equipment that many of them had gone without.[69]

## Bogged Down with Polemics

By the middle of 2003, it was clear that the United States was up against an insurgency. On June 16 General Abizaid, the newly installed CENTCOM commander, stated that the U.S. now faced a "classical guerilla-type warfare." Two days later Wolfowitz conceded, "There is a guerilla war there, but . . . we can win it." However, by the end of the month, Rumsfeld was contradicting both of them, when he stated that the "evidence from Iraq 'doesn't make it anything like a guerilla war or an organized resistance.'"[70] Two days later, Bush made his famous "Bring them on" remark about the insurgents. They did.

In September 2003, Rumsfeld flew to Iraq to assess the possibility of cutting back on troop strength. When he arrived in Iraq, he complained, "I just don't see a steady line of advance. Maybe we need better metrics . . . a more efficient way to measure how we're meeting our goals."[71] To some, this sounded very much like a request for the body count, something the military did not want any part of, given the Vietnam experience. Bremer was livid. They could barely hold the pieces together with the number of troops they had. Rumsfeld obviously did not understand anything about the insurgency. On September 12, Abizaid received a memo from Rumsfeld ordering him to "ramp up the Iraqi numbers." In other words, the Pentagon wanted to withdraw U.S. troops, so the commanders should find a way to get more Iraqis trained for their army.[72] Rumsfeld called Bremer the next day, telling him that he supported the idea of giving sovereignty to the Iraqi Council or some other organization as soon as possible. Bremer flatly disagreed. Rumsfeld replied, "Well then, send me a paper giving me your reasons."[73] During the third week of September, Bremer had a teleconference call with Rumsfeld, Wolfowitz, and Abizaid. Rumsfeld suggested that Iraqi forces replace Coalition forces. Bremer responded, "Mr. Secretary, . . . we have to be realistic. . . . I got the impression that nobody in the conference wanted to hear this assessment."[74] Rumsfeld then said that they would have to speed up the training programs, to which Bremer responded that was exactly what they were doing. Rumsfeld was apparently worried about his position in the administration. There were rumors that his standing had gone down. After all, Iraq was not much of a success.[75]

Bremer's battle with Rumsfeld continued. On October 3, 2003, Lieutenant General Ricardo Sanchez, the commander of Multinational Forces in Iraq, gave a briefing to Bremer on the feasibility of replacing U.S. troops with Iraqis. In the meantime, Rumsfeld asked Bremer to find "some newsworthy, 'interim steps' that we could take to 'mitigate' political authority to the Iraqis. 'We've got to show some forward motion on the political front,

Jerry',"" Rumsfeld warned.[76] Bremer knew that language was vintage Feith. Turning to the issue of security, Bremer reported, "'Mr. Secretary, I have to be frank,' I said. 'You're seeing inflated numbers on police rosters. We shouldn't kid ourselves thinking that the Iraqis are better prepared than they are. We need a professional police force here, one that's trained to high standards.'"[77]

Bremer was not Rumsfeld's only critic. In September many members of Congress were blaming Rumsfeld for the mess in Iraq. He had demanded full authority over the process, yet it had failed. The United States was facing mounting casualties, and the war was costing more than $1 billion a week.[78] Rumsfeld fired back, arguing that current policy was working. He noted that the U.S. did not flood Iraq with thousands of troops—in fact only a few more than 100,000 troops were on the ground. This "restraint" helped the United States save lives, and U.S. actions made clear that we fought a war against a regime, not a people. He went on to claim progress:

> We have made solid progress. Within two months, all major Iraqi cities and most towns had municipal councils—something that took eight months in Germany. Within four months a new Iraqi police force was conducting joint patrols with coalition forces. Within three months, we had begun training a new Iraqi army—and today some 56,000 are participating in the defense of their country. By contrast, it took 14 months to establish a police force in Germany and 10 years training to begin training a German army.[79]

By October, Rumsfeld was claiming, "The progress has been so swift that . . . it will not be long before [Iraqi Security Forces] will be the largest and outnumber U.S. forces, and it shouldn't be too long thereafter that they will outnumber coalition forces combined."[80] Where Rumsfeld obtained his remarkable information is unknown. Of course, secretaries have to issue public statements to justify the administration's policies. That is true of all administrations. But it is important that they be credible. The veracity of Rumsfeld's claims were questionable in light of comments General Sanchez made on October 6: "Resistance to the occupying troops was strengthening and [he] warned Americans to brace themselves for more casualties."[81]

Concerned about the criticism of the Iraq War, and the tendency to focus on Rumsfeld and his handling of it, on October 6, 2003, Bush gave Rice more authority to deal with that country. She would lead four groups: counterterrorism, economics, communications, and politics. Called the Iraq Stabilization Group, it "will be run one rung higher on the bureaucratic ladder, consisting of undersecretaries who have some policy making authority."[82] While some in the Defense Department tried to downplay the importance of this interagency group, Rumsfeld was concerned enough to give an interview to newspapers in Europe in which he "showed his disdain for the White House power grab quite clearly. . . . He said he had known nothing of the reorganization until he read about it in the news."[83] In essence, Rice was now the president's point person on Iraq. Theoretically, she had operational control. The real question was, Would it fundamentally change Rumsfeld's power over events in Iraq?

## Handling Moqtada al-Sadr

Many Americans in Iraq, especially in the CPA, dismissed the importance of Moqtada al-Sadr, an ayatollah popular among the impoverished Shiites in Baghdad. In fact, the CPA hated him, and he returned the favor.

On October 10, 2003, over 300 of Sadr's men attacked a patrol of the U.S. Second Armored Cavalry Regiment, which was responsible for security in what has been dubbed "Sadr City," a slum where more than 2 million people lived. The next day, Sadr announced that he had formed "an alternative government, complete with ministers, in a direct challenge to the Governing Council.[84] Bremer sent a memo to Rumsfeld recognizing the extent of the problems, but saying that he felt that the United States could not sit by and permit him to set up a government. Recognizing the danger that arresting Sadr could have—riots all over the Shiite part of Iraq, Bremer nevertheless felt that it was critical to act. He argued that the United States must "get the Iraqi police to arrest him and the others named on the August arrest warrant."[85] Violence against Americans was clearly spreading. On October 16 the CPA learned that Sadr's people had killed three more Americans, this time in Karbala. The suspects had escaped.

On October 20 the U.S. and the Iraqi forces launched a joint operation to capture the fugitives, who were hiding in a mosque. The operation was successful. The Iraqi Civil Defense Forces asked those holed up in the mosque to surrender. They refused, so the Iraqi forces went in with the Americans backing them up. There was no resistance, and the action was publicly portrayed as an Iraqi victory.

## Cut Troop Strength

As 2003 drew to a close, General Casey and Rumsfeld were developing a plan to cut back troop levels. By mid-October there were 130,000 troops in Iraq. The idea was to begin to withdraw forces in spring 2004, so that by summer there would only be 100,000 U.S. troops in Iraq. Washington was focused on the upcoming 2004 presidential and congressional elections, and there was concern that if something wasn't done, the president might have to mobilize more of the National Guard, a politically suicidal move during an election year. For his part, Bremer felt the military was playing with numbers, and he was determined that the United States not leave until Iraq had a professional police force, which was a long way off in his mind.[86]

Meanwhile, during one of Bremer's trips to Washington, the president asked to meet privately with him. Bush inquired about working with Rumsfeld. Bremer responded that he was a micro-manager, but said he had found ways to work with him. When Rumsfeld heard about the private meeting he was furious. He told Andrew Card, the president's chief of staff, "He works for me!" "No," Card responded, "He's the presidential envoy."[87]

Despite the ongoing attacks on U.S. troops, Rumsfeld continued to maintain that progress was being made. In early November, on the bloodiest day for U.S. troops in seven months, Rumsfeld insisted that the administration's policy for improving security in Iraq was "on track." He argued that more than 100,000 Iraqi forces had been trained and that by September 2005 the number would double.[88] Ignoring Bremer's latest report, Rumsfeld clung to the rosy picture of an increasingly stable and well-trained Iraqi security force.

Meanwhile, there was a military–political split between General Abizaid and Bremer. The general strongly opposed using former Iraqi officers to build the new Iraqi Army. Abizaid told Bremer that he had opposed Bremer's move to disband the army, but that he had kept his opinion to himself. But he had grown tired of reading articles in U.S. newspapers by Walt Slocombe, who was back in Washington and opposed the hiring of former Iraqi officers.[89] The relationship worsened to the point that Abizaid would complain about Bremer in January stating, "I can't talk to him."[90] The relationship between Bremer and the military—especially between him and General Sanchez, would get so bad that it would impact policy during the battle for Fallujah.

## White House Tries to Retake Control

The White House was concerned. Progress toward stability was too slow. It was beginning to look like the Iraqi uprising was going to last forever. So White House staff unveiled the "November 15 Agreement." According to this arrangement, there would be a number of deadlines and steps to get Iraq to the point where it had a permanent government. The Governing Council would draft and approve an interim constitution by February 28, 2004. It would be ratified in a national referendum, so that elections could be held by December 31, 2005, for a permanent Iraqi government. From

June 30, 2004 until December 31, 2005, authority would be in the hands of an interim government. Unfortunately, to many Iraqis this plan, like others, was made in America.

Rumsfeld paid an important visit to Baghdad on December 6, 2003. Bremer noted he was in an irritable mood, the reason for which soon became clear. According to Bremer, the conversation went as follows:

> "Look," Rumsfeld said, "it's clear to me that your reporting channel is now direct to the president and not through me.". . .
>
> "Condi has taken over political matters." he said. "I think that's a mistake. The last time the NSC got into operational issues, we had Iran-Contra. But she seems to have jumped into this with both feet."
>
> "She certainly is on top of things Don," I said, addressing him by his first name as usual in private.
>
> "Well," he said with a tight smile. "I'm bowing out of the political process. Let Condi and the NSC handle things. It might make your life a little easier."[91]

Rumsfeld's power and influence was on the decline, especially on Iraq. According to Bremer, "Rumsfeld was clearly unhappy that Rice had stepped in and taken control of policy."[92] Others, no doubt, breathed a sigh of relief.

Meanwhile, according to a 2006 interview with Bob Woodward, Rumsfeld claimed that from May 2, 2003, until the end of the year, a number of decisions were made "that weren't visible to him."[93] While the one cited by Rumsfeld in this interview was the appointment of General Sanchez to command the critical Iraqi ground command, it suggests that throughout the remainder of 2003, Rumsfeld was only peripherally involved in operational matters. His task now was to defend the Iraqi operation on the Hill, to the media, and to the American people.

As the insurgency drew on, it increasingly became obvious that the army was faced with its worst nightmare—some were concerned that it could be a repeat of Vietnam. The heavily armed insurgents would pop out of nowhere with their AK-47s, rocket-propelled grenades, and roadside explosives to attack and kill Americans. Then they would blend back into the population. All of America's vaunted technological superiority was counting for naught. The army and Marine Corps were suffering from their lack of language and cultural knowledge.[94] The soldiers were doing what they were trained to do, but many of the officers and civilians leading them were not sensitive to problems of counterinsurgency. Tom Ricks quotes one general as saying, "Tactically, we were fine. Operationally, usually we were okay. Strategically—we were a basket case."[95] To a large degree, this was the military's own fault.

## Abu Ghraib Shatters Illusions

The lax discipline erupted into scandal regarding the Abu Ghraib prison, west of Baghdad. A handful of U.S. military police stationed at this prison forced detainees to simulate homosexual acts. A female soldier boasted of making at least one prisoner crawl around on the floor with a dog's leash around his neck, while a U.S. animal handler reportedly set his dog on a detainee to the point that the detainee was in fear of his life. To make matters worse, digital images were made of these actions and widely distributed. The illusion of the Iraqi population greeting the Americans as liberators had finally burst. To many Iraqis the Abu Ghraib scandal was a national humiliation brought on them by their "liberators."

A blue ribbon panel that investigated the incident directly criticized the way Rumsfeld and his colleagues conducted the war. First, the United States did not deploy enough troops and interfered with complicated sequencing procedures. For the prison that meant too few guards, and guards who were not properly trained. Instead of mobilizing a military police unit that could be properly trained, individuals from different units with little or no training were thrown together. Second, the Pentagon did not adequately plan for occupying the country.[96] The consequence was a lack of MPs in general. And then there were reports (denied by Rumsfeld and unproven) that the secretary had authorized the mistreatment of prisoners in an effort to get intelligence from them.[97] The report, however, faulted senior military officers to a much greater degree than it did the secretary. It is somewhat ironic, given the complaints from military officers about the lack of troops, that the report "was most critical of the top officers in Iraq. . . . who should have appealed to higher headquarters for additional assets and taken stronger action to strengthen leadership. . . . "[98] While both of those are valid complaints, especially the second one, for a general to ask Rumsfeld for more troops could well have resulted in his recall and possibly the end of his career. Generals like Abizaid and Sanchez both knew the secretary was trying to withdraw troops, and they also knew that there was a major problem in finding new ones to send to Iraq.

Meanwhile, in terms of troops, the army began to undertake one of the most ambitious troop transfer projects in recent years. The army intended to replace all of the U.S. troops in Iraq who had served for a year with fresh ones. Not only was that a logistical nightmare, it also meant that battle-tested troops were being replaced by new, often raw troops.[99] This took place just prior to Rumsfeld's announcement that he was invoking emergency powers that would authorize the Pentagon to grow by 30,000 troops above its congressionally approved limit of 482,000.[100] The next month,

General Myers was asked to predict how long U.S. forces might remain in Iraq, and he wisely answered, "I really do believe its unknowable."[101] The administration had no rational planning model for Iraq. "Washington also failed to recognize the differences between reserve or national guard troops and regulars in terms of their training. There was a tendency to assume they were interchangeable."[102]

## Conclusion

Bremer's arrival marked a decline in Rumsfeld's influence on Iraq policy. The White House was getting increasingly concerned about the situation in Iraq and—much to Rumsfeld's displeasure—was turning to National Security Adviser Rice for leadership and an infusion of rationality into U.S. policy.

Nevertheless, while much of policy went through the White House, Rumsfeld remained a major player. The idea of abolishing three key entities—the Iraqi government, the Baath Party, and the Iraqi Army—was designed in the Pentagon, primarily, it appears, by Feith. Rumsfeld approved the decisions and he continued to interact and work with Bremer during his time in Iraq. Unfortunately, their interaction did far more harm than good.

Admittedly, he could have done it more diplomatically, but it is hard to criticize the logic of Bremer's argument. Turning Iraq over to the G-7, a group of exiles, should have never been on the drawing board. If Feith and others had not been so close to Chalabi, that notion probably would never have seen the light of day.

It is harder to endorse the dissolution of the Iraqi Army and the de-Baathification policy so easily, however. Both policies were opposed by almost anyone who knew anything about Iraq, and both did far more harm than good. Trying to carry out a policy of de-Baathification with young Americans who know next to nothing about the country and its language was absurd. Yet, that was the policy.

The same is true of the end of the army. There was no doubt that there were many in the army who were opportunists or Saddam loyalists. While it would have made sense to disband the Special Guards and the Republican Guard, the whole army is another matter. Bremer made that decision at a time when it was clear from both civilians and the military that there were thousands of former soldiers available. He made no effort to call them back or to find out what kind of officers and NCOs were involved. Instead, he gratuitously alienated those who understood weapons and conflict. To use a military phrase, it was as if Bremer decided to "shoot himself in the foot."

Before taking the job, Bremer should have insisted that he and Rumsfeld agree on what kind of individuals would be sent to join his "team." The idea that young individuals with no special skills or familiarity with Iraq could be accepted with just the conservative Heritage Foundation's recommendation that they were good, conservative Republicans seems absurd, although fully in line with the way Feith operated. As a former FSO, Bremer should have realized that poor staffing had condemned his operation to failure. Bremer apparently did not push to have more FSOs sent to Iraq.

Meanwhile, Rumsfeld continued to try defend U.S. policy in Iraq. To be convincing the arguments must be credible, but he would invent figures to show that the Iraqi police or military forces were increasing daily, when everyone knew that was not the case.

Finally, it is unfortunate that Bremer did not bring the military in closer to his planning and implementation procedures. The military can be very frustrating to deal with at times, but leaving them out is not sound bureaucratic politics. There is always the worry about the camel having its nose under the tent, so to speak, but at least then the camel—or in this case the military leadership—understands what is going on and can react immediately.

# 8
# *Rumsfeld Is Fired*

President Bush and his top advisors have consistently substituted wishful
thinking for analysis and hope for strategy.
   *Peter Galbraith*

The first six months of 2004 would be difficult ones for the U.S. military in
Iraq. The United States would be forced once again to deal with the firebrand
Ayatollah Muqtada al-Sadr and a major uprising in Fallujah. Not surprisingly,
there were calls for Secretary of Defense Donald Rumsfeld's head, and Rumsfeld even offered his resignation. Yet President George W. Bush expressed his
continued confidence, and Rumsfeld remained at the Pentagon. The secretary would see his operational powers somewhat circumscribed, but he
would continue to do his best to influence events in Iraq. As time went on,
Rumsfeld would be continually attacked—increasingly by former military
officers who were deeply involved in fighting and planning the Iraq War and
who had witnessed firsthand the disastrous impact of his decisions.

   It would also be a difficult time for the professional military. Officers
would struggle with the question of whether it was right to openly criticize the commander in chief. The line between being a military officer and
criticizing the decisions of political superiors began to blur over dilemmas
such as, Does a retired officer have the right to criticize the president or the
secretary of defense? At first glance the answer might be no, but they had
seen "up close and personal" the results of political interference in military
operations and wanted it to stop. In the end, Rumsfeld would be fired[1] and
a difficult chapter in U.S. civil-military relations would draw to a close.

## Command Confusion

*Al-Sadr*

By March 2004, Muqtada al-Sadr was becoming an increasingly serious problem. At times, it seemed as if parts of Iraq had two governments—Sadr's Shiite Mehdi Army and the interim government. The United States had to do something, especially since political power would be handed over to the Iraqis in July. Coalition Provisional Authority (CPA) director Paul Bremer moved to shut down Al Hawza, Sadr's newspaper, which was clearly inciting violence and rebellion. Bremer had assumed that if Sadr lashed back, General John Abizaid and Lieutenant General Ricardo Sanchez would quickly suppress him and his thugs. Unfortunately, within hours he had ordered a full mobilization of his followers, and protestors began flooding the traffic circle in front of the newspaper's office. Bremer called Sadr an "outlaw" that the United States would not tolerate. Sadr responded, "I have the honor to be termed an outlaw by the occupation." Furthermore, he warned that if U.S. forces moved against holy sites in the cities of Najaf or Karbala, "We will be human time bombs which would explode in their faces."[2]

Sadr soon became even more brazen. He took over the main mosque in Kuraas, sister city of Najaf, where Muhammad's son-in-law had reportedly led worshipers in the seventh century.[3] By March 13, 2004, Sadr's Mehdi Army was setting up roadblocks across the south—as well as kidnapping and raping women. Brutalities committed by the Mehdi Army became commonplace, and Bremer called on General Abizaid to retaliate. But the Americans were forced to hold back for several weeks while hundreds of thousands of religious pilgrims visited Najaf and Karbala to celebrate a religious holiday. By April 11 it seemed that bloodshed was imminent as U.S. troops began massing for an attack. Shia clerics defused the situation by getting Sadr, whose army had suffered significant casualties, to pull back. But much to Washington's chagrin, Sadr remained free.

*The Battle for Fallujah—Round One*

On March 23, 2004, the Marine Corps took over command of Fallujah, a city 43 miles west of Baghdad, from the Army's 82nd Airborne. Mindful of its efforts to get close to the local populace in northern Vietnam in the 1960s, the Marines decided to focus primarily on counterinsurgency. They would fight the bad guys if necessary, but would try to win the hearts and minds of the locals in the meantime. Accomplishing the latter makes defeating the former much easier. Unfortunately for the Marines and everyone else involved, it would be a long time before they would get a chance to apply their counterinsurgency methods. Most observers believed that the idea of pacifying Anbar province—where the city of Fallujah is located—would never be realized. The Marines simply did not have a sufficient number of troops.

The Marines were experiencing most of the same problems as the army, but their lines of command were even more tangled. When the Joint Task Force issued an order, for example, it did not say what the Marines were supposed to do. They did not have an operational document laying out their mission. Little help came from the State Department, which should have been coordinating with other Coalition members and consulting with the Iraqi Governing Council. By this point in time, the process should have been bureaucratized to the point that such actions were almost routine.[4] But Rumsfeld did his best to keep State out of the governing process in Iraq.

Coordination problems inside Iraq were also monumental. The CPA evidenced so much confusion and hostility toward the military that it is doubtful it could have liaised with the Marines (and the army that was dealing with al-Sadr at about the same time) if it had wanted to. Ambassador Bremer would claim control and seek to improve coordination by setting up a joint briefing room. Unfortunately, while both the CPA and the military used it, the CPA was briefed at 0700, the military a half hour later. There were also fights over turf. General Ricardo Sanchez and Bremer did not get along.[5] One had worked his way up from a poor Mexican family in Texas, while the other belonged to the East Coast elite and graduated from Ivy League universities. And while Bremer would claim he was the senior officer in Iraq reporting to the president, Sanchez was not about to take orders from him. Consider this example: Jeffery Oster, who served as Bremer's chief of staff, asked for a briefing on the next steps after the CPA had been driven out of Kut. "'That's military business,' a colonel told Oster, 'not to be shared with the CPA. LTGEN Sanchez does not work for the ambassador.'"[6] Bremer also did not see military traffic and, unless told by Sanchez what was happening on the operational front, he remained in the dark. On the working level, the lines of authority were even more confused and the idea of creating a joint political-military planning unit to prepare to deal with an event of this kind never seemed to dawn on Bremer.

Marine patrols were roaming Fallujah making themselves familiar with the city, talking to people, trying to get to know them. But their increased visibility was actually making the situation worse, as the insurgents were warning the populace to get prepared to fight the Americans. Then on May 31, four U.S. contractors from Blackwater Security were driving through

Fallujah and took a wrong turn. They were attacked, their car burned, and their bodies were mutilated, burned, and drug through the streets. Two corpses were hanged from a bridge.

Strangely enough, General James Conway, the Marine commander in Fallujah, wanted to continue his counterinsurgency strategy of blending into the local scene and avoiding a wider conflict. Conway's advice to General Sanchez was to wait a few days, figure out who the culprits were, and then mount a targeted operation to seize them. Bing West noted that while the troops were "watching TV in a mess hall outside Fallujah. . . . The Marines had the names and addresses of those responsible."[7] Conway's recommendation was conveyed up the chain of command until General Myers passed it along to Rumsfeld. According to one source, Rumsfeld and Myers decided that "it was unsatisfactory to have parts of the country that were not under control"[8] and they wanted action.

The next day Rumsfeld, accompanied by General Abizaid, went to the White House to meet with the president. Both men believed that, given the international coverage that the incident had received, the United States had to respond decisively. However, as often occurred, Rumsfeld refused to share the views of the general on the spot with the president. Instead, Rumsfeld came up with an order to mount "a specific and overwhelming attack to seize Fallujah."[9] Rumsfeld went way beyond just ignoring General Conway's advice. He told the president that an attack on Fallujah "was something they could do with a relatively low level of civilian casualties."[10] Bush told Abizaid, "Get ready to go," adding, "If this isn't resolved in 48 hours, you go."[11] Later, Sanchez told Conway, "The president knows this is going to be bloody."[12] Clearly, there was a disconnect somewhere. Either Rumsfeld or Abizaid did not pass an accurate statement of what was said to Sanchez or the latter was freelancing. The idea that a professional military officer in either position would mis-transmit a presidential statement seems very unlikely. Another possible explanation is that Rumsfeld wanted an attack on Fallujah, and, as he had on other occasions, he took the information he wanted, embellished it, and ignored anything that he did not like.

The Pentagon's refusal to follow General Conway's advice was raised by the media with Pentagon spokesman Lawrence DiRita. He was asked if Conway's views had been made known all the way up the chain of command. "'All the way to Rumsfeld,' an official said. But Rumsfeld and his top advisors didn't agree, and didn't present the idea to the president. 'If you're going to threaten the use of force, at some point you're going to have to demonstrate your willingness to actually use force.'"[13] It is not clear from this statement who the "top advisors" were, but when a battlefield commander makes a recommendation through his chain of command, even when his senior civilian officials disagree, it would seem only prudent to make the president aware that there were dissenting points of view—especially when they came from the man who knew the situation on the ground best.

The Marines were ordered to launch an attack on a town of 240,000 people. However, their orders did not state what they were expected to accomplish. This was one of the worst possible violations of military culture: confusion in lines of command or authority. It is not clear who was responsible for this confusion—Rumsfeld or General Sanchez. If it was Rumsfeld's fault, then Sanchez should have provided the kind of conceptual clarity that was lacking. The Marines were eventually told that the task of the operation was to "pacify" Fallujah.

In an effort to avoid a clash, Marine commanders met with local religious leaders and demanded that they condemn the killings of the contractors. At Friday services, the imams pointed out that Islam forbids desecrating bodies, but they refused to denounce the killings. When Sanchez subsequently ordered the Marines to "clobber people" in Fallujah, General Conway objected and asked to speak to General Abizaid, who told him the order had come "from high up." Later, Conway would say publicly, "We felt like we had a method that we wanted to apply to Fallujah; that we ought to let the situation settle before attacking out of revenge."[14] Meanwhile, the commander of the First Marine Division, General James Mattis, protested, "'This is what the enemy wants.' He had been preparing to take Fallujah for months, but he didn't want to do it this way—hastily, clumsily, acting in anger rather than cool detachment. He was ordered nevertheless, to attack Fallujah within seventy-two hours. He requested that order in writing but didn't get it."[15] So the United States went on the offensive.

To assist the Marines, a 620-man battalion from the Iraqi Army, a unit made up primarily of Kurds that had just finished basic training, was sent Fallujah, but they refused to join the fight. This episode highlighted a major problem with the training program, even though on January 6, when the unit finished boot camp, Rumsfeld had called it a major part of the new Iraq.[16] While there were some problems in the way they had been handled and informed of their mission, it was a severe setback for the U.S. training program. Despite optimistic comments from Washington, the troops were not performing as expected. There were good reasons for the problems, and they were not only linguistic or cultural.

The refusal also revealed major flaws in the U.S. training effort. Some Iraqi police and soldiers felt let down by the U.S. effort to equip and train them. A subsequent report by the GAO found that in March 2004, the provisioning of the Iraqi Civil Defense Corps was "months behind schedule," with the result that "no Iraqi Civil Defense Corps units possessed body armor, and many were using Saddam-era helmets for protection." In addition, as of late April, many units were still awaiting the delivery of the most basic equipment—uniforms, helmets, vehicles, radios, rifles, ammunition, and night-vision gear.[17]

The United States, in the words of General John Keane, the former deputy chief of staff of the army, had "lost about a year, to be frank about it," in training Iraqi forces.[18]

On April 4, 2,000 Marines converged on Fallujah and began attacking the next day. They ran into stiff resistance. Following standard procedures, the Marines responded with a heavy barrage of bombs, mortars, and gunfire. It was a major combat operation, which Rumsfeld had not expected. Five Marines and an unknown number of civilians and insurgents died. The secretary had been convinced that the mere thought of an attack would cause the town's leading citizens to turn over whomever had killed the American contractors. Alternatively, Rumsfeld thought that if conflict became necessary, he could go back to the world of high technology and use "smart bombs" to achieve his ends. As the Marines were fighting their way into the city they were at the same time fanning the flames of anti-U.S. feelings among the local Sunnis. Once again, the United States had failed to understand the depth of the animosity toward the American occupation of Iraq.

The Marines were off balance when they attacked. They had not been given time to conduct formal reconnaissance or to collect intelligence. They were simply told to attack. And they did, first with small teams in an effort to seize high-value targets, then with the mass of Marines, backed up by some tanks and armored personnel carriers. The fighting was very difficult and prolonged. Meanwhile, the Arab press was engaged in sensationalistic reporting, which radicalized the Arab population throughout the region.

Meanwhile, members of the Governing Council were becoming worried. They were well aware of the level of popular outrage because of the Marines' actions. This was especially true of the Sunni members of the Council. They had met separately and were threatening to resign if the CPA did not declare a cease-fire. To make matters worse, the UN was threatening to pull out of Iraq. Bremer was also becoming concerned, while Washington's best ally, U.K. Prime Minister Tony Blair, was putting pressure on the White House to call a cease-fire. Bremer stated in his memoirs that he believed that if the conflict had continued, it "would result in the collapse of the entire political process and force the postponement of Iraqi sovereignty."[19]

Bremer met with members of the Governing Council on the evening of April 8. Generals Abizaid and Sanchez were also present. By the end of the meeting, Abizaid had agreed that the battle was undermining Iraqi political stability, so he ordered the Marines to suspend the offensive.

While the delicacy of the diplomatic situation is easy to understand, it would be an understatement to suggest that the Marines were "upset." Rather, they were incensed. They had not been in favor of attacking Fallujah. But Washington and Baghdad had ordered them to attack, so they did. In the process they and their colleagues had put their lives on the line, and what was their country doing? Even members of the CPA who were in the field with the Marines thought the battle should go on. They were fighting some very bad people, and they were winning. One-third of the city was under the control of the U.S. Marines, and the rest would be in only another few days. But Bremer suddenly declared a cease-fire. As General Conway stated, "Once you commit, you've got to stay committed."[20] One well-known retired Marine expressed what every Marine was thinking: "We have been challenged. . . . If we back off on this thing, we are sending a strong signal that the Americans will not be able to control the situation."[21]

In an effort to find a working solution to the problem of Fallujah, the Marines startled everyone by coming up with a new idea. General Conway authorized the creation of a brigade of Iraqis—a force of locals—who would police the city. However, this innovation again demonstrated the problems inherent in a divided chain of command. Conway had gotten permission from Sanchez and Abizaid to negotiate such an arrangement. From a military standpoint, that was all he needed. But no one had said anything to Bremer or the Iraqi Governing Council. Predictably, Bremer was furious and did his best to have the idea overturned. But with Washington focused on the Abu Ghraib scandal there was little he could do to get rid of this seemingly crazy Marine idea. The Iraqi defense minister was also upset at being left out of the loop. From the standpoint of the civilians in the Pentagon, this arrangement was tantamount to handing over control of the city to the insurgents. This was exactly the question Wolfowitz raised when he remarked, "Have we turned Fallujah over to the old regime?"[22] If that were not confusing enough, General Myers, the chairman of the Joint Chiefs of Staff, endorsed the deal, calling it "a microcosm of what we want to happen all over Iraq."[23]

On the afternoon of April 30, 200 Sunni security personnel were assembled in formation. The Marines were warned to stay 300 meters away, while a representative ceremoniously handed control of the city over to Jassim Saleh, a former general in Saddam's army. It was hoped that putting forward a Sunni unit would demonstrate to the local populace that the United States was genuinely interested in letting the Iraqis run Iraq. After all, the Iraqis had repeatedly told the Americans during the siege that the problem was that the citizens of Fallujah wanted to run their own affairs; now they had the opportunity.

In fact, General Conway's idea turned out to be a flop. After a few weeks of cooperation the Marines realized that the Sunni brigade was becoming the heart of a new Fallujah resistance army. The brigade worked together with the local police, the imams, and the insurgents to take over control of the city. By the end of June, it was becoming clear that Fallujah was returning to the dangerous insurgent stronghold it had been prior to the Marine attack. By the fifth day of Bremer's ceasefire, West reported that the insurgents were probing Marine lines and firing at anything that moved.[24] Indeed, to the Marines on the front lines, the only difference between the period prior to the ceasefire and after it was that instead of moving forward, the Marines were remaining in their positions, keeping the insurgents from pushing them back.

In the meantime, General Abizaid had realized that the new Iraqi troops were not doing the job. Perhaps in months or years they might be proficient, but for now, they were not up to the task. In fact, he called them "a great disappointment." Abizaid had to fight the war, and since he could not count on Iraqi troops to pick up the slack, he asked the Joint Chiefs of Staff for the equivalent of 7,000–10,000 troops—"if not more." This request was made one week after more than 20,000 troops were told their rotations were being extended. When Rumsfeld was asked about the Fallujah operation and what part he had in the misadventure, he responded, "I certainly would not have estimated that we would have had the number of individuals lost . . . that we have had lost in the last week."[25] One of his first and only admissions of a "mistake."

## Confusion Grows

*Training the New Army*

As problems training the Iraqi Army continued, Rumsfeld did his best to interject himself into the debate. For example, in February 2004, General Abizaid suggested at an NSC meeting that U.S. forces be embedded in Iraqi military units. The president seemed pleased, but Rumsfeld spoke up: "Oh, Mr. President, I haven't approved that yet."[26] Regardless of what authority Rice might or might not formally have over events in Iraq, Rumsfeld was determined to keep control of the Pentagon and its part in the war. The real problem was that introducing these forces into the Iraqi Army might seem to make good sense from an American standpoint—it would demonstrate that the United States was shifting combat to the Iraqis. However, the Iraqi point of view was very different.

From the Iraqi perspective, the scenario was as follows: Iraqis would be recruited and go through boot camp under U.S.-trained contractors (mostly retired U.S. soldiers and Marines). When they finished, they would be assigned to U.S. Army units. But the Iraqis had never met these American officers and there was no special bond between them, something that is very important in Arab cultures. There would be little time to build these bonds, because the U.S. officers were only scheduled to be there for a year. The Iraqis felt like that they were fighting for a foreign army. It was difficult enough to get the average soldier to rise above his ethnic and religious identity in order to get him to focus on being an Iraqi. But expecting him to work closely with Americans with whom he had little in common would not work.[27]

The Americans and the Iraqis also clashed over the concept of how to build an army. It was clear that the new Iraqi Army was not meeting its challenges during the early period. Instead of fighting, the units continued to dissolve. The Americans argued that it was a lack of leadership, a point that the Iraqis accepted. In order to deal with the desertion problem, Iraqis suggested finding senior Iraqi officers who, after being vetted, could lead the Iraqi soldiers. The idea was to build an army from the top down. The general would build a division, and he would find the divisional staff as well as the brigade and battalion staffs. In the United States it was meritocracy that was supposed to drive movement from the bottom to the top. That was important too in Iraq, but personal relationships and time constraints counted even more. However, this nuance was something the civilians in the Pentagon like Feith did not want to hear and would not endorse.

From a political standpoint, the main problem continued to be Rumsfeld. Despite Wolfowitz's best efforts, he could not get the secretary to focus on the matter. Rumsfeld seemed to believe that only Special Forces could train Iraqi troops. Wolfowitz, however, argued that it could also be done by regular Marines or army personnel. He had tried to get Rumsfeld to send a study mission to Iraq to look at the real requirements for training Iraqis, but Rumsfeld kept putting him off. Rumsfeld finally agreed, and, as discussed above, General Karl Eikenberry, who had built the new army in Afghanistan, was sent to Iraq. Upon his return, he filed a report calling for the creation of a unified command to deal with the training mission. Then in April 2004, Lieutenant General David Petraeus was sent again to Iraq, this time to head up the training of Iraqi forces.

*The Brass Doubts the War*

It is common for military officers to complain about how a campaign is being run, not only by their own officers, but by politicians. However, in most cases, the complaining takes place in private between colleagues. Very seldom does criticism from senior officers regarding the secretary of defense or his deputy become public.

However, on May 9, 2004, an article appeared in the *Washington Post* noting the views of Major General Charles Swannack, commander of the 82nd Airborne. He argued publicly that the situation in Iraq was a mess. Asked if the United States was winning, he replied, "I think, tactically, we are, I think operationally maybe we are. But strategically, we are not."[28] A number of officers were saying privately that the first step toward changing strategy would be for Rumsfeld to resign. To them, he was responsible for a whole series of blunders ever since the United States went into Iraq. Ricks cited two active duty officers who directly and indirectly criticized Rumsfeld. One, a colonel on terminal leave at the National War College, called for more coherence in U.S. policy. Another unidentified general pointed "directly at Rumsfeld and Deputy Defense Secretary Paul D. Wolfowitz."[29] The bitterness toward Rumsfeld came through in a comment by another unidentified general. "'Like a lot of senior Army guys, I'm quite angry with Rumsfeld and the rest of the Bush administration,' . . . He listed two reasons. 'One is, I think they are going to break the Army.' But what really incites him is, 'I don't think they care.'"[30] What was really surprising was to see public criticism directed at the chairman of the Joint Chiefs. Speaking about General Myers, one unidentified general commented, "Had someone like Colin Powell been the chairman [of the Joint Chiefs of Staff], he would not have agreed to send troops without a clear exit strategy."[31] Another officer was more direct. Retired Army Colonel Robert Killebrew, a frequent Pentagon consultant, said, "'The people in the military are mad as hell.' He said the chairman of the Joint Chiefs of Staff, Air Force General Richard B. Myers, should be fired."[32] Clearly, animosity toward Rumsfeld and Wolfowitz—and Myers—was growing on the part of serving officers.

Military officers were not the only ones getting tired of Rumsfeld's actions and inactions. On July 15, 2004, Steve Herbits, who had worked closely with Rumsfeld for many years, wrote a memo that blasted Rumsfeld, calling him "indecisive," refusing to believe that other people could be smarter than him in some areas, saying he was "abrasive," and ending with the question: "Did Rumsfeld err with the fundamental political calculation of this administration: not getting the post-Iraq rebuilding process right within 18 months?"[33] It was a damning criticism from a close colleague. By November, complaints were being heard from the CIA, stating they "are mad at the policy in Iraq, it's a disaster, and they're digging the hole deeper and deeper," according to one intelligence analyst, while an army staff officer who served in Iraq and stayed in touch with his colleagues reported, "It just seems that there is a lot of pessimism flowing out of theater now. There are things going on that are unbelievable to me."[34] There was a growing consensus among Americans working on Iraq that Rumsfeld and his civilian colleagues were a disaster. According to one report, Andrew Card, the president's chief of staff, was so worried about the negative impact that Rumsfeld was having on the administration that he suggested Bush replace Rumsfeld with former secretary of state James A. Baker III. Bush reportedly thought about it, but Cheney and Karl Rove, White House deputy chief of staff, convinced him to leave Rumsfeld in his job.[35] After all, replacing a secretary of defense during an election year might be seen as an admission of failure. By December, Senator John McCain (R-AZ), a former Vietnam POW, would state that he had no confidence in Rumsfeld.[36] Then a bit later, two other very important Republican senators, Trent Lott of Mississippi and Chuck Hagel, a Vietnam vet from Nebraska, blasted Rumsfeld. Lott commented, "I don't think he listens enough to his uniformed officers," while Hagel stated, "I don't like the way he has done some things. I think they have been irresponsible."[37]

## Number of Troops

The issue of troop numbers topped the agenda during May and June of 2004. On May 17 Bremer met privately with General Sanchez to discuss the issue. Bremer said he asked the general what he would do if he had more soldiers. Sanchez replied, "I'd control Baghdad." He said he needed an additional 30,000–40,000 troops. Sanchez also mentioned the problem of controlling Iraq's borders and the difficulties he faced in maintaining the lines of communications, especially in the area of logistics.

The next day Bremer told National Security Adviser Condoleezza Rice that he was going to ask Rumsfeld for more troops. That afternoon he sent Rumsfeld a message in which "I stressed that while I did not think our mission was on the brink, I felt we were in a dangerous situation," and called for one or two more divisions.[38] According to the *New York Times*, the Pentagon acknowledged Bremer's request but claimed that General Meyers and the Joint Chiefs had looked at the situation and decided that additional forces were not required.[39]

Meanwhile, the issue was getting attention at the highest level of the army in particular. Chief of Staff General Peter Schoomaker noted that the army was "stressed." To relieve the pressure, he suggested temporarily adding

30,000 troops. However, recruiting more troops is very costly. The Congressional Budget Office estimated that an additional 10,000 troops would add $1 billion to the annual defense budget.[40] Finally recognizing that Iraq was a long-term commitment, the army estimated it needed 140,000 troops in Iraq through January 2007.[41]

A September congressional hearing focused on the question of troop levels. Senator John McCain again attacked Rumsfeld, noting, "It's clear, at least to most observers, that we don't have sufficient personnel." Rumsfeld was unmoved. Defense was doing a number of things, especially with the army, to increase frontline forces in Iraq.[42] By October, the Army's Chief of Staff stated, "We are planning 12 months boots on the ground until the level of effort goes down."[43]

## Interim Government and Turf Wars

The creation of the Interim Government in June 2004 meant the end of the Coalition Provisional Authority. This inevitably raised the question of who was in charge of U.S. personnel (civilian and military) working in Iraq. Secretary Powell argued that it should be the State Department, since the country would now have a U.S. ambassador, who was the president's personal representative. Rumsfeld maintained that with 130,000 troops in Iraq, the Department of Defense should still be in charge. National Security Adviser Rice had had enough of being in the middle trying to be neutral; she wanted a clear decision—and she got one. This time, Powell won. "On May 11, 2004, Bush signed National Security Presidential Directive (NSPD-36). The three-page directive, classified SECRET, formally shifted responsibility for Iraq from the Pentagon to the State Department after the termination of the Coalition Provisional Authority."[44] Ambassador John Negroponte, the Embassy's chief of mission from the Department of State who took over from Bremer, would be in charge.

Despite the continued insurgency, the new Iraqi government took over the reins of power on June 2, 2004. Interim Prime Minister Iyad Allawi took the oath of office on a red Koran and called on Iraqis to rally behind the new, temporary government. He pledged to hold elections for a new government by the January 31, 2005, the deadline set by the coalition.[45] With the dissolution of the CPA, most of its responsibilities were transferred to the new Interim Government. The new U.S. Embassy, headed by Ambassador Negroponte, would still have a major say in matters—at least as long as thousands of U.S. troops remained in the country. Immediately after the conclusion of the handover ceremony, Paul Bremer went to the airport and left for the United States—his job was done.

Allawi maintained that the creation of the Interim Government marked a major shift in U.S. policy in Iraq. It signaled a reduction in the power of people like Rumsfeld, Wolfowitz, and especially Feith in Washington. The Interim Government included a number of senior Baathists who had been reinstated, as well as a number of nationalists and secularists. Rather than permitting the Iraqis to go only for ideological purity in personnel and policy decisions, Allawi stated that it was now clear that Washington was looking for a new approach and sanctioned Baghdad's decision to branch out "by appeasing and empowering" more of its "moderate" political base.[46] But, despite these steps, the insurgency raged on.

*Enter General Casey*

In July 2004, General George Casey replaced General Sanchez as commander of the Multinational Forces in Iraq.[47] He had been to multiple meetings in Washington with senior members of the administration, including Rumsfeld, and understood that one of the major problems facing the United States in Iraq was the lack of a common strategy. Each division commander was following his own approach in dealing with problems in his area. One of the first things that Casey did was to put everyone on the same page. "The centerpiece . . . was that we were going to transition to the Iraqi security forces. . . . The political strategy was to stand up a representative democracy, a representative government, as quickly as possible." The problem, however, as General Keane noted, was that Casey lacked a strategy to defeat the insurgency. "We were resting on a political military strategy that would hopefully stem the violence because the Sunnis would come into the political process and therefore seek a political solution to the confrontation."[48] As far as Casey was concerned, his primary task was get "out of Iraq as soon as possible, and that had always been the president's strategy; it has always been Secretary Rumsfeld's approach, and it was the approach that General Abizaid and General Casey had."[49] In the meantime, he focused on creating security.

This left U.S. forces in a difficult situation. First, authority was split between Casey and Ambassador John Negroponte. Then as Keane pointed out, the main problem was that the United States had failed to provide security in the major cities. In retrospect, given Casey's inability to get Rumsfeld to add troops—assuming he were to request them—his options for developing a meaningful military strategy were limited.[50] The other problem was that CENTCOM lacked an understanding of the way political and military factors must interact in such a situation. As it was, U.S. forces were more or less running in place, trying to impose security while waiting for the Iraqis to take over, but it was becoming increasingly clear that the latter was not going to happen.[51] Whether or not General Casey understood this problem in depth and whether or not he tried to get Abizaid or Meyers to raise it with Rumsfeld is unclear.

## Fallujah, Round Two

What to do with Fallujah remained a serious problem for the Interim Government. The continued shelling from Fallujah, and the danger that the various insurgents—especially al-Qaeda, which had made it their home—might take nearby Samara, increased pressure to begin another assault. Clearly, if the insurgent stranglehold over the city were to be broken, U.S. troops would have to do the heavy lifting.

In June the insurgents began to push against Marine lines—trying to open up paths outside the Fallujah city limits. It was also becoming increasingly clear that the police were working for the insurgents. On June 5, for example, six Shiite truck drivers became upset at an insurgent checkpoint and ran to a police station. "The police took them to a mosque, where they were handed over to insurgents. They were executed and their bodies mutilated."[52] The Marines remained steadfast in holding their lines, but nothing serious was done by the U.S. side to attack the insurgents. The situation remained a stalemate, even though Prime Minister Allawi had pledged not to permit Fallujah to keep drifting. Something clearly had to be done. The city had turned into the car-bomb capital of Iraq. The insurgents would plan attacks, and then ex-filtrate with weapons and personnel only to return to their safe haven in Fallujah. Some observers were referring to the "Talibanization" of Fallujah.[53]

Unlike the first go-around in Fallujah, senior U.S. and Iraqi officers had since taken the time to carefully plot out how they were going to attack the city. For example, they had stockpiled huge amounts of food, fuel, weapons, and ammunition. They had enough to support full-scale operations for a full fifteen days.[54] Toward the end of October, U.S. warplanes were bombing targets in Fallujah on a daily basis, and a major effort was launched to convince civilians to leave the city. Most did, as did a considerable number of the more senior insurgents. All water and electricity to the town was turned off, and no man under the age of 45 was permitted to leave the city.

Then on November 7, all hell broke loose. Some 6,500 Marines, 1,500 soldiers with tanks, along with two Iraqi units with a total of 2,000 troops, attacked. There were even 2,500 naval personnel serving in support roles.[55] Rumsfeld praised the troops, noting, "They'll take as long as they take."[56]

It was a house-to-house battle with U.S. and Iraqi troops digging the insurgents out and, more often than not, killing them because the Islamic extremists preferred martyrdom to surrender. It was a brutal battle, according to one observer, "probably the toughest battle the U.S. military had seen since the end of the Vietnam War."[57] In many ways it was comparable to the 1968 Tet Offensive in Vietnam. By November 9, the city was in U.S. and Iraqi hands, although fighting continued until the middle of the month. According to Interim Prime Minister Allawi, while a number of insurgents had left the city, about half of them stayed to fight and die. They tried to set up sniper teams and other units to slow up the Americans. However, given the overwhelming firepower used by the Americans, there was no doubt about the outcome. Unfortunately, in the process, the city was almost completely destroyed.

## Rumsfeld Faces the Troops

With his reputation and job already on the line, Rumsfeld did something very characteristic—but very unwise. He went to Kuwait in late 2004 in an effort to show the U.S. public that he cared deeply about its fighting men and women. During a question-and-answer period, he was asked by a young soldier from the Tennessee Army National Guard, "Why do we soldiers have to dig through local landfills for pieces of scrap metal and compromised ballistic glass to up-armor our vehicles?" Rumsfeld's rather cold response was, "You go to war with the army you have." Instead of expressing concern and talking about what Washington was doing to solve the problem, the young man was basically told, "suck it up, you have what you have."[58] The answer was silly, because what the soldier was really asking was: the United States had more than a year to prepare for this war, why didn't you do it? Rumsfeld did not have an answer.

## Leadership Changes

### The January 2005 Iraqi Election

On January 30 Iraqis were to elect a National Assembly that would appoint an acting government and draft a constitution. The Sunnis were strongly opposed to the election. They saw this process as a way for the more numerous Shiites to take control of the country. Even the UN representative, Lakhdar Brahimi, sent messages to Bush asking him to delay the vote. However, the president remained committed to holding the election on January 30. He also ordered the CIA and the State Department to remain absolutely neutral.

Despite concern by officials that there would be a very low turnout, some 8.4 million Iraqis went to the polls—about 58 percent of the population. The main Shiite party won 48 percent of the votes, while the Kurdish Party placed second with 25.7 percent.[59] For Bush, it was a vindication of his policy, of his belief that the United States could export democracy and that people around the world wanted it, and would vote for it if given an opportunity. The only downside was that the Sunnis had boycotted the election—some 20 percent of the population had voluntarily disenfranchised themselves.

Despite the Joint Chiefs' changes, there was no end in sight of the many problems facing the U.S. military. For example, the officers and NCOs who had dealt with Iraqi trainees had very little good to say about them. The Iraqis claimed the Americans didn't trust them and they were right. Others argued that they lacked courage and would not fight. In one case, an entire Iraqi unit left and went home because their company commander was killed in a car bombing. Half of them did not seem to know why they were fighting.[60] Marine Major General Stephen T. Johnson, commander in Western Iraq, "said yesterday that there are 10,000 Iraqi soldiers in his sector, but no unit is able to conduct operations on its own."[61] No one was even sure that they would *ever* be able to carry their load.

The situation facing Rumsfeld was not getting any better. According to Woodward, sometime after Thanksgiving 2005, White House Chief of Staff Card again approached Bush with the suggestion that Rumsfeld be fired. He was almost impossible to deal with—something Card was hearing from Republicans and Democrats alike. "He was more arrogant and unresponsive than ever." Bush's response suggested that he did not understand the depth of the problem. "Bush reminded him that they were at war. Rumsfeld was transforming the military, hadn't been insubordinate, and needed to get the new Pentagon budget approved.[62] Replacing him would be disruptive.

## Pace Becomes Chairman

On September 30, 2005, General Peter Pace was named to replace Myers as chairman of the Joint Chiefs. He had fought in Vietnam and worked his way up to the top by holding all of the key jobs. The problem, in the minds of many of his colleagues, was that he was too much like Myers: selected because Rumsfeld believed he would not stand up to him. Pace might disagree with him on issues, but he would not go to the mat when he believed the secretary was wrong.

During the middle of July 2005, General Jim Jones, a Marine serving as the NATO Commander, met with his old service friend Pace. Jones asked

Pace why he would even want to be chairman of the Joint Chiefs. "You're going to face a debacle and be part of the debacle in Iraq." He said he was so worried about Iraq and the way Rumsfeld ran things that he wondered if he himself should resign in protest. Pace responded that someone had to be chairman, and he didn't know who else would do it. Jones responded, "'Military advice is being influenced on a political level,' he said. The JCS had improperly 'surrendered' to Rumsfeld. 'You should not be the parrot on the secretary's shoulder.'"[63] After he became chairman, Pace spoke with a number of people, including Admiral Vern Clark, chief of naval operations. Clark spoke of the need to set a goal for his time as chief and then rattled off other recent chairmen, noting their accomplishments. Turning to the most recent four years, he said "he would not be so unkind as to ask Pace to sum up how Dick Myers had done." Finally, with an eye toward Goldwater–Nichols, he told Pace that he "should reassert his legal responsibility as chairman. You should have something to say about it when the guy sitting one deck up refuses to forward your assessment to the Congress for 13 months. Thus is fundamentally not just a breakdown in the system. That is a breach of faith."[64]

The job definition had to go beyond what Rumsfeld decreed or wanted. The few authorities under the law given to the chairman, including a requirement that the Chairman's Program Assessment be sent directly to Congress, had been neutered by Rumsfeld. Though it was just one report, it was symbolic. Rumsfeld had refused to let it go to Congress for over a year.[65]

The Goldwater–Nichols Act made the chairman of the JCS the primary military adviser to the secretary of defense and the president. It would be up to Pace to reclaim that authority and use it. For example, it was clear that the generals in Iraq desperately needed more troops—they told everyone who visited how they were undermanned for the mission they had been assigned. They wanted someone to get through to the secretary. But no one believed that Pace would go toe-to-toe with the secretary to represent military interests. He would mention them, even argue in favor of them, but that was it.

In May 2006, Pace met with the combatant commanders, the chiefs, and the top civilians in the Pentagon. General Jones spoke up. He was concerned about Rumsfeld's control of just about everything that happened at Defense. Control is fine, he maintained, but when it gets to the point where alternative views are not being carefully considered, there is a serious problem. The problem, as Woodward pointed out, was that, "no one seemed willing to take on the secretary of defense."[66]

By the end of 2005, there had been a major change in political leadership in Washington. Wolfowitz and Feith had left the Pentagon to pursue other options. Their departure would have a critical impact on U.S. policy toward Iraq; namely, the ideological purity and rigidity that both had insisted on were no longer an overriding concern for their successors. The key question, however, was whether their interference had so undermined the U.S. effort to pacify the country that there was little their successors could do to save Rumsfeld's job or reverse course in Iraq.

## Rice versus Rumsfeld

There was a fundamental difference between Rumsfeld and Rice, who had replaced Powell as secretary of state in January 2005, after he decided to leave the government. Like the CEO he had been, Rumsfeld was convinced that the proper way to handle Iraq was to give its leaders a chance to fail. If they could not stand on their own, that was their problem. This is why Rumsfeld was so opposed to a strategy of counterinsurgency. He saw it as another form of state building, something he believed the military should avoid. It should focus on fighting wars, not on finding ways to help Shiites and Sunnis get along.

Meanwhile, Rice was increasingly coming to the conclusion that Rumsfeld's strategy would not work. The United States could not simply pack up and leave. There was a real danger of a civil war if U.S. troops suddenly left, not to mention the possibility that the conflict could spread to include other parts of this volatile region. Rice believed the United States had to come up with an "exit strategy," i.e., a more comprehensive approach to the problem.[67] In essence this meant a counterinsurgency strategy, one she called, "Take, Clear, Build."[68] Under this approach, U.S. troops would take an area, clear it of the enemy, and then hold it so the enemy would not return while the U.S. helped Iraqis rebuild it. Rumsfeld was fine with the first idea, but he opposed the second and third steps. When Rice testified before the Senate on October 19, 2005, she repeated her view that "our political-military strategy has to be clear, hold and build, to clear areas from insurgent control, to hold them securely and to build durable Iraqi institutions." Zelikow recalls that this speech was "very consciously written as an effort to articulate a strategy for success in Iraq."[69]

Rumsfeld was reportedly furious. In his mind, she had already stolen the policy portfolio from him and given it to State; now she was elbowing her way into what Rumsfeld considered purely military matters. It was his job to determine what kind of a strategy the U.S. military would follow in Iraq. Besides, he believed that her comments were inaccurate, because they suggested that what was happening was a joint partnership between the United States and the Iraqis. That was wrong. The U.S. government was trying to get the Iraqis to stand on their own two feet.[70] While Rumsfeld may have reigned supreme in the Pentagon, and while he was able to inflict his will on the generals running the show in Iraq, Rice would continue to haunt him.

The battle continued. Bush was scheduled to speak on Veteran's Day 2005 and the draft of his speech had the phrase "Take, Clear, Build." Rumsfeld was upset and called Card, asking that it be taken out. He was not moved by Card's reply that it was the focal point of the speech. Rumsfeld saw Rice's fingerprints on the document and continued to protest, but the language remained in the speech.

In December 2005 President Bush attended an NSC meeting. The issue was Iraqi oil exports—there were problems. Rumsfeld continued to argue that it was a problem for the Iraqis to solve, not one for the U.S. government. The military could not guard thousands of miles of pipeline. Rice disagreed. Protecting and helping get the pipeline running smoothly was part the U.S. counterinsurgency strategy, she explained. According to Woodward, "Card was struck by the tension between Rice and Rumsfeld. It was not new, but it had a sharper edge."[71]

## Iraq's December 2005 Election

In December 2005, Iraqis voted for the first assembly formed under the new constitution. One author called the December vote "a watershed in Iraq's history."[72] The Sunnis did not boycott it, instead they recognized the silliness of their action in January. This time they went to the polls. Almost 80 percent of the voters turned out—11 million in all. Bush was encouraged, as democracy seemed to be working. But so was the insurgency. Despite the successful election, the insurgents kept on killing Iraqis and Americans whenever they got the chance.

On February 22, 2006, al-Qaeda attacked the Shiite shrine in Samara, an action that had a major impact on the insurgency. The goal, as Michael Gordon put it, was to provoke "an overreaction on the part of the Shiites and [make] Iraq essentially ungovernable and chaotic and an entity that the Americans can no longer control."[73] They were convinced that faced with such a situation, the United States would withdraw. Within Iraq, sectarian violence worsened. Somewhat disingenuously General Peter Pace commented, "Well, the Iraqis walked up to the precipice. They saw what civil war could mean for them, and they walked back."[74] General Casey made similar comments.[75] Although the generals' comments further undermined their credibility with many of their colleagues, they had little choice but to echo Rumsfeld's view.

Card has wondered why the generals did not stand up to Rumsfeld when they knew the situation was getting worse. Indeed, he was very critical of the behavior of the generals throughout the Iraqi invasion. According to Woodward, "Card put it on the generals—Myers and Pace in the Pentagon, Abizaid and Casey in Iraq. If they had come forward and said to the president, 'it's not worth it' or 'The mission can't be accomplished,' Card was certain the president would have said, 'I'm not going to ask another kid to sacrifice for it.'"[76] Rumsfeld had made sure that he would not have to put up with strong-minded generals who disagreed with him. He carefully selected only those who might raise an objection in private, but would never consider going to the president and give him the kind of message suggested by Card. Fortunately, there were other generals who were more than ready to stand up to Rumsfeld.

## Stability Operations

There were officers in the U.S. Army who were well aware of the military's shortcomings in the Iraq War. The military officers were certainly aware of the importance of counterinsurgency. For example, General Peter W. Chiarelli, who had commanded the First Calvary Division and would take over as commander of Multinational Forces in January 2006, wrote an article in *Military Review,* a journal primarily intended for military officers. In it, he noted that it was time for the army to pay more attention to factors such as building sewers, schools, water lines, or other infrastructure work to help win over the Iraqi people. He was not the only one interested in the topic; other officers were also discussing its importance.[77]

Eventually this led to the drafting of a new manual, *The U.S. Army/Marine Corps Counterinsurgency Field Manual.*[78] One of the most important changes in procedure was that the new document did not talk about Phase III or Phase IV. As the military had learned in Iraq, one could not separate the two because they occurred *simultaneously.* For example, it would be impossible to separate reconstruction and combat, in either Afghanistan or Iraq. The new document, together with comments from some of the key players, also brought up a long-term military concern—how to get U.S. civilian agencies involved on the battlefield. As it was, everything was being left to the military. Why not transfer money to the Department of State "to enable civilian professionals to deploy alongside military forces in stabilization and reconstruction operations."[79] The final DOD Directive 300.05 read as follows: "Stability Operations are a core U.S. military mission. . . . They should be given priority comparable to combat operations and be explicitly addressed and integrated across all DoD activities, including doctrine, organization, training, education, exercises, material, leadership, personnel, facilities and planning."[80]

This was not the only area where the army locked horns with Rumsfeld on an issue that was vital to counterinsurgency operations in Iraq. Rumsfeld's next battle was over civil affairs and psychological operations: Who should have responsibility for them, Special Forces or the regular army? Rumsfeld wanted them to be under the command of regular army forces. His reasoning was that the reassignment would help the regular army because it was not doing a good job in that area. For exactly that reason, the Civil Affairs units did not want to make the move. Rumsfeld believed that the regular army did not understand them or their work, so they were usually shunted aside. In addition, many Special Operations soldiers were worried that this was just another example of Rumsfeld's efforts to get them to focus primarily on attack missions, instead of training foreign militaries and winning the hearts and minds with their aid projects. Rumsfeld formally raised the issue in January 2004 and pushed it throughout the year, but the army refused to back down.[81]

## The Crisis in Iraq is Exposed

### The Attack of the Generals

On March 19, 2006, Major General Paul Eaton, U.S. Army (Ret.) wrote an op-ed piece in the *New York Times* in which he bluntly stated, "Donald Rumsfeld is not competent to lead our armed forces." He blasted the secretary, calling him "incompetent strategically, operationally and tactically." He was accused of being a "bully," "of trying to intimidate people." And in his strongest statement he argued, "Donald Rumsfeld demands more than loyalty. He wants fealty. And he has hired men who give it."[82] From the military standpoint, the last comment was particularly damning for Meyers and Pace. After all, it was Rumsfeld who hired both men.

Then on April 9, Lieutenant General Greg Newbold, U.S. Marine Corps (Ret.), who had resigned prior to the beginning of the war because he could not stand Rumsfeld's manipulation of intelligence data and his refusal to listen to anyone in uniform, came out with a piece in *Time*. Newbold called the Iraqi invasion plan "fundamentally flawed," and said it was a "plan executed for an invented war." U.S. troops were committed for that war with "a casualness and swagger that are the special promise of those who have never had to execute missions, or bury the results."[83] He also blasted his former colleagues and seniors on the Joint Staff. "When you look around at how many people were in positions to raise their voices, senior military leaders who had a duty to object, and how many did—I'm having trouble counting how many did."[84]

Several days later, Major General Charles Swannack (Ret.), who, as noted above, had spoken previously against Rumsfeld, stated in an interview, "I really believe that we need a new secretary of defense because Secretary Rumsfeld carries way too much baggage with him. . . . Specifically, he has micro-managed the generals who are leading our forces there."[85] On the same day, Tony Zinni blasted Rumsfeld for "throwing away 10 years worth of planning,"[86] while Major General John Batiste, who had been a military assistant to Paul Wolfowitz, and who had been offered but turned down a promotion to lieutenant general to be commander of the U.S. occupation forces in Iraq, also entered the fray. As he put it, "The trouble with Don Rumsfeld, . . . is that he's contemptuous, he's dismissive, he's arrogant, and he doesn't listen."[87] He also later commented that he and his colleagues had *always* asked for more troops, despite denials from the Pentagon and the White House that the generals were getting whatever they asked for.[88]

A day later, Major General John Riggs jumped in. Riggs was in charge of developing the lighter, more mobile army that was to be built around future combat systems, the kind of high-tech futuristic general who presumably would get along well with Rumsfeld. However, he "told NPR that Rumsfeld had helped create an atmosphere of 'arrogance' among the Pentagon's top civilian leadership. . . . They only need military advice when it satisfies their agenda. I think that's a mistake, and that's why I think he should resign."[89]

Such an outpouring of criticism by retired senior officers had not been seen since the days of McNamara, and it made clear that there was a deep sense of animosity and betrayal on the part of the military toward Rumsfeld. David Ignatius reported that when he asked an army officer, who had extensive experience in Iraq, how many of his colleagues wanted to see Rumsfeld fired, he said 75 percent.[90] Other sources reported the same situation: "There is now a group of officers who feel an obligation to speak out more aggressively and I think that has to have been influenced by the Vietnam experience."[91]

When asked about the generals' criticism, Rumsfeld brushed it aside, commenting that there were thousands and thousands of retired admirals and generals, so it was not surprising if two or three disagreed with him.[92] The absurdness of this statement was that there were no retired admirals or air force generals who had been involved on the ground in Iraq. There were also a limited number of army and Marine generals who were involved either on the ground or in Washington in dealing with Iraq. Thus five or six generals going public was a significant part of those who had dealt with Iraq up to that time.

To be fair, there were generals who came to Rumsfeld's defense. In addition to Franks and Myers,[93] Marine Lieutenant General Michael DeLong, who had been Franks's deputy, commented, "When we have an administration that is currently at war, with a secretary of defense that has the confidence of the president, has done well—no matter what grade you put there, he has done well—to call for his resignation right now is not good for the country."[94] Myers also criticized the generals who had publicly attacked Rumsfeld, arguing, "My whole perception of this is that it's bad for the military, it's bad for civil-military relations, and it's potentially bad for the country, because what we are hearing and what we are seeing is not the role the military plays in our society."[95] He further added, "In our system, when it's all said and done . . . the civilians make the decisions."[96] For his part, Pace came out with a strong endorsement in which he claimed, "We had then, and we have now, every opportunity to speak our minds, and if we do not, shame on us because the opportunity is there."[97] Pace, Myers, Franks, and DeLong clearly belong to that segment of the officer corps who believe that after giving whatever advice they believe necessary, it is their task to fall in line and carry out the secretary's decision, regardless how repugnant or dangerous for the country they might consider those decisions to be. It also appears that the senior officers supporting Rumsfeld were in the minority. Another unidentified officer made the problem very clear—"'You saw what happened to Shinseki,' said the officer, who requested anonymity for fear that he might be disciplined for publicly supporting Rumsfeld's opponents. 'It's suicide to come out against your boss. I understand why they waited until they retired.'"[98] In fact, the Pentagon's media department launched a press blitz, with a memorandum claiming that U.S. military leaders "are involved to an unprecedented degree in every decision-making process in the Department of Defense."[99]

While the media offensive from the Pentagon was predictable, the military's response to Rumsfeld's first six years as secretary of defense suggested that the public relations department in the Pentagon was overplaying its hand. Besides, the fact that six retired generals were prepared to do something few senior officers had done in the past—go public with criticism of their boss, an action that could easily mean an end to Pentagon contracts for the companies they worked for—indicates that their feelings against Rumsfeld's were deep, very deep.

Perhaps the most interesting comment on this topic came from Colin Powell, who resigned as secretary of state after the 2004 presidential election. He told an audience that the "administration had 'made some serious mistakes' after the fall of Baghdad." For example, he pointed out, "We didn't have enough troops on the ground. We didn't impose our will." As a result of the Pentagon's failure to plan for Phase IV in the Iraqi operation, "an insurgency got started, and . . . it got out of control."[100] Given Powell's well-known tendency to not criticize the president and to avoid polemics against anyone, that was a rather brutal statement. He stated clearly that the United States had made major mistakes—and Rumsfeld was running the Pentagon at the time. To a military man, the verdict was clear: Rumsfeld bears full responsibility for the mess in Iraq.

As expected, Bush again issued a strong statement endorsing Rumsfeld. "I reiterated my strong support for his leadership during this historic and challenging time for our Nation. . . . I have seen first-hand how Don relies upon our military commanders in the field and in the Pentagon to make decisions about how best to complete these missions. . . . he has my full support and deepest appreciation."[101]

## Rumsfeld and Rice—Again

The secretaries of defense and state crossed swords again in April 2006. While visiting Berlin, Rice commented, "'I know we've made tactical errors, thousands of them I'm sure,' but the big strategic decision to take down Saddam Hussein will be seen by future historians as correct."[102] Rumsfeld audaciously responded, "I don't know what she was talking about, to be perfectly honest." He then went on to explain how sides need to change tactics during a war, but he never really addressed Rice's comment head on. She was right, the United States had made many tactical errors in Iraq, but as Thomas Friedman pointed out, none as big as the strategic mistake that Rumsfeld made "by not deploying enough troops to control Iraq's borders and fill the security vacuum."[103] The point was that Rumsfeld was losing power, and his retort was just the latest sign of his tender ego.

In June, there was a meeting at Camp David that included the president. According to Zelikow—who was not present but was involved in planning the meeting—the goal of the meeting was to get the president directly involved "in a real war council to take a hard, roots-up look at what we're doing in Iraq."[104] It was clear to some that Washington had to change strategy in the aftermath the Samara bombing. Iraq had held elections, but the situation was continuing to deteriorate. The conflict was changing from what might have been called an insurgency to a civil war, which required a reevaluation of U.S. strategy. No longer was it just a matter of reducing troops. Indeed, as Kagan noted, "There was a recognition that things were not moving in the right direction, especially after the mosque bombing and violence was picking up."[105]

## Back to the War

The war in Iraq was worsening, and General Casey still did not seem to understand the nature of threat he was facing. For example, when he returned to Washington in June, he had a plan—a plan that was "another version of his plan to draw down American forces in Iraq."[106] Fewer troops were not the solution—not in the face of a major, growing insurgency. Weeks later the United States deployed an additional 7,000 troops, giving the impression of confusion—if not chaos—in the upper ranks of the national security bureaucracy. Then in August, the chief of intelligence for the Marine Corps in Iraq filed a report in which he stated that prospects for victory in Anbar province were slim at best. One of the main reasons was the lack of combat troops. This report flew in the face of the optimistic reports from General Casey's headquarters in Iraq. Here was a senior officer telling it like it was, similar to the kind of reports that the CIA had been filing but, more often than not, ignored by the Pentagon and the White House. According to the author of this secret report, the only thing that could improve the situation would be an infusion of troops and resources.[107]

Toward the end of August, Rumsfeld used a speech to the American Legion's annual convention to condemn critics of the Bush administration, those who sought to "appease the Nazis before World War II." He also warned that the country was faced with a "new type of fascism."[108] It was his most explicit attack on his critics to date. He maintained that some in the United States had not learned history's lesson. "It seems that in some quarters, there is more of a focus on dividing our country than acting with unity against gathering threats."[109] The Democrats responded with a letter signed by a dozen leading members of Congress to the president, urging him to change leadership in the Pentagon. Their point was that such an action would demonstrate to the public that he understood the problems that Rumsfeld's policies created "in Iraq and elsewhere."[110]

## Continuing to Build an Iraqi Army

Both the U.S. military and the politicians in Washington were frustrated by the failure to build a new, effective, combat-ready Iraqi army. A former Green Beret and retired army colonel who visited Iraq came back stating that the newly trained forces he saw showed "a lack of willingness to fight for something." The problem, he maintained, was that while there were units prepared to fight alongside the Americans, many of them appeared more loyal to their tribes than to the Iraqi Army. And this was supposed to be the key to U.S. withdrawal—stability in Iraq backed up by a combat ready, diverse military ready to defend the regime against enemies both domestic and foreign. In September, the Pentagon announced that the army had extended the combat tours of 4,000 soldiers who had been scheduled to return home.[111] Furthermore, non-deployed brigades were getting low readiness ratings primarily because of a lack of weapons and equipment. The entire concept for training the Iraqi Army was unrealistic.

General Casey testified before Congress and then appeared on television on October 5 with Tim Russert. He noted that there were close to 200,000 Iraqi security forces in the field, adding "I'm optimistic." Later during the month he predicted that the Iraqi Army could take over control of the country in twelve to eighteen months.[112] Behind the scenes, however, it was obvious that the brass was anything but optimistic. For example, when pressed by his friends to tell them the strategy for winning, Abizaid made it clear just how little the army thought of Rumsfeld.

> What's the strategy for winning? They pressed him.
> "That's not my job," Abizaid insisted.
> No, it is part of your job, they insisted. Abizaid was the articulate one. He could talk for an hour and it sounded great, better than anyone.
> "No," Abizaid said. Articulating strategy belonged to others.
> Who?
> "The President and Condi Rice because Rumsfeld doesn't have any credibility anymore," he said.[113]

By October, Casey was described as "more concerned." "His concern was that Iraqis are not standing up quickly enough to take this mission," according to a person who knew him.[114]

The problem was that the White House continued to believe in the inevitable triumph of democratic forces in Iraq, while the army and the rest of the military was becoming increasingly pessimistic. Their leader, Rumsfeld, was also becoming increasingly irrelevant, thereby leaving a leadership vacuum at an extremely critical time.

Meanwhile, matters were not progressing much better on the Iraqi political front. By September, U.S. officials expected some progress on the part of Iraqi officials in resolving the problems facing them—for example, to create a new investment law, to decide how to allocate oil revenues, to agree on how to handle former Baathists, and to hold local elections.

## Endgame

### The Pressure Intensifies

According to Michael Gordon, Rumsfeld did not "realize that he's a short-timer."[115] However, on November 6, 2006, there was an editorial in the *Army, Navy, Air Force,* and *Marine Times* that argued that it was one thing when the majority of Americans believed that Rumsfeld had failed. "But when the nation's current military leaders start to break publicly with their defense secretary, then it is clear that he is losing control of the institution he heads." And it continued, "For two years, American sergeants, captains, and majors training the Iraqis have told their bosses that Iraqi troops have no sense of national identity, are only in it for the money, don't show up for duty and cannot sustain themselves. . . . And all along, Rumsfeld has assured us that things are well in hand." The editorial concluded by noting that regardless of which party wins the upcoming election, it is time "to face the hard and bruising truth: Donald Rumsfeld must go."[116] None of these four newspapers are owned by the Pentagon—they are independent. Nevertheless, while they sometimes take positions in opposition to the Pentagon, this kind of blanket opposition is very unusual and very damaging. These are the newspapers that the average officer and enlisted personnel see and read on a weekly basis, and to have them publicly calling for the ouster of the country's secretary of defense was not something that could be ignored.

Equally surprising was the blast Rumsfeld received from Richard Perle. The long-time conservative and previous Rumsfeld supporter commented that, had he seen where things were going to go in 2003, "I would probably have said, 'Let's consider other strategies for dealing with the thing that concerns us most, which is Saddam supplying weapons of mass destruction to terrorists.'"[117] If that were not enough, Kenneth Adelman, a well-known conservative and former Reagan administration official, said he was deeply bothered by the failure to stop the looting, and "by Rumsfeld's casual dismissal of it, with the phrase 'stuff happens.'" All in all, he argued, the Bush national security team "has proved to be 'the most incompetent' of the past half century."[118] Bush responded by vowing to support Rumsfeld and emphasized that he wanted him to remain in his post.[119]

## The Resignation

On November 6, one day prior to the off-year election, Rumsfeld submitted his letter of resignation. Interestingly, the letter made no mention of the words "war" and "Iraq."[120] Perhaps Rumsfeld believed mention of either would have been embarrassing, given his responsibility for the Iraq War. For the president, with the magnitude of the election losses staring him in the face, and the belief on the part of many Republicans that Rumsfeld's presence in the government was one of the main reasons for the Republican debacle, Bush had no choice but to accept Rumsfeld's resignation. He announced that he was replacing Rumsfeld because "a fresh perspective is needed to guide the war in Iraq."[121]

There were two very different but accurate "political obituaries" on Rumsfeld's time in office that did an excellent job of noting the reasons for his failure. First, the *New York Times* ran an especially hard hitting editorial blasting Rumsfeld on November 9:

> Mr. Rumsfeld, you remember, was absolutely certain that Iraq could be transformed with less than half the troops that a generation of senior generals had thought necessary. He was wrong, but it was the Army's top general who lost his job. Similar travesties played out over postwar planning and over reconstruction contracts. At some point, people must have stopped telling Mr. Rumsfeld what was really going on, fearing his wrath or retaliation.[122]

Then one from the *Armed Forces Journal,* a journal that is read regularly by many officers in all of the services.

> In the end, it has been Rumsfeld's greatest strengths—his self-confidence, his managerial expertise and insistence on efficiency, his faith in technology, his problem-solving—practicality—that have equally been his weaknesses. These are uniquely American quirks, the strengths and weaknesses of the traditional American way of war. The secretary of defense's failures are a symptom of our approach to strategy, not the disease itself.[123]

In any case, Rumsfeld was gone, much to the happiness of thousands of officers and non-commissioned officers. They were hopeful that Robert Gates, the new secretary of defense, would listen to their ideas and advice. Stephen Cambone, Rumsfeld's assistant and the top intelligence officer in the Pentagon, left the Pentagon on December 31, 2006. His departure marked the end of Rumsfeld's closest confidants on military transformation and Iraq from the Pentagon.

## Conclusion

The last two years of Rumsfeld's reign at the Department of Defense were as difficult and full of problems as the previous four, if not more so. He had to sit back and watch while Condoleezza Rice slowly but surely took over greater and greater control of U.S. policy toward Iraq. It infuriated him. He was a supporter of social Darwinism; he wanted to force the Iraqis to sink or swim. But what would have happened had the United States done as he suggested, and hundreds of thousands of Iraqis began to slaughter each other?

One characteristic of Rumsfeld that continued to manifest itself was his refusal to deal with his military subordinates in a forthright manner. The first Fallujah incursion was a perfect example. CPA Director Paul Bremer was clearly responsible for the lack of coordination, but so was Rumsfeld. And then the secretary went to the president and failed to relay General James Conway's recommendation. There is no doubt he had the authority to so, but it was another insult to the military—no respect for their point of view. Observers could not help but ask why General Myers did not say anything. The president should hear both sides of an issue. Rumsfeld, or Myers, could have easily said, "The commander on the ground believes we should be patient, but General Myers and I believe we need to take immediate action." But neither spoke up.

The decision to form the Fallujah brigade would turn out to be a poor one, but this was another incident where a joint political-military authority, staffed with officers who understood the Arab world and working closely with the Marines, might have come up with a better idea. Then as the city began to move closer to becoming the Taliban capital of Iraq, it was clear that the something had to be done. Fortunately, the second attack would be far more successful. It was carefully planned out, and with the cooperation of army troops and navy support, the city was neutralized.

Training Iraqis was another example of the lack of preparation for Phase IV. The State Department-sponsored study had warned of problems—cultural problems would be a concern in training Arabs. But Washington was caught flat-footed and forced to send contractors to train the new Iraqi Army. A lack of equipment, few instructors who understood Iraqis, and wholly different training methods ensured problems—as demonstrated by the brigade that refused to fight at Fallujah.

While Myers or whomever may not have passed on the commanders' request for more troops, it was clear to everyone serving in Iraq that they were desperately needed. But the administration wanted to keep the numbers as small as possible. One might have expected Peter Pace, the new JCS chairman, to be more forthcoming in fighting for the military's interests, but few officers anticipated anything like that from him, and they were right. He had been selected primarily because Rumsfeld was convinced that he could control him. Another violation of military culture—find a chairman who will do what he is told without defending military interests.

Meanwhile, pressure for Rumsfeld to resign was growing. The retired generals made the headlines. Seldom had the country seen so many senior officers blasting the secretary of defense. Behind the scenes, fine, but not in public, even though they were retired and had the right to speak out. Few made use of it. But these men, most of whom had been directly involved in the war, were prepared to do so. Rumsfeld seemed to make a specialty out of alienating everyone he dealt with, not just the military. Rice, for example, was getting tired of him and his games. He was becoming a negative for the Bush administration. Even insiders like Card were privately calling for him to be replaced.

Finally, the president let Rumsfeld go. Bob Gates was a welcome change for many, if not most in uniform. Pace was informed that he was being replaced by Admiral Michael Mullen as chairman, and his deputy would be General James Cartwright, a Marine. Casey was reassigned to the Pentagon as chief of staff of the army, and Abizaid retired. A new approach was clearly needed. Frederick Kagan and General John Keane helped convince the president of the advisability of moving to a counterinsurgency strategy—the approach Rice had argued in favor of for over a year. To implement this new strategy Gates brought in General David Petraeus, the former commander of the 101st Airborne and author of the army's counterinsurgency strategy, gave him a fourth star, and sent him off to Iraq to implement the policy. The United States now had an officer at the top who understood Iraq and who was dedicated to charting a new course for fighting the insurgency. The Bush administration had made a complete break with the Rumsfeld regime.

# Conclusion

Shinseki was right.
*John Abizaid*

Donald Rumsfeld will go down in history as one of the worst U.S. secretaries of defense since the end of World War II. His arrogance and assumed omnipotence led him to destroy the existing cooperative relationship between the U.S. military and the Department of Defense. Rumsfeld dominated the Pentagon to such an extent that often his voice was the only one heard. He excluded the military from important meetings, ignored their advice, and surrounded himself with civilian sycophants and officers who were prepared to play the game of Pentagon politics the way Rumsfeld wanted it played. When General Eric Shinseki stood up to him, Rumsfeld did his best to isolate him, and tried to get the general to resign his position as the army's chief of staff, but Shinseki held his ground. Rumsfeld will be remembered for the problems he caused for the military, problems that will haunt it for years to come. However, Rumsfeld did not achieve this level of destruction alone. Other civilians also played key roles.

## President George W. Bush

In the larger sense, Bush was responsible for what Rumsfeld did to the military. He was the president, and he could have removed Rumsfeld at any time. Rumsfeld offered his resignation twice, but Bush turned it down and instead heaped praise on Rumsfeld.

**193**

Bush's leadership style played a major role in this Pentagon circus. Bush governed as the country's chief executive officer, the first CEO president in the history of the United States. Thus, it is not surprising that he would assume that an individual who had been successful in the corporate world would be able to "shake up" the Pentagon and move it to the high-tech world he praised in his 2000 stump speech at the Citadel. Bush's leadership style put him above the bureaucratic politics in the various departments. Consequently, since he liked Rumsfeld and believed that Rumsfeld was doing a good job of moving the Pentagon down the road of military transformation, he retained him as secretary of defense and refused to get involved in internal Pentagon political-military politics.

## Vice President Cheney

Vice President Cheney's role in the Pentagon mess is the most difficult to nail down. He was clearly the most active in policy circles of any vice president since World War II. That translated into a major role in the lead up to the Iraqi War, if for no other reason than he constantly went out of his way to undercut Secretary of State Colin Powell. He clearly had no respect for the United Nations, and his office was deeply involved in the effort to create evidence sufficient to convince Capitol Hill and the American people to go to war against Saddam Hussein. Based on what little information is available, Cheney consistently sided with Rumsfeld when it came to Iraq. He appeared uninterested in issues like military transformation—that was Rumsfeld's area.

## Donald H. Rumsfeld

The biggest reason Rumsfeld had a difficult relationship with the military was his approach in dealing with them. During his six years in office, he violated almost every canon of military culture. From his first day in office Rumsfeld made it very clear that he had little or no respect for America's military leaders. He held his first staff meeting without them, and he then proceeded to exclude senior military officers from his newly convened study groups on the future of the military. These meetings dealt with issues of vital importance to all of the services, but he was not interested in what they had to say. Apparently he did not value the professionalism and expertise they had gained from over thirty years of military service. He knew the answers before he heard the questions. Regardless of whether he was being overly enthusiastic in carrying out the president's order or if transformation was his own idea, he insulted the military, especially the army, time after time. Indeed, Rumsfeld's alienation of the military was so bad that most people expected him to be the first cabinet officer to leave the administration. However, 9/11 provided a respite, but the situation between the secretary and the military did not improve.

Rumsfeld's treatment of General Shinseki was disgraceful. As army chief of staff, Shinseki had a legitimate concern. The army was already stretched thin; indeed, while Rumsfeld made it clear that he intended to get rid of two army divisions, Shinseki said he believed it actually needed two *more* divisions just to carry out the missions currently assigned to it. Shinseki did what the law required him to do—he spoke openly and honestly to Congress on the number of troops required for Iraq, and he stood up to Rumsfeld on the issue of transformation. Indeed, Rumsfeld missed a great opportunity by refusing to work with Shinseki, as he was already pushing the process of transformation in the army. But Rumsfeld was not interested in cooperation—he wanted control. He was not interested in working with Shinseki or Secretary of the Army Thomas White. One of the reasons Rumsfeld fired White was his enthusiastic support of Shinseki. If Rumsfeld had deigned to work with Shinseki, he would inevitably have been forced to make compromises—perhaps to even accept the Crusader artillery system. In many ways, what made Rumsfeld's rejection of the Crusader so harmful to civil–military relations was not just its rejection, but the abusive way in which Rumsfeld handled the matter. First, Deputy Secretary Paul Wolfowitz told the army it had a month to prove its case for acquisition, then Rumsfeld abruptly canceled it. It is not surprising that many in the army turned to the media and industry to plead their case.

## Micromanagement

When I asked General Richard Myers about Rumsfeld's role in the Iraq War, he commented, "Secretary Rumsfeld was deeply involved at the strategic level on Iraq issues throughout my tenure. He was never involved in the tactical, day to day operations."[1] While that is accurate in one sense, it is misleading in another. Rumsfeld interfered with the TPFDD deployment algorithm, which seriously affected the kinds of forces the combatant commander had in place to fight the war. Second, his micromanagement of troop numbers also represented interference at the operational and tactical levels. There is nothing wrong with a civilian official asking hard questions, but in this case it represented constant badgering by Rumsfeld to force the combatant commander to adopt his approach to fighting the war in Iraq.

Third, Rumsfeld refused to send the First Cavalry Division to Iraq—a decision that General Franks reluctantly accepted. Proving Rumsfeld's theory of military transformation—i.e., small numbers of troops relying on high-tech weapons that were maneuverable and versatile—had greater priority than providing troops to take care of reconstruction operations.

### No Post-Combat Planning

Because of Rumsfeld's insistence on small numbers of troops, the Coalition forces, and especially the United States, arrived in Iraq with far too few soldiers and Marines to secure the country. Furthermore, little or no advance planning was done on post-combat operations. As a consequence, soldiers and Marines were walking around Baghdad watching the rampant looting, but their orders were only to guard the Oil Ministry. Yet, the work the State Department had done with Iraqi émigrés showed clearly the kinds of problems the U.S. military would face once it took over Iraq. Even more surprising was the incompetent way that Jay Garner's Office for Reconstruction and Humanitarian Assistance was handled. If Rumsfeld was such a military expert, he should have known that nothing would get done on a battlefield unless the military was ordered to do it, especially if it was something out of the ordinary like giving priority to reconstruction efforts. Sending Garner to Iraq with minimal support preordained his effort to failure.

Then Rumsfeld took three other actions that defy logic. First, he selected L. Paul "Jerry" Bremer to be his pro-consul in Baghdad. As almost every military officer and Iraqi who worked with him would testify, Bremer's arrogance rivaled that of Rumsfeld. He quickly moved to subvert any chance of creating an Iraqi government. To make matters worse, Rumsfeld agreed to a de-Baathification order drafted by Under Secretary Douglas Feith. This order put significant parts of the Iraqi population out of work. He either did not understand, or did not care to know that Baath Party membership in Iraq was much like Communist Party membership in the former USSR. For many jobs it was *sine qua non.*

But even worse than the de-Baathification order, Rumsfeld fired the Iraqi military. The armed forces were disbanded overnight at a time when Iraqi soldiers were telling U.S. civilian and military personnel, not to mention the media, that despite the destruction to their facilities, they were prepared to return to their barracks.

With these three orders, Rumsfeld probably did more than anyone else (except, perhaps, Bremer) to get the insurgency started. As far as the Iraqis were concerned, the Americans had made it clear that they had little interest in rebuilding the country. They had just put thousands of people out of work with the de-Baathification order, while the elimination of the army put hundreds of thousands of soldiers on the streets. And these soldiers not only knew where the weapons were located—they knew how to use them.

I disagree with people who suggest that everyone involved in the invasion of Iraq shares responsibility for that action.[2] In the abstract, of course, that is true. However, under the military's concept of accountability, the person in charge is accountable for what those under his or her command do. Rumsfeld was in charge of the Pentagon, and it was Rumsfeld's subordinates who were directly involved in manipulating intelligence data. It was Rumsfeld who interfered in military planning to the point that nothing was done to deal with Phase IV. It was also Rumsfeld who, with Vice President Dick Cheney's assistance, pushed hard for the war in part so he could prove the validity of his military transformation thesis. And it was Rumsfeld whose actions forced the military to deal with an insurgency that it was unprepared for.

Having played a major role in getting the United States into a hopeless situation trying to control or at least pacify a country that was increasingly slipping toward civil war, Rumsfeld continued to influence policy. Rumsfeld did everything he could to sabotage Condoleezza Rice's effort to move in the direction of counterinsurgency. Many military officers that I have spoken with believe that, had a policy of counterinsurgency been followed immediately after the invasion with enough troops to make it work, the situation currently confronting the United States in Iraq would be quite different. The fact that it took so long to get a counterinsurgency policy working remains one of Rumsfeld's "achievements." He wanted to pass the ball to the Iraqis and then have the United States exit. Leaving aside the catastrophic impact such an action would have had on Iraq and the region, it would have also placed the United States in a difficult situation. The key to any exit strategy, of course, is to come up with a well-trained, reliable Iraqi Army. But despite Wolfowitz's pleas, Rumsfeld was slow to act.

## Arrogance

Toward the end of his tenure, Rumsfeld saw his power ebbing away. His vaunted claim that he would force military transformation on the military rang hollow. True, the modularization of the army was an important step forward as was the Stryker armored vehicle, but both of these developments would probably have happened if he had not been secretary. Indeed, the army and the Marine Corps might have been further along the road of transformation if Rumsfeld had left them alone.

Another example of Rumsfeld's arrogance was his refusal to pay attention to the six retired generals who went public with their criticism. Of course he was not going to humbly announce that they were right and he was wrong, but this revolt was almost unprecedented in post–World War II America. True, several admirals had spoken out on Capitol Hill against President Harry Truman's effort to cancel a carrier, MacArthur was fired, and the Joint Chiefs almost resigned under Lyndon Johnson—but those occurred under different circumstances. These were six former senior officers—many of whom had led troops in Iraq. They gave up their careers and special contacts with the Pentagon to speak out against the secretary, an action for which they were criticized. Unfortunately, Rumsfeld either did not understand the military or did not care what they thought. While it is difficult to determine to what degree the comments of the six had on Rumsfeld's position in the government, he was clearly becoming more vulnerable.

## Deputy Secretary Wolfowitz

Paul Wolfowitz was not concerned about military transformation. Instead, his attention was focused on foreign policy, in general, and Iraq, in particular. He was a convinced believer in the idea that it was Washington's "manifest destiny" to introduce democracy around the world through regime change—by military force, if necessary. Further, Wolfowitz belonged to a group that believed that the United States would be welcomed with open arms by the downtrodden of the world, oppressed peoples who were just waiting to be liberated. Wolfowitz's ideological blinders were especially obvious after 9/11.

Wolfowitz was the first to suggest that the United States should not worry about Afghanistan in the aftermath of 9/11. Instead, he pushed for Washington to initiate immediate military action against Iraq. He was also a strong supporter of Ahmed Chalabi, an émigré Iraqi of questionable moral background. Chalabi aspired to be the new leader of Iraq, and he hoped the United States would install him in that position after it got rid of Saddam Hussein. Indeed, Wolfowitz's ideological fervor for the unilateral use of U.S. military power in support of regime change became something of a joke among other key policymakers. Rumsfeld dispatched Wolfowitz to counter Shinseki's suggestion that it would take "several hundred thousand" troops to take Iraq. Such a comment was "wildly off the mark," Wolfowitz stated. He was also a strong supporter of the decision to get rid of the Iraqi Army and introduce a policy of de-Baathification. Wolfowitz also appears to have been the brains behind the creation of the Office of Special Plans under Feith. The office's primary function was to find data or information that would justify an invasion of Iraq. It did not matter what the other intelligence agencies in the government thought, because Wolfowitz believed they could not be trusted, so with Rumsfeld's approval this special office was set up.

Meanwhile, Rumsfeld gradually marginalized Wolfowitz, perhaps because he was too ideological and too ambitious. According to Woodward, in 2004, Rumsfeld canceled several of his subordinate's trips to Iraq.[3] His explanation was that there was too much work to do in Washington, but Wolfowitz's private complaints about Rumsfeld's failure to jump on the issue of training the new Iraqi military might have played a factor.

## Under Secretary Feith

Despite his much publicized intellectual brilliance, Douglas Feith, under secretary for defense policy, turned out to be one of Rumsfeld's worst personnel decisions. While he may have impressed people in the academic world, Feith's policy sense was abysmal, which was especially clear in his dealings with the army. Most senior officers considered him totally incompetent and believed his ability to deal with real world problems was also nonexistent. Feith had one advantage; he was a dedicated believer in the same world of democracies that Wolfowitz believed in and just as dedicated to creating a democratic world in the Middle East—beginning with Iraq. He was convinced that the parts of the world that did not enjoy the blessings of U.S.-style liberty were just waiting for an invitation to become a U.S.-style democracy. It didn't matter if democracy was brought to them via the barrels of U.S. guns.

Aside from Rumsfeld, Feith had the most policy autonomy of all the civilians in the Pentagon. True, he would have to justify his policy actions and choices to Wolfowitz and Rumsfeld, but in many areas he was the one in charge, especially when it came to Iraq. The fact that Rumsfeld and Wolfowitz were prepared to delegate that much power to a subordinate when it came to dealing with military affairs and Iraq seems unexplainable. Feith was a man who knew nothing of the practical world (let alone the military), and who had pronounced sympathy for Israel. Yet Wolfowitz liked him and Rumsfeld was impressed by him, even if the military was not. In fact, the disdain that the military held for Feith may have been one of the reasons Rumsfeld and Wolfowitz admired him.

An inventory of Feith's actions reveals the harm he did regarding the invasion of Iraq. First, he worked hard to have the State Department excluded from the invasion. To the maximum degree possible, he cut ties with State and had nothing but contempt for its Future of Iraq Study. Feith played the primary role in manipulating data to prove the existence of a connection between Saddam Hussein and al-Qaeda, a conclusion that the vast majority of the intelligence community considered spurious. When the CIA, State, and other parts of the intelligence community complained, he ignored them and took his "dog and pony" show around Washington. Unfortunately, too many people—including perhaps, the president—were persuaded by him. It was a disaster from a policy standpoint. After he resigned, Feith testified on the Hill where he was strongly criticized by Senator Carl Levin (D-MI) who charged, "Senior administration officials used the twisted logic produced by Feith's office in making the case for the Iraq War."[4]

Even more upsetting, the Department of Defense's Inspector General undertook a review of the actions of Feith's Office of Special Plans and concluded:

> The Office of the Under Secretary of Defense for Policy developed, produced, and disseminated alternative intelligence assessments on the Iraq and al-Qaida relationship, which included some conclusions that were inconsistent with the consensus of the intelligence community, to senior decision-makers. While such actions were not illegal or unauthorized, the actions were, in our opinion, inappropriate given that the intelligence assessments were intelligence products and did not clearly show the variance with the consensus of the intelligence community.[5]

Feith claimed that he was on top of things. He assured everyone that going to war with Iraq would not be a problem, that he was ready for the post-hostilities period. In fact, little or nothing had been done to prepare for the post-invasion situation. Feith preferred to believe Chalabi, who claimed that Coalition troops would be welcomed as liberators, and that the Iraqis would quickly set up a new, democratic government. There was no need for a lengthy occupation and reconstruction process. The United States would only have to stay in Iraq for several months and could then go home secure in the knowledge that it had brought democracy to Iraq.

Incredibly, Feith, with all of his knowledge of Israeli politics, did not seem to understand anything about political culture—that political attitudes are shaped by things such as language, history, and culture. To suggest that the Iraqis were just waiting for the Americans to come and make Western-style democracy a reality was not only idealistic—it was absurd. Iraq had not had a democratic regime for at least a thousand years, and perhaps it never enjoyed that kind of a political system.

Furthermore, Feith naively believed that Iraq's three main factions, the Shiites, Sunnis, and Kurds, would quickly adapt to a democratic political system. The majority Shiites had been subjected to decades of brutal rule by the Sunnis and were just waiting for an opportunity to pursue their own interests. The Kurds in the north wanted nothing to do with either group. They had a quasi-independent government already and were perfectly prepared to become independent if that became an option. While it was true that Chalabi had assured Feith that these ethnic and religious splits were meaningless, a good policy officer looks beyond the comments of a single person, especially if that individual had a special interest in the subject. An analyst is obligated to investigate fully and hear all sides before making a decision. But Feith apparently believed he had the answers to the questions before they were even asked. The U.S. military paid a heavy price for Feith's inability to plan for the post-invasion period.

There also were organizational issues; specifically, how to implement a post-invasion policy once it became clear that the United States was intent on invading Iraq. In theory, Jay Garner and his group were sent to Iraq to facilitate the transfer from Saddam Hussein's totalitarian regime to a Western-style democracy. Unfortunately, this process was so mishandled that it would have been a miracle if anything had worked out positively. The Pentagon was so dismissive of Garner that not only did he have to beg to get his personnel to Kuwait, once they were there, he had to figure out how to get them to Baghdad. The only reason they were eventually able to make the flight was because Garner had personal ties with General Franks. When they finally arrived, it became clear that neither Feith nor Wolfowtiz, nor most importantly Rumsfeld, had made Garner's mission a priority. Feith has never explained why he did not ask Wolfowitz or Rumsfeld to make Phase IV reconstruction a priority when it became obvious that Garner's people were experiencing major problems. The military took their cue from the Pentagon, and if the Pentagon did not make it a priority, neither would they.

Feith also had a hand in disrupting the de-Baathification process. He made sure that individuals sent to work for the CPA were, first and foremost, politically loyal to his version of the president's policy. He arranged for the conservative Heritage Foundation in Washington to run the ideological check, and anyone who passed got a ticket to Iraq. Substantive qualifications for a position were secondary. Not only did this have an adverse impact on the reconstruction process, 22-year-old college graduates were put in charge of ministries dealing with issues far outside their major. They were also the ones who carried out the de-Baathification process. When it became obvious that the young Americans were not competent to handle the vetting process, Chalabi, a Shiite, was put in charge. He made it nearly impossible for Sunnis who had been party members to join the new Iraqi government.

Feith eventually left the Defense Department, but the effect of his decisions would live on to haunt the United States as it struggled to bring order and stability to Iraq. A significant portion of the insurgents are believed to be former members of the military, and one of the key issues facing the Iraqi parliament has been its inability to agree on a de-Baathification process. Had the Iraqi military been reconstituted, and had lower-level members of the Baath Party not been ousted from their jobs, the chances of creating a stable government would have increased, even if had not been as democratic as the West might have wished.

## Jerry Bremer

As the top civilian in Iraq, Bremer was a disaster from the beginning. Rumsfeld liked him, perhaps because he was as arrogant as the secretary and possibly because he paid little or no attention to the people who worked for him. That was especially evident in Iraq. Indeed, Bremer seemed to pay more attention to Feith and Rumsfeld than to others in the government. He went to Iraq determined to make a "big splash" and was convinced that the best way to do that was to tell the Iraqis that he was putting off the idea of a transitional government in favor of the Coalition Provisional Authority. Then he further irritated the Iraqis by bungling the de-Baathification process and by issuing the order to abolish the Iraqi Army—in the face of almost unanimous disagreement on the part of his advisers and the U.S. military.

## Civil–Military Relations and the Introduction of Change

One of the key tasks facing civilian policymakers is getting the conservative military to change the ways it plans for and fights wars. There is always a tendency on the part of generals and admirals to fight the last war. After all, they know how it turned out, and they, or their subordinates, most likely have studied it in some detail.

This study and Rumsfeld's desire to convince the military to change could be a case study for future secretaries of defense on what *not* to do when it comes to introducing change.

## Respect the Organization

First, keep in mind that the secretary is an outsider coming into the Pentagon. Do not make major changes without involving the military in the process. Similarly, the military is different from most other organizations in terms of its cohesion, conservatism, bureaucracy, hierarchical structure, dedication to the institution it serves, and feeling that it should handle its own matters without outside, civilian interference.

Perhaps the biggest mistake the Bush administration made was in expecting that it could make radical changes in the U.S. military in a relatively short period of time. Instead, leaders must assume that a bureaucracy as large and complex as the armed forces will resist change. The more one attempts to force change from outside, the more resistance will grow. That is what happened with Rumsfeld and his colleagues when they decided to skip a generation of weapons and reform the army (in particular), its missions, equipment, and personnel policies. Change is possible, but slow, steady progress is more secure than a mad dash to the finish line.

Some Washington observers think that the best way to get a bureaucracy moving is to bring in a hard-charging CEO and let him or her shake up the Pentagon. In fact, during the two times that kind of a CEO has become secretary of defense in the post–World War II period and tried to make radical changes in the military, they failed miserably. The business world has a very different organizational culture than that which exists in the armed forces.

Surprisingly, the CEO of a large organization has considerably *more power* to introduce change than does a senior military officer or the secretary of defense. A person like Rumsfeld was an excellent choice to get the Searle Corporation back on its feet. He was prepared to fire people, change procedures, and restructure overnight. And because it was a private business, he got away with it. Furthermore, for a businessman the top priority is the bottom line—is the firm making or losing money? If the firm is profitable, no one cares about the CEO's leadership style. If it is not, he was expected to do whatever it took to get the firm back on its feet. He could slash the staff, change the company's product line, or do whatever seemed appropriate.

Unfortunately, no one told Rumsfeld that a secretary of defense has *far less* authority to make changes than does a CEO. In addition to having Congress and industry looking over his back, he was dealing with a very cohesive and bureaucratic organization, and he was an outsider looking in. Men and women who serve in the military and face the dangers of combat together have a greater sense of cohesion than most business co-workers.

There is a commitment to the service, to the hierarchy, and to each other that is seldom seen in the civilian world.

The military is not likely to sit still if the secretary comes in and attempts to make sweeping changes while ignoring its senior officers. It will fight back when its interests are attacked, and if the attack is serious, it will attempt to mobilize its friends on the Hill and engage the media in the form of leaks. Those are problems that a hard-charging CEO rarely has to worry about in the business world. If a new secretary of defense's first action is to "shake things up" the way Rumsfeld did, the military will immediately go to battle stations. Rumsfeld could have gotten his point across by bringing the senior officers into his office and making clear what he expected and asking them for their input and voluntary cooperation.

## Understand Personnel

Human resources issues are quite different in the military. Few organizational promotion systems are as tight and inflexible as the military. Academy and ROTC graduates start out as ensigns or second lieutenants and gradually work their way up the promotion ladder. In most cases, the officer will not rise above 05 or 06 (Lieutenant Colonel/Commander or Colonel/Captain). The idea that an admiral can pull up a lieutenant and make him a captain is absurd. Of course a senior officer can make life much easier by giving a young officer a sterling fitness report or by seeing that he or she gets the right job. The road to promotion is one of holding certain jobs, including command, and gradually working one's way up to the top. While I have heard of cases where an individual "lucks out" because he or she has a friend on the promotion board, the process is strictly run and every effort is made to keep everything that happens at a promotion board secret and anonymous—with the focus on performance, not politics.

Actions like those taken by Rumsfeld to promote individuals he believed agreed with him were guaranteed to turn an organization like the military against him. Senior officers expect the secretary to select someone he gets along with, but to choose someone primarily because he seems to be a malleable yes-man is guaranteed to upset the military. Furthermore, the idea that the secretary of defense will approve all promotions from two-star and above raised questions in the eyes of the services concerning the competency of the officers involved. Were they promoted for their performance or because they supported Rumsfeld's policy? Too often, it appeared to be the latter.

As a civilian, the secretary of defense should surround himself with senior officials who understand the military. Its vocabulary and way of thinking and acting are often quite different from what a civilian is used to. That does not mean that the secretary should necessarily be "pro-military" or be prepared to give in to the military. Secretary of Defense William Perry (1994–1997) was very knowledgeable when it came to military issues, and the generals and admirals knew it. They respected him in a way that the generals and admirals who met with Under Secretary Stephen Cambone did not. They immediately realized that he had no idea what he was talking about. He was just Rumsfeld's mouthpiece.

### Appear Neutral

To get the best from the military in terms of advice, the secretary should encourage different points of view, keeping his own opinions to himself until the military has presented a range of views. He should expect those presenting different positions to answer hard questions, and he should not put up with cliché answers. Bureaucracies have a tendency to provide whatever answer is already on the shelf. In this sense, Rumsfeld's questioning of the assumptions underlying policies or battle plans was right. The problem came when he gave the impression that he was not really interested in their opinions.

Change will come much easier if the secretary can convince senior officers of the value of change. Obviously, not all officers will agree with everything the secretary wants, but political power is more often than not the "power to persuade." If Rumsfeld had been willing to work with General Shinseki by supporting what he was trying to do in the army, the process of transformation might have gone further than it has. If the secretary showed that he respected and took into careful consideration the ideas of senior officers, they would have been more likely to support him. Support by senior officers is invaluable. It does not take very long for subordinates to discover whether or not their superiors are having input into the process. If they are, and if they appear to support the policy, support from below will be strengthened.

## Military–Civil Relations and the Introduction of Change

Every officer must decide personally what approach to take toward officership. Do they keep their criticisms to themselves or make them public? As Fred Kaplan explains, "The ethical codes are ambiguous on how firmly an officer can press an argument without crossing the line."[6] Generals Myers, Pace, and Casey decided that they would keep their views private, between themselves and the secretary. They believed that officers like Colin Powell, while chairman of the Joint Chiefs, had crossed the line when he openly opposed President Bill Clinton on the issue of gays in the military. Unlike Shelton, Myers was not prepared to go to the president privately without involving the secretary, even though such access was guaranteed to the chairman by the Goldwater–Nichols Act. The position taken by Myers, Pace, and Casey is a rational and honorable one, but it has significant consequences. It is one of the factors that is leading to a hemorrhage of junior officers from the armed forces, particularly the army.[7] The generals did not stand up to Rumsfeld and insist that more troops were needed in Iraq. Many junior officers, according to Colonel Don Snider, a professor at West Point, see the current "high op tempo as stemming from the failure of senior officers to speak out."[8] The junior officers see policies that are not achieving a specific goal, but are costing the lives of their troops. They are the ones who have to write the letters to the next of kin. The junior officers and their troops are risking their lives, but many generals and admirals do not want to risk their careers.

General Myers offers an explanation in a 2007 *Foreign Affairs* article. He argues that officers in the military are in a unique position when it comes to resigning. "Professionals can resign, but a military leader sworn to defend the country would be abandoning it, along with the people under his or her command." Furthermore, he maintained, "Even the hint of resignation would encourage civilians to choose officers more for compliance and loyalty than for competence, experience, intelligence, candor, moral courage, professionalism, integrity, and character."[9] He worries that if senior officers really had stood up to Rumsfeld, the secretary would have completely ignored the military and gone off on his own. This may be true, but there are many officers who believe that this was more of less what he did regarding with military transformation and Iraq anyway. Furthermore, it is important to keep in mind that many junior and mid-level officers maintain that such behavior could compel the administration to rethink its policies.

Perceptions are critically important. Neither Myers, Pace, nor Casey were prepared to stand up to Rumsfeld in a way that showed the troops that they were protecting their interests, even if they sometimes lost. They may have done so behind closed doors, but many junior and mid-level officers I have spoken with believe the senior officers should, at a minimum, have followed the example of Lieutenant General Greg Newbold, who resigned. Newbold, however, suggested that he should have taken the next step at the time and spoken publicly about Rumsfeld's efforts to create phony intelligence to justify an invasion.[10] However, there is an important qualifier. No one expects or wants the chairman or the Joint Chiefs of Staff or any other senior officer to take such a step just because he disagrees with the secretary. There is no excuse for being reckless. But there comes a point when senior officers must be prepared to resign rather than follow orders they know to be dangerous and counterproductive.

The Joint Chiefs of Staff nearly resigned *en masse* over President Lyndon Johnson and Secretary of Defense Robert McNamara's interference in military operations in Vietnam. Given the way they were treated—and ignored—by both Johnson and McNamara, it is surprising that they decided not to. If they had, the United States might have left Vietnam much earlier and with less loss of life.

This is a very difficult problem that officers must struggle with. The issue of resigning or speaking against a civilian superior is a matter of conscience for any officer, retired or on active duty. No respectable officer wants to be put into a position of taking an action that would show disapproval of a civilian authority. Such an action would be seen by the overwhelming majority of officers as a last resort. Shinseki gained tremendous respect for his opposition to Rumsfeld, but he did *not* disobey an order. The easiest way to avoid such a situation is for civilian authorities not to put senior officers in such a position. Senior officers expect civilian leadership. They also expect civilian officials to respect their views when the lives of their troops are at stake.

## Recovering from Rumsfeld

Rumsfeld was no sooner gone than the army announced that it was in process of rewriting the "Full Spectrum Operations" manual. The new version included a section that stated, "In addition to defeating the enemy, military units must focus on providing security for the local population, even during the heat of battle." This was a new approach, no doubt influenced by the combination of Phases III and IV. The most important change, however, was a section that stated, "If a unit does not have the forces to conduct stability operations after an offensive mission, it is the commander's obligation to request more manpower."[11] This means that if a commander is put in a position like Franks put his army and Marine commanders in during the invasion of Iraq, the commander has an obligation to tell his superiors that he cannot carry out the mission without more personnel. This goes against the centuries old "can-do" policy of carrying out the mission no matter what the cost. Equally significant, top army generals began talking about the "urgent need to replenish and expand the armed forces." They were no longer afraid to express their opinions, even publicly.[12] The other reason this new language is important is because it means that the army has at long last begun to realize that those who have argued in favor of counterinsurgency for years were right: it is not just a matter of linear combat. It is also now a case of winning hearts and minds.[13] The army simply outlasted Rumsfeld and his colleagues.

## Conclusion

Politics in the United States is built around conflict; that is the way the founders of this country wanted it. Conflict is inevitable in civil–military relations and cannot be eliminated. The task, rather, is to find a way to regulate conflict—to create structures, procedures, and organizations that can mediate differences. The generals will always want more tanks, armored cars, trucks, etc., than the secretary can approve. All of the services are pushing to fund their pet projects, but the secretary has to make the final decision.

Rumsfeld did not create processes to regulate conflict and thereby gain the benefits of a more cooperative relationship. Had he done so, the limits of military transformation—given current commitments—would have become clear early on. Similarly, the tremendous problems involved with regime change in Iraq would have become clear. The invasion might have never taken place. But instead, Rumsfeld delegated authority to individuals like Feith, who had little or no idea what was happening in the national security realm. He also permitted his suspicion of the CIA to cloud his judgment and saw Iraq as a laboratory to prove the validity of his approach to military transformation.

In the end, it was General Shinseki who was right, not Rumsfeld. Shinseki was honorable and respectful in the way he dealt with Rumsfeld. I suspect that Rumsfeld's attacks on him hurt. Shinseki was reportedly encouraged to go public when the generals publicly criticized Rumsfeld. But Shinseki refused to do that, despite Rumsfeld's verbal attacks. The general remained quiet.

It was hard for a CEO like Rumsfeld to relate to Shinseki. Rumsfeld tried to goad Shinseki into resigning by leaking the name of Shinseki's successor, but his ruse failed. Shinseki finished out his tour as army chief of staff and then quietly left the scene. That was the kind of devotion to "duty, honor, country" expected of a West Point graduate. If Rumsfeld had adopted a more cooperative approach in dealing with officers like Shinseki, the United States would probably not be in Iraq four years after the invasion, and military transformation would have been a much smoother process—and perhaps Washington would have been even further down the line in creating the army's future combat systems.

Unfortunately, Rumsfeld had his own ideas of how to run the U.S. military and would not listen to others. As a result, the country is still paying a high price for his arrogance in terms of money and casualties. This is hardly the kind of legacy that any soldier would want.

# Appendix:
# A Note on Methodology

One of the rules of political science—a discipline to which I belong—is to try to be as objective as possible in evaluating events in the political arena. Sometimes that is very difficult, especially when dealing with an emotionally charged topic such as Donald Rumsfeld's time as secretary of defense and its implications for the U.S. military. While it would be wrong to maintain that an author can analyze an event with a methodology that is 100 percent objective, the burden on the scholar is to try to be as objective as possible.

## Sources

There are a number of sources for information on the events that occurred in the Pentagon during the first six years of the Bush administration. First, there are interviews. One can speak directly to the key players and get their perspective on events. That is a useful approach. There are problems with it, however, as it is often very difficult to get access to key decision makers.

Furthermore, if the memoirs and interviews that have appeared on Rumsfeld's years in the Pentagon are any indication, these individuals more often than not distort the situation in order to present themselves in a positive light while, at the same time, avoiding discussion of events that might make them look bad. There were exceptions, however. The interviews done by PBS's *Frontline*, for example, turned out to be very enlightening. Meanwhile, I used personal interviews in a number of cases—most generally with serving military officers. In almost every case, their comments were very useful. After all, they were the ones who witnessed the events first hand; in some cases sitting in the room where decisions were taken.

Speaking with military officers raises the question of verifiability. Can the scholar make the sources—or a transcript of the conversations—available to others? The answer is no. In almost all cases, these officers spoke on the condition that they *not* be identified in this book. As career military officers, most of them feared that their comments—if they were made public and if they were critical of the administration—could have a very negative impact on their careers.

A second source of information was the many books written on Rumsfeld, as well as on the Afghan and Iraq wars. In many cases, these books were written by journalists. They were full of details of what happened on this date, in that place. Were they always right? No, no more than this book can claim to be "always right." The journalists, like everyone on the outside, looked "through a glass darkly." However, their analyses and insights were often very useful and enlightening.

There were also a number of excellent articles and books written by scholars—whether military or civilian. In many instances, they were critical in enabling a nonspecialist to understand the complexities of military hardware or operations. For example, it would have been very easy to throw up my hands when faced with the complexity of the army's future combat systems. This was new territory for me. However, because of articles published in military journals such as *Parameters*, as well as several books written by scholars in think tanks or former military officers, I was able to understand the debates.

A third source was newspaper articles. Following the events covered in this book from the end of 2000 to the latter part of 2006 from a variety of news outlets provided the building blocks upon which events could be analyzed. "But," one critic said to me, "the newspapers are all biased. What good are they in analyzing events?" Similarly, some of my historian friends argued that the only way a valid study of a period such as Rumsfeld's tenure at the Defense Department can be usefully carried out is to wait ten to twenty years after he leaves office—when the files from the period are opened up. They are right. Any study carried out in twenty years will have the benefit of a complete or almost complete collection of documents from the Pentagon, White House, CIA, and other sources. It is bound to be more authoritative. But what about in the meantime? Do we ignore these events and the lessons they may have for civil-military relations for ten or twenty years? My answer is no. A well-researched, albeit imperfect, study based on what is available can be very useful and may provide us with some insights into how to create an environment more conducive to better civil-military relations.

## Organization

This book is organized using a combination of a time line and the identification of key events. A time line beginning prior to the Bush administration was noted, and then key events were identified. The events were fit on this time line and to the highest degree possible, events were discussed as the time line dictated. For example, material covering the generals' attack on Rumsfeld were considered when they occurred as was the war in Afghanistan. There were, however, exceptions. Some categories were dealt with in several chapters, either because the events discussed took place in different time periods or because one dealt with the issue of transformation, while the other was integral to a discussion of the Iraq War. The role of General Eric Shinseki is one that comes to mind. His role in military transformation was important, as was his role in the decision to invade Iraq. Similarly, Douglas Feith's role was limited to the invasion of Iraq, but he was important throughout almost all events related to the invasion of Iraq, so he appears when his actions had an important impact on policy.

## Objectivity

Having collected the data, organized and evaluated it, the next challenge is to ensure a sense of objectivity, given the lack of primary documents. To me, the key question is whether there is enough information available to enable generalizations about trends in U.S. civil–military or military–civil relations, however tentative those generalizations might be. I believe it is possible. After going through the numerous speeches, books, newspapers, articles, memoirs, and interviews on specific events and if they all tell more or less the same story, then I have what my colleague Joe Aistrup called "a preponderance of data." For example, Rumsfeld or Wolfowitz or Feith may claim that they did not interfere in military operations in Iraq, but if a preponderance of information from other sources—including foreign sources—tells the same story, then I think it is fair to say that a preponderance of the evidence points to the conclusion that they interfered in military operations.

Unfortunately, there are gaps and unanswered questions in this study. I am certain that in time another study will correct this or that part of my analysis. However, that is what scholarship is supposed to do. Those of us who look at such events, try to be as objective as possible thereby enabling others to build on—and correct—our analyses. In the process, the goal is to provide the scholar and the policymaker with some insights to problems related to civil–military and military–civil relations in the United States.

# Notes

## Abbreviations

| | |
|---|---|
| LAT | Los Angeles Times |
| NYT | New York Times |
| WP | Washington Post |
| WT | Washington Times |
| USAT | USA Today |

## Introduction

1. John A. Nagl, *Counterinsurgency Lessons from Malaya and Vietnam: Learning to Eat Soup with a Knife* (Chicago: University of Chicago Press, 2003), 3.

2. The following comments about the U.S. military are based, in part, on my experience teaching at the National War College in Washington, D.C., as well as my very close interaction with military officers for the past forty years.

3. Adam Clymer, "Sharp Divergence Found in Views of Military and Civilians," *NYT* (September 9, 1999): A1. See also Ole R. Holsti, "A Widening Gap between the U.S. Military and Civilian Society," *International Security* 23, 3 (Winter 1998/1999): 5–42; and Mark J. Eigelberg and Roger D. Little, "Influential Elites and the American Military after the Cold War," in *U.S. Civil-Military Relations: In Crisis or Transition?* ed. Don M. Snider and Miranda A. Carlton-Carew (Washington, DC: Center for Strategic and International Studies, 1995), 34–67.

4. H. R. McMaster, *Dereliction of Duty: Johnson, McNamara, the Joint Chiefs of Staff, and the Lies that Led to Vietnam* (New York: Harper, 1998).

5. Michael Desch, "Bush and the Generals," *Foreign Affairs* 86, 3 (May/June 2007): 99.

6. Cited in ibid.

7. J. William Fulbright, *The Arrogance of Power* (New York: Random House, 1968). Fulbright's focus was the Vietnam War and actions the United States took in pursuit of victory in that war. Here the focus is on Rumsfeld's actions vis-à-vis the U.S. military.

8. U.S. General Accounting Office, "Military Transformation: Army Has a Comprehensive Plan for Managing Its Transformation but Faces Major Challenges," Report to Congressional Committees, November 2001.

9. Samuel P. Huntington, *The Clash of Civilizations and the Remaking of the World Order* (New York: Simon and Schuster, 1996).

10. Nagl, *Counterinsurgency Lessons from Malaya and Vietnam*, xiii.

11. Michael R. Gordon and Bernard E. Trainor, *Cobra II: The Inside Story of the Invasion and Occupation of Iraq* (New York: Pantheon, 2006); Bob Woodward, *Bush at War* (New York: Simon and Schuster, 2002); idem, *Plan of Attack* (New

York: Simon and Schuster, 2004); idem, *State of Denial: Bush at War, Part III* (New York: Simon and Schuster, 2006) (the last book was especially helpful); Thomas E. Ricks, *Fiasco: The American Military Adventure in Iraq* (New York: Penguin Press, 2006); Michael Isikoff and David Corn, *Hubris: The Inside Story of Spin, Scandal, and the Selling of the Iraq War* (New York: Crown, 2006); Rajiv Chandrasekaran, *Imperial Life in the Emerald City: Inside Iraq's Green Zone* (New York: Knopf, 2006); Bing West, *No True Glory: A Frontline Account of the Battle for Fallujah* (New York: Bantam, 2005); James Fallows, *Blind into Baghdad: America's War in Iraq* (New York: Vintage, 2006); Andrew Cockburn, *Rumsfeld: His Rise, Fall, and Catastrophic Legacy* (New York: Scribner, 2007); Tom Clancy and Tony Zinni, *Battle Ready* (New York: Putnam, 2004).

12. Ali A. Allawi, *The Occupation of Iraq: Winning the War, Losing the Peace* (New Haven, CT: Yale University Press, 2007).

13. Frederick W. Kagan, *Finding the Target: The Transformation of American Military Policy* (New York: Encounter Books, 2006).

14. L. Paul Bremer, *My Year in Iraq: The Struggle to Build a Future of Hope* (New York: Simon and Schuster, 2006); Tommy Franks, *American Soldier* (New York: Regan, 2004); David L. Phillips, *Losing Iraq: Inside the Postwar Reconstruction Fiasco* (Boulder, CO: Westview, 2005); Peter W. Galbraith, *The End of Iraq* (New York: Simon and Schuster, 2006); Michael DeLong, *Inside CENTCOM: The Unvarnished Truth About the Wars in Afghanistan and Iraq* (New York: Regency, 2004); George Tenet, *At the Center of the Storm: My Years at the CIA* (New York: HarperCollins, 2007); Larry Diamond, *Squandered Victory: The American Occupation and the Bungled Effort to Bring Democracy to Iraq* (New York: Times Books, 2005).

15. Karen DeYoung, *Soldier: The Life of Colin Powell* (New York: Knopf, 2006).

## Chapter 1. The New Administration and Military Transformation

1. Charles A. Stevenson, *SECDEF: The Nearly Impossible Job of Secretary of Defense* (Dulles, VA: Potomac Books, 2006), 160.

2. Nixon had appointed Ford vice president in December 1973, following the resignation of Vice President Spiro Agnew over charges of tax evasion.

3. Jeffrey Krames, *The Rumsfeld Way: Leadership Wisdom of a Battle-Hardened Maverick* (New York: McGraw-Hill, 2002), 30.

4. Andrew Cockburn, *Rumsfeld: His Rise, Fall, and Catastrophic Legacy* (New York: Scribner, 2007), 30. See also James Mann, *The Rise of the Vulcans: The History of Bush's War Cabinet* (New York: Viking, 2004), 61, 66–67. It should be noted that Schlesinger brought Ford's wrath on himself. See Dale Herspring, *The Pentagon and the Presidency: Civil-Military Relations From FDR to George W. Bush* (Lawrence: University Press of Kansas, 2005), 233–234.

5. Stevenson, *SECDEF*, 162.

6. Elaine Sciollino and Eric Schmitt, "Defense Choice Made Name as Infighter," *NYT* (January 8, 2001): A1.

7. Ibid.

8. Midge Decter, *Rumsfeld: A Personal Portrait* (New York: HarperCollins, 2003), 82.

9. Ibid., 102.

10. Krames, *The Rumsfeld Way*, 189.
11. Ibid., 39; Decter, *Rumsfeld*, 130.
12. Jonathan Weisman, "A Warrior in One Battle, Manager in Another," *USA Today* (December 21, 2001): A6.
13. Cockburn, *Rumsfeld*, 103.
14. Ibid., 105.
15. Rowan Scarborough, "Rumsfeld Makes No Apology; Answers Critics Who Say He's Rude," *WT* (January 30, 2003): A1.
16. Doyle McManus, "Pentagon Reform Is His Battle Cry," *LAT* (August 17, 2003): A1.
17. George Tenet, *At the Center of the Storm: My Years at the CIA* (New York: HarperCollins, 2007), 138.
18. Cited in Mann, *The Rise of the Vulcans*, 201.
19. Ibid., 202.
20. Ibid., 236.
21. He was under secretary from July 2001 until he resigned on August 8, 2005.
22. The report is available from the Institute for Advanced Strategic and Political Studies at http://www.iasps.org/strat1.htm (last accessed October 15, 2007).
23. Jeffrey Goldberg, "A Little Learning," *The New Yorker* (May 9, 2005), available at http://www.newyorker.com/archive/2005/05/09/050509fa_fact (last accessed October 15, 2007).
24. Ibid.
25. Ibid.
26. For a discussion of this act, see Herspring, *The Pentagon and the Presidency: Civil-Military Relations from FDR to George W. Bush*, 292–295.
27. Robert R. Tomes, *U.S. Defense Strategy from Vietnam to Operation Iraqi Freedom* (New York: Routledge, 2006), 136.
28. Ibid.
29. Cockburn, *Rumsfeld*, 107–108.
30. Ibid., 108.
31. Thomas E. Ricks, "Rumsfeld on High Wire of Defense Reform: Military Brass, Conservative Lawmakers are Among Secretive Review's Unexpected Critics," *WP* (May 20, 2001): A1.
32. Vernon Loeb and Thomas E. Ricks, "Rumsfeld's Style," *WP* (October 16, 2002): A1.
33. Bryan Bender, "Rumsfeld's Battles with Pentagon Have Long History," *Boston Globe* (April 24, 2006): A1.
34. Bob Woodward, *State of Denial: Bush at War, Part III* (New York: Simon and Schuster, 2006), 73.
35. Cockburn, *Rumsfeld*, 110. I have researched the first meetings between the Joint Chiefs and almost all presidents since 1940, and this kind of behavior was clearly unusual. See Herspring, *The Pentagon and the Presidency*.
36. Thom Shanker and Eric Schmitt, "Rumsfeld Seeks Leaner Army, and a Full Term," *NYT* (May 11, 2005): A1.
37. Bob Woodward, *Plan of Attack* (New York: Simon and Schuster, 2004), 14–15.
38. Woodward, *State of Denial*, 38.
39. Rowan Scarborough, "Defense Secretary Criticizes Top Staff: Says Joint Chiefs Overdo Reports," *WT* (January 24, 2003): A1.

40. Ibid.

41. Woodward, *State of Denial*, 24.

42. Cockburn, *Rumsfeld*, 112.

43. Herspring, *The Pentagon and the Presidency*, 121.

44. Decter, *Rumsfeld*, 125.

45. Paul Richter, "Bush's Defense Secretary Goes on the Offensive," *LAT* (May 22, 2001): A1.

46. Woodward, *State of Denial*, 38.

47. Cockburn, *Rumsfeld*, 111.

48. The following is based on Lieutenant Colonel H. R. McMaster's excellent essay, "Crack in the Foundation: Defense Transformation and the Underlying Assumption of Dominant Knowledge in Future War," Student Issue Paper, Center for Strategic Leadership, U.S. Army War College vol. S03-03 (November 2003), 27, available at http://www.carlisle.army.mil/usacsl/Publications/S03-03.pdf.

49. Ibid., 20.

50. Frederick Kagan, "A Dangerous Transformation," *Opinion Journal* (November 13, 2003).

51. Ian Roxborough, "From Revolution to Transformation: the State of the Field," *Joint Forces Quarterly*, no. 32 (2002): 69.

52. Kagan, "A Dangerous Transformation."

53. Jonathan Weisman, "Rumsfeld and Myers Defend War Plan," *WP* (April 2, 2003): A19.

54. Ibid.

55. Walter Fairbanks, "Implementing the Transformation Vision," *Joint Forces Quarterly* 42, 3 (2006): 31.

56. General Myers published an article on the topic that followed the lines noted by Rumsfeld above. Richard B. Myers, "A Word from the Chairman: Understanding Transformation," *Air and Space Power Journal* 17, 1 (Spring 2003).

## Chapter 2. Rumsfeld Pushes Transformation

1. Michael Duffy, "Rumsfeld: Older but Wiser?" *Time* (August 27, 2001): 22–27.

2. Thomas Mahnken and James R. Fitzsimonds, "Tread-Heads or Technophiles? Army Officer Attitudes toward Transformation," *Parameters* (Summer 2004): 60.

3. As quoted in Andrew Cockburn, *Rumsfeld: His Rise, Fall, and Catastrophic Legacy* (New York: Scribner, 2007), 99.

4. Terry M. Neal, "Bush Outlines Defense Plan in Address at the Citadel," *WT* (September 24, 1999): A3.

5. Thomas E. Ricks, "Rumsfeld, Bush Agendas Overlap Little," *WT* (January 11, 2001): A4.

6. Paul Richter, "For the Military, Bush Is Not Yet All That He Can Be," *LAT* (February 14, 2001): A1.

7. David E. Sanger, "Bush Details Plan to Focus Military on New Weaponry," *NYT* (February 14, 2001): A1.

8. Ibid.

9. Michael Noonan, "The U.S. Quadrennial Defense Review and Defense Policy, 2006–2025," *E-Notes*, Foreign Policy Research Institute (March 9, 2006).

10. Frederick W. Kagan, *Finding the Target: The Transformation of American Military Policy* (New York: Encounter Books, 2006), 234.

11. Philip Shenon, "Pentagon Urges Trims in Military and More Base Closings," *NYT* (May 20, 1997): A18.

12. The report is available at the National Defense Panel web site: www.dtic.mil/ndp/.

13. NDP quotes are from Ibid. The latter quote is from Kagan, *Finding the Target*, 239.

14. Midge Decter, *Rumsfeld: A Personal Portrait* (New York: Regan Books, 2003), 107.

15. Ibid., 110.

16. As cited in Kagan, *Finding the Target*, 258. Much of the following discussion is based on Kagan, 258–265.

17. Ibid., 259–260.

18. As cited in Ibid., 261.

19. Frederick Kagan, "A Dangerous Transformation," *Opinion Journal* (November 12, 2003).

20. Gordon R. Sullivan and Lieutenant Colonel James M. Dubik, "Land Warfare in the 21st Century," manuscript, February 1993, available at: http://www.strategicstudiesinstitute.army.mil/pubs/display.cfm?pubID=247.

21. Ibid., xvii.

22. Ibid., xxvi.

23. Ibid.

24. Ibid., xxvii.

25. Kagen, *Finding the Target*, 207.

26. Ibid.

27. Douglas MacGregor, *Breaking the Phalanx* (New York: Praeger, 1997).

28. General Eric Shinseki, "Address to the 45th Annual Meeting of the Association of the United States Army," October 12, 1999.

29. "Press Conference by Secretary of the Army Louis Caldera and Chief of Staff of the Army, General Eric Shinseki," transcript, Association of the United States Army, Washington, DC, October 12, 1999.

30. David Jablonsky, "Army Transformation: A Tale of Two Doctrines," in Conrad Crane, ed. *Transforming Defense* (Washington, DC: Strategic Studies Institute, 2001), 52.

31. Bruce R. Nardulli and Thomas L. McNaugher, "The Army: Toward the Objective Force," in *Transforming America's Military*, ed. Hans Binnendijk (Honolulu, HI: University Press of the Pacific, 2003), 108.

32. Thom Shanker, "Army Chief Seeks Changes to Improve Lives," *NYT* (May 29, 2001): A13.

33. Army Development System Task Force, "Army Development System, XXI Final Report," manuscript, August 2001.

34. Colonel Gregory Fontenot, Lieutenant Colonel E. J. Degen, and Lieutenant Colonel David Tohn, *On Point: The United States Army in Operation Iraqi Freedom* (Annapolis, MD: Naval Institute Press, 2005), 20.

35. Ibid., 21.

36. Andrew Krepinevich, "The Army and Land Warfare: Transforming the Legions," *Joint Force Quarterly* (Autumn 2002): 77.

37. Ibid., 54.

38. Frank Gibney, "The General Who Got It Right on Iraq," *LAT* (December 26, 2004): M3.

39. Paul Richter, "Bush Defense Secretary Goes on the Offensive," *LAT* (May 22, 2001): A1.

40. Peter Boyer, "A Different War," *New Yorker* (July 1, 2002): 54.

41. Andrew Cockburn, *Rumsfeld: His Rise, Fall and Catastrophic Legacy* (New York: Scribner, 2007), 155.

42. Steven Lee Myers, "Military Chief Seeks Money, Saying Forces are Strapped," *NYT* (December 15, 2000): A26.

43. Thomas E. Ricks, "Rumsfeld on High Wire of Defense Reform; Military Brass, Conservative Lawmakers Are among Secretive Review's Unexpected Critics," *WP* (May 20, 2001): A1.

44. Richter, "For the Military, Bush Is Not All That He Can Be."

45. Thomas E. Ricks, "Rumsfeld Outlines Defense Overhaul," *WP* (March 23, 2001): A1.

46. Ibid.

47. Quoted in Ibid.

48. Ricks, "Rumsfeld on High Wire of Defense Reform."

49. Ibid.

50. Ibid.

51. Charles A. Stevenson, *SECDEF: The Nearly Impossible Job of Secretary of Defense* (Dulles, VA: Potomac Press, 2006), 167.

52. Ricks, "Rumsfeld on High Wire of Defense Reform."

53. Ibid.

54. Ibid.

55. James Kitsfield, "Army Shell-Shocked in Face of Rumsfeld Reforms," *National Journal* (June 11, 2001): 1.

56. James Gerstenzang and Paul Richter, "Bush Appeals for More Agility, 'Forward Thinking' by Military," *LAT* (May 26, 2001): A2

57. Kitsfield, "Army Shell-Shocked," 1.

58. Thomas E. Ricks, "Pentagon Puts Money Where the People Are," *WP* (June 28, 2001): A31.

59. Ibid.

60. "Rumsfeld Rejects Linchpin Force Structure Findings in Major Review," *Inside the Pentagon* (July 19, 2001): 1.

61. Ibid., 2.

62. Ibid., 3.

63. Thomas E. Ricks, "Review Fractures Pentagon: Officials Predict Major Military Changes Far Off," *WP* (July 14, 2001): A1.

64. "Rumsfeld Rejects Linchpin Force Structure," 4.

65. Ricks, "Review Fractures Pentagon."

66. Andrea Stone, "Rumsfeld Rejects Pentagon Report. Differing Visions of Armed Forces' Future Expose Rift with Military Leaders," *USA Today* (July 19, 2001): A13.

67. Thomas E. Ricks, "For Military, 'Change Is Hard'; Rumsfeld Indicates His Review is Running into Resistance," *WP* (July 19, 2001): A16.

68. Ibid.

69. Bill Keller, "The Fighting Next Time," *NYT Magazine* (March 10, 2002): 32ff.

70. Cockburn, *Rumsfeld*, 114.

71. Ibid.

72. Donald Rumsfeld, "Transforming the Military," *Foreign Affairs* 81, 3 (May/June 2002): 22.

73. Duffy, "Rumsfeld: Older but Wiser?"

74. Thom Shanker, "Military Scuttles Strategy Requiring '2-War' Capability," *NYT* (July 13, 2001): A1.

75. Thom Shanker, "Rumsfeld Sees Discord on Size of Military," *NYT* (July 19, 2001): A18.

76. Cockburn, *Rumsfeld*, 115.

77. Ricks, "For Military, 'Change Is Hard'; Rumsfeld Indicates His Review Is Running into Resistance."

78. Thomas E. Ricks, "Rumsfeld Warned Not to Cut Size of the Army," *WP* (August 3, 2001): A8. The letter was signed by thirty-four of sixty members.

79. Rowan Scarborough, "Troops-cut Plan Faces Wide Opposition: Civilian Secretaries, Joint Officers to Argue against Reduction in Forces," *WT* (August 13, 2001).

80. Ibid. See also Michael R. Gordon and Bernard E. Trainor, *Cobra II* (New York: Pantheon, 2006), 9.

81. Thomas E. Ricks, "Rumsfeld Mulls Two Options: Status quo or 10% Military Cut; Secretary Wants to Match Armed Forces, New Strategy," *WP* (August 9, 2001): A4.

82. Thom Shanker, "Defense Chief May Leave Size of Field Forces Up to Services," *NYT* (August 17, 2001): A12.

83. "The Infighter Who Tried to Change the Pentagon and Has Failed So Far. Here's Why," *Inside Politics*, CNN.Com, August 20, 2001.

84. Vernon Loeb, "Rumsfeld May Let Military Branches Decide Cutbacks," *WP* (August 17, 2001): A5.

85. Shanker, "Defense Chief May Leave Size of Field Forces Up to Services."

86. Ibid.

87. Bob Woodward, *State of Denial: Bush at War, Part III* (New York: Simon and Schuster, 2006), 53–70. I spoke with several four-star officers who were interviewed for the job. All of them commented that it was clear that Rumsfeld was not interested in having an independent chairman. As one put it, "Mr. Secretary, if you say it is snowing in July, I will publicly back you up, but privately, I will tell you what I think." "Then, I don't want you," replied Rumsfeld.

88. Ibid., 71. As far as General Myers and General Peter Pace (who became the new vice chief) are concerned, several fellow officers commented, "Two of the nicest and most decent officers around, but neither of them are likely to take a position independent of Rumsfeld. They may argue a bit, but in the end it will be Rumsfeld's way."

89. Ibid., 72.

90. Gordon and Trainor, *Cobra II*, 4.

91. Thomas E. Ricks, *Fiasco: The American Military Adventure in Iraq* (New York: Penguin Press, 2006), 89.

92. Cockburn, *Rumsfeld*, 111.

93. Ibid., 70.

94. When asked about rumors that Myers did not make use of Goldwater–Nichols as Shelton did to provide "independent" advice, Myers responded, "When I was chairman, I encountered quite the opposite. The secretary insisted I make my

views known to the President and the National Security Council, especially when they differed from his. And remember, while the chairman is the principal military adviser, the other joint chiefs are advisers as well. I know of no issue with any of the joint chiefs not being able to provide their advice in a timely manner to the President or National Security Council." E-mail from General Myers to the author, August 28, 2007.

95. Cockburn, *Rumsfeld*, 89.

96. Lou Dubose and Jake Bernstein, *Vice: Dick Cheney and the Hijacking of the American Presidency* (New York: Random House, 2006), 167.

97. U.S. Department of Defense, Speech, "DOD Acquisition and Logistics Excellence Week Kick-off—Bureaucracy to Battlefield"; transcript available at: http://www.defenselink.mil.

98. Ryan Henry, "Defense Transformation and the 2005 Quadrennial Defense Review," *Parameters* (Winter 2005/2006): 10.

99. "Quadrennial Defense Review Report" (September 30, 2001), 17, available at: http://www.dod.mil/pubs/qdr2001.pdf.

100. Kagen, *Finding the Target*, 283, emphasis in the original.

101. Ibid.

102. The second half of this book will deal with Afghanistan and Iraq, so both are dealt with here only tangentially to make a point about the policy of transformation.

103. "President Speaks on War Effort to Citadel Cadets," White House Press Release (December 11, 2001).

104. Robert Tomes, *U.S. Defense Strategy from Vietnam to Operation Iraqi Freedom* (New York: Routledge, 2007), 139.

## Chapter 3. Rumsfeld, Reform, and Shinseki

1. Mike Allen and Thomas E. Ricks, "Bush Seeks Major Defense Boost," *WT* (January 24, 2002): A1.

2. Thom Shanker, "Rumsfeld Asserts Forces Must Take Risks and Think Creatively to Prepare for New Challenges," *NYT* (February 1, 2002): A10.

3. Ibid.

4. Thomas E. Ricks, "Bush Backs Overhaul of Military's Top Ranks," *WP* (April 11, 2002): A1.

5. Ibid.

6. Thomas E. Ricks, "General with a Key Pentagon Role to Retire," *WP* (May 2, 2002): A13.

7. Robert Schlesinger, "Rumsfeld, Army Leaders in Discord," *Boston Globe* (September 1, 2003): A1.

8. See Dale R. Herspring, *The Pentagon and the Presidency: Civil-Military Relations from FDR to George W. Bush* (Lawrence: University Press of Kansas, 2005), chapters 5 and 6.

9. Thom Shanker and Eric Schmitt, "Joint Chiefs Chairman Is a General but Also a Diplomat," *NYT* (May 6, 2002): A18.

10. Ibid.

11. Vernon Loeb and Thomas E. Ricks, "Rumsfeld's Style, Goals, Strain Ties in Pentagon," *WP* (October 16, 2002): A1.

12. James Fallows, "Blind into Baghdad," *Atlantic* (January 2004): 17.

13. Esther Schrader and Nick Anderson, "A Cross-Fire of Visions for a New U.S. Military," *LAT* (May 12, 2002): A18.

14. Scott Shuger, "Outgunned: What the Crusader Cancellation Really Means to the Army," *Slate* (May 23, 2002), available at http://www.slate.com/id/2066158/.

15. Schrader and Anderson, "A Cross-Fire of Visions for a New U.S. Military."

16. Ibid.

17. Shuger, "Outgunned."

18. Andrew Cockburn, *Rumsfeld: His Rise, Fall and Catastrophic Legacy* (New York: Scribner, 2007), 156–157.

19. Greg Miller and John Hendren, "Arms Issue May Sink Army Chief," *LAT* (May 3, 2002): A16.

20. "Army Chief Digs in Over Flap," *LAT* (May 7, 2002): A30.

21. Vernon Loeb and Ellen Nakashima, "Rumsfeld Backs Army Secretary," *WP* (May 8, 2002): A2.

22. John Hendren, "House Approves Big Defense Bill, Setting up Showdown," *LAT* (May 10, 2002): A28.

23. Donald Rumsfeld, "A Choice to Transform the Military," *WP* (May 16, 2002): A25.

24. Warren Vieth, "Rumsfeld, Army Chief at Odds on Weapons System," *LAT* (May 17, 2002): A20.

25. Ibid.

26. Ibid.

27. Ibid.

28. David Shaw, "The Fall of Enron," *LAT* (January 26, 2002): A1.

29. This will be dealt with in the second half of this book.

30. Esther Schrader, "Army Secretary Resigns: Leadership Vacuum Seen," *LAT* (April 26, 2003): A18.

31. Thomas E. Ricks, "Air Force's Roche Picked to Head Army," *WP* (May 2, 2003): A29.

32. Steven Lee Myers, "Army's Armored Vehicles Are Already behind Schedule," *NYT* (November 18, 2000): A10.

33. Jack Kelly, "Rumsfeld Ruffles Feathers; Pentagon Complaints Show He's Doing a Good Job," *Pittsburgh Post-Gazette* (October 20, 2002).

34. Sean Naylor, "Rumsfeld Plan Has Army Officials Crying Foul," *Defense News* (October 21, 2002): 36.

35. Vernon Loeb, "Army Shows Off Its New Strykers," *WP* (October 17, 2002): A19.

36. Thom Shanker, "Army Takes on Critics of an Armored Vehicle," *NYT* (October 29, 2002): A25.

37. Ibid.

38. John Hendren, "Army Holds Its Own in Ground Battle with Rumsfeld," *LAT* (November 29, 2002): A1.

39. Steve Fainaru, "Soldiers Defend Faulted Strykers," *WP* (April 3, 2005): A21.

40. Tina Sussman, "Stryker Team Key to Iraq Security Plan," *LAT* (February 24, 2007).

41. The actual invasion will be discussed in the second half of the book.

42. According to the man who led one of the units that used horses, only one member of the unit had ever sat on a horse before—and the troops "were forced

to learn how to ride at a gallop." Private conversation between the author and the commander of these troops, February, 2007.

43. Donald Rumsfeld, "Transforming the Military," *Foreign Affairs* 81, 3 (May/ June 2002): 28.

44. Ibid., 30.

45. Frederick Kagan, "A Dangerous Transformation," *Opinion Journal* (November 12, 2003).

46. Thomas Ricks and Vernon Loeb, "Bush Developing Military Policy of Striking First, *WP* (June 10, 2002): A1.

47. "Future Combat Systems—Background," available at http://www.global security.org/military/systems/ground/fcs-back.htm. I have spoken to a number of army officers, especially those at field grade level who very skeptical. As one officer put it, "Most of this is nonsense."

48. Ed Grabianowski, "How Future Combat Systems Will Work," http://science .howstuffworks.com/fcs1.htm.

49. Kagen, *Finding the Target*, 251.

50. Ibid., 113.

51. Andrew Feickert, "The Army's Future Combat System (FCS): Background and Issues for Congress," *CRS Report for Congress* (April 28, 2005), i.

52. Thom Shanker, "Military Spending Proposals Envision Changing Battlefield," *NYT* (November 22, 2002): A18.

53. Ibid.

54. Rowan Scarborough, "Rumsfeld Bolsters Special Forces," *WT* (January 6, 2003): A1.

55. I will argue in the second part of this book that one of the reasons Rumsfeld went out of his way to support this war was because he saw it as a way to prove the validity of his new approach to warfare.

56. As cited in Kagan, *Finding the Target*, 346.

57. Donald Rumsfeld, "Testimony before the Senate Armed Service Committee," July 9, 2003, printed manuscript.

58. As cited in Kagan, *Finding the Target*, 348.

59. Ibid., 348–349.

60. Stephen Biddle et al., *Toppling Saddam: Iraq and Military Transformation* (Carlisle, PA: Strategic Studies Institute, U.S. Army War College, April 2004), v.

61. Gregory Fontenot, E. J. Degen, and David Tohn, *On Point: The United States Army in Operation Iraqi Freedom,"* (Annapolis, MD: Naval Institute Press, 2005), 417.

62. Ibid.

63. Kagan, *Finding the Target*, 353.

64. Vernon Loeb, "Rumsfeld Turns Eye to Future of Army," *WP* (June 8, 2003): A12.

65. This issue is discussed in greater detail in the second part of this book.

66. Associated Press (June 11, 2003). "William I. Nash, a retired major general and veteran of the Gulf War and the Bosnian mission, said of General Shinseki, 'He is as fine a soldier I've ever served with, and his key characteristics are loyalty and professional competence.'" Bernard Weintraub and Thom Shanker, "Rumsfeld's Design for War Criticized on the Battlefield," *NYT* (April 1, 2003): A1.

67. While Keane claimed that he was retiring for personal reasons, several individuals I have spoken with who knew him claim that the real reason was that he

could not stand the way Rumsfeld had treated Shinseki and had no intention of taking any more abuse from Rumsfeld.

68. Bradley Graham, "Retired General Picked to Head Army: Rumsfeld's Choice of Schoomaker Expected to Rankle Many in Uniform," *WP* (June 11, 2003): A9.

69. Feicker, "The Army's Future Combat System," 3. According to Stephen Biddle, this program was labeled "spiral development." Conversation with Biddle at the Council on Foreign Relations, June 7, 2007.

70. Dan Morgan, "House Approves $369 Billion for Defense Spending," *WP* (July 9, 2003): A4.

71. Vernon Loeb, "Army Will Face Dip in Readiness," *WP* (December 6, 2003): A1.

72. Vernon Loeb, "Pentagon Plan Seeks Annual Budget Boost of $20 Billion," *WP* (January 31, 2003): A4.

73. Carl Hulse, "Both Houses Back More Military Spending," *NYT* (May 23, 2003): A21.

74. Esther Schrader, "Army Cancels Comanche Helicopter," *LAT* (February 24, 2004): A10.

75. Ibid.

76. Tom Philpott, "The Army's Challenge," *Military Officer* 11, 11 (November 2004): 62.

77. Thom Shanker, "New Chief Sets Out to Redesign a Stretched Thin Army," *NYT* (January 28, 2004): A19.

78. Les Brownlee and Peter J. Schoomaker, "Serve a Nation at War: A Campaign Quality Army with Joint and Expeditionary Qualities," *Parameters* (Summer 2004): 13.

79. Brad Knickerboxer, "How Will Iraq Change U.S. Military Doctrine," *Christian Science Monitor* (July 2, 2004): 2.

80. Thomas E. Ricks and Josh White, "Scope of Change in Military is Ambiguous," *WP* (August 1, 2004): A6. Vice Admiral Arthur K. Cebrowski (Ret.) was head of the Office of Force Transformation from 2001 to 2005.

81. Josh Sherman, "Rumsfeld Taps Six Panels to Oversee Quadrennial Defense Review," *Inside the Pentagon* (March 3, 2005).

82. Michael P. Noonan, "The Quadrennial Defense Review and U.S. Defense Policy, 2006–2025," Foreign Policy Research Institute *E-Notes* (March 9, 2006).

83. David S. Cloud, "Pentagon Review Calls for No Big Changes," *NYT* (February 2, 2006): A17.

84. Fred Kaplan, "Is Rumsfeld Bored or Tired?" *Slate* (January 12, 2006).

85. See Fred Kaplan, "Rumsfeld Surrenders: The QDR Dashes his Dreams of Military Transformation," *Slate* (February 3, 2006).

86. "The Flawed Plane Congress Loves," *NYT* (March 24, 2005).

87. "Future Combat Systems," GlobalSecurity, org. (November 14, 2006), available at: http://globalsecurity.org/military/systems/ground/fcs.htm.

88. Ibid.

89. Jason Sherman, "Army Defends Future Combat System Costs," Military.com (July 20, 2006).

90. Fred W. Baker, III, "Future Combat Systems Restructuring a 'Balancing Act,'" American Forces Press Service (February 8, 2007), available at http://www.spacewar.com/reports/Future_Combat_Systems_Restructuring_A_Balancing_Act_999.html.

91. Thom Shanker and David S. Cloud, "Rumsfeld Shift Lets Army Seek Larger Budget," *NYT* (October 8, 2006): A1.

92. Michael O'Hanlon, "Transformation Reality Check," *Armed Services Journal* (March 2007): 22.

93. Matt Kelley, "Pentagon Dithering Turned U.S. Forces into Sitting Ducks," *USAT* (July 17, 2007): A1. As the author noted, "Perhaps it's no coincidence that the month after the Pentagon chief was forced out of his job in November 2006, the Joint Chiefs of Staff suddenly reversed course and approved construction of 4,060 MRAPs."

## Chapter 4. Rumsfeld's War in Afghanistan and Preparations for Iraq

1. As cited in Michael Isikoff and David Corn, *Hubris: The Inside Story of Spin, Scandal, and the Selling of the Iraq War* (New York: Crown, 2006), 77.

2. Lewis D. Solomon, *Paul D. Wolfowitz: Visionary Intellectual, Policymaker, and Strategist* (Westport, CT: Praeger, 2007), 70.

3. *Iraq Liberation Act of 1998*, HR 4664, 105th Cong., 2nd sess., *Congressional Record* (October 1, 1998): H9274. It is perhaps worth noting that during the 2000 presidential campaign Al Gore "promised to support groups working to unseat Saddam Hussein." James Fallows, *Blind into Baghdad: America's War in Iraq* (New York: Vintage, 2006), 49.

4. George Tenet, *At the Center of the Storm: My Years at the CIA* (New York: HarperCollins, 2007), 303. Woodward lists the figure at $97 million. Bob Woodward, *Plan of Attack* (New York: Simon and Schuster, 2004), 10.

5. Thomas E. Ricks, *Fiasco: The American Military Adventure in Iraq* (New York: Palgrave, 2006), 19.

6. Ibid., 20.

7. Bob Woodward, *Bush at War* (New York: Simon and Schuster, 2002), 9.

8. Ibid., 22.

9. David L. Phillips, *Losing Iraq: Inside the Postwar Reconstruction Fiasco* (New York: Basic Books, 2005), 63.

10. Ibid., 64.

11. Ali A. Allawi, *The Occupation of Iraq: Winning the War, Losing the Peace* (New Haven, CT: Yale University Press, 2007), 22.

12. James Fallows, "Blind into Baghdad," *Atlantic* (January 2004): 49.

13. Tom Clancy with General Tony Zinni, *Battle Ready* (New York: Putnam, 2004), 20.

14. "Post-Saddam Iraq: The War Game," *National Security Archive Briefing Book*, No. 207 (November 4, 2006), available at http://www.gwu.edu/~nsarchiv/NSAEBB/NSAEBB207/index.htm.

15. Ibid.

16. Clancy and Zinni, *Battle Ready*, 20.

17. Eric Schmitt and James Dao, "Iraq Is Focal Point as Bush Meets with Joint Chiefs," *NYT* (January 11, 2001): A20.

18. Karen DeYoung, *Soldier: The Life of Colin Powell* (New York: Knopf, 2006), 315.

19. Ibid., 216.

20. Tenet, *At the Center of the Storm*, 303.

21. DeYoung, *Soldier*, 317.

22. Bob Woodward, *State of Denial: Bush at War, Part III* (New York: Simon and Schuster, 2006), 49.

23. Tenet, *At the Center of the Storm*, 153.

24. Andrew Cockburn, *Rumsfeld: His Rise, Fall, and Catastrophic Legacy* (New York: Scribner, 2007), 9.

25. Tenet, *At the Center of the Storm*, 160.

26. E-mail from General Myers to the author dated August 27, 2007.

27. Tenet, *At the Center of the Storm*, 171.

28. Woodward, *Bush at War*, 98.

29. Ibid., 305.

30. Stephen F. Hayes, *Cheney: The Untold Story of America's Most Powerful and Controversial Vice President* (New York: HarperCollins, 2007), 352.

31. Isikoff and Corn, *Hubris*, 80.

32. Woodward, *Bush at War*, 49.

33. Fallows, *Blind into Baghdad*, 50.

34. Tommy Franks, *American Soldier* (New York: Regan Books, 2004), 232.

35. Tenet, *At the Center of the Storm*, 175.

36. Franks, *American Soldier*, 250.

37. Ibid., 251. Emphasis in original.

38. Michael DeLong, *Inside CENTCOM* (Washington: Regenery, 2004), 23.

39. Ibid., 83. Another author suggests that, during a break, Wolfowitz spoke with the president and "that the broad outline of Wolfowitz's ideas stuck with Bush." Solomon, *Paul D. Wolfowitz*, 78.

40. Michael R. Gordon and General Bernard E. Trainor, *Cobra II: The Inside Story of the Invasion and Occupation of Iraq* (New York: Pantheon Books, 2006), 17.

41. Tenet, *At the Center of the Storm*, 309. Emphasis in the original.

42. Ibid., 178. Emphasis in the original.

43. Woodward, *Bush at War*, 99.

44. Ibid., 208.

45. The best study of CIA operations is by Gary C. Schroen, who led the team. *First In: An Insider's Account of How the CIA Spearheaded the War on Terror in Afghanistan* (New York: Ballantine, 2005).

46. Glenn Kessler, "U.S. Decision on Iraq Has Puzzling Past: Opponents of War Wonder When, How, Policy Was Set," *WP* (January 12, 2003): A1.

47. Schroen, *First In*, 25.

48. See Ryan Henry, "Defense Transformation and the 2005 Quadrennial Defense Review," *Parameters* 35, 4 (Winter 2005/2006): 6.

49. Myers and Pace took over as chairman and vice chairman, respectively, on October 1, 2001.

50. Franks, *American Soldier*, 263.

51. Woodward, *Bush at War*, 43.

52. Ibid., 63.

53. Ibid., 150.

54. Thomas E. Ricks, "Rumsfeld's Hands-On War: Afghan Campaign Shaped by Secretary's Views, Personality," *WP* (December 9, 2001): A1.

55. Franks, *American Soldier*, 276.

56. DeLong, *Inside CENTCOM*, 28.

57. Franks, *American Soldier*, 277. Emphasis in original.

58. Ibid., 48.

59. Frederick W. Kagan, *Finding the Target: The Transformation of American Military Policy* (New York: Encounter, 2006), 296. See also Woodward, *Bush at War*, 288.

60. Woodward, *Bush at War*, 237.

61. Franks, *American Soldier*, 280.

62. Ibid., 245.

63. Tenet, *At the Center of the Storm*, 216.

64. Based on a discussion with an army officer who led one of the Special Forces teams into Afghanistan.

65. Tenet, *At the Center of the Storm*, 216.

66. DeLong, *Inside CENTCOM*, 55.

67. "President Speaks on War Effort to Citadel Cadets," White House Press Release (December 11, 2001).

68. Woodward, *Bush at War*, 321. Wolfowitz made similar statements. See Solomon, *Paul D. Wolfowitz*, 81–82.

69. Stephen Biddle, "Afghanistan and the Future of Warfare: Implications for Army and Defense Policy," U.S. Army War College, (November 2002): 6. This is an excellent in-depth analysis of the Afghan campaign and makes a very strong argument against the uniqueness of the Afghan campaign for military transformation.

70. Kagan, *Finding the Target*, 208.

## Chapter 5. Finding a Reason to Overthrow Saddam: The Die Is Cast

1. Glenn Kessler, "U.S. Decision on Iraq Has Puzzling Past: Opponents of War Wonder When, How Policy Was Set," *WP* (January 12, 2003): A1. See also Michael R. Gordon and Bernard E. Trainor, *Cobra II: The Inside Story of the Invasion and Occupation of Iraq* (New York: Pantheon, 2006), 18.

2. Bob Woodward, *State of Denial: Bush at War Part III* (New York: Simon and Schuster, 2006), 81.

3. There is some confusion. Gordon and Trainor suggest that Rumsfeld flew to Tampa to deliver the message (pp. 21–22), while Franks says he received a phone call on November 21. See Tommy Franks, *American Soldier* (New York: HarperCollins, 2004), 315.

4. Franks, *American Soldier*, 315.

5. Bob Woodward, *Plan of Attack* (New York: Simon and Schuster, 2004), 8.

6. Gordon and Trainor, *Cobra II*, 24. Franks does not mention this, although by and large his memoirs were written to avoid overcriticism of the secretary.

7. Woodward, *Plan of Attack*, 37.

8. Thomas E. Ricks, *Fiasco: The American Military Adventure in Iraq* (New York: Penguin, 2006), 33.

9. Ibid.

10. Gordon and Trainor, *Cobra II*, 22.

11. Peter W. Galbraith, *The End of Iraq* (New York: Simon and Schuster, 2006), 89.

12. Ricks, *Fiasco*, 34.

13. Franks, *American Soldier*, 330.

14. Communication from General Tony Zinni, July 17, 2007.

15. Woodward, *Plan of Attack*, 41.

16. Gordon and Trainor, *Cobra II*, 29.

17. Ibid.

18. Franks, *American Soldier*, 337.

19. Woodward, *Plan of Attack*, 57.

20. Gordon and Trainor, *Cobra II*, 32. Woodward gives the numbers of 105,000 to start the war, and 230,000 by the end. Woodward, *Plan of Attack*, 58.

21. Woodward, *Plan of Attack*, 63.

22. Franks, *American Soldier*, 351–352.

23. Ibid., 362.

24. Ibid., 367.

25. Woodward, *State of Denial*, 86. See also Karen DeYoung, *Soldier: The Life of Colin Powell* (New York: Knopf, 2006), 368.

26. Woodward, *State of Denial*, 86.

27. DeYoung, *Soldier*, 370.

28. Woodward, *Plan of Attack*, 85–86.

29. Ricks, *Fiasco*, 35.

30. DeYoung, *Soldier*, 377.

31. Michael Isikoff and David Corn, *Hubris: The Inside Story of Spin, Scandal, and the Selling of the Iraq War* (New York: Crown, 2006), 195.

32. Gordon and Trainor, *Cobra II*, 36.

33. Woodward, *Plan of Attack*, 96.

34. Ibid., 99; Franks, *Soldier*, 370.

35. James Fallows, "Blind into Baghdad," *Atlantic* (January/February 2004), 9–10.

36. Ibid., 6; Woodward, *Plan of Attack*, 132.

37. Fallows, "Blind into Baghdad," 3. Anyone, including myself, who has served in the Pentagon quickly realizes that the military is the organization least likely to push for the use of military force. People die when that happens, and most senior officers want to be convinced that it is critical to the U.S. national interest. That does not mean they will not carry out orders, even some silly ones. It means that it is usually civilians who push for the use of force.

38. Ricks, *Fiasco*, 40–41.

39. Ibid.

40. Thomas E. Ricks, "Some Top Military Brass Favor Status Quo in Iraq. Containment Seen Less Likely than Attack," *WP* (July 28, 2002): A1.

41. Thomas E. Ricks, "Timing, Tactics on Iraq War Disputed," *WP* (August 1, 2002): A1.

42. Ricks, "Some Top Military Brass Favor Status Quo in Iraq."

43. DeYoung, *Soldier*, 399.

44. Walter Pincus, "Memo: U.S. Lacked Full Postwar Iraq Plan," *WP* (June 12, 2005): A1; "The Secret Downing Street Memo," *Sunday Times* (July 23, 2002): A1.

45. Pincus, "Memo: U.S. Lacked Full Postwar Iraq Plan."

46. Glenn Frankel, "From Memos: Insights into Ally's Doubts on Iraq War," *WP* (June 28, 2005): A1. The British were not the only ones who were getting that impression. According to Tenet, Feith told U.S., British, French, and German officials on September 6 that "war is not an option." Tenet, *At the Center of the Storm*, 310.

47. Alastair Campbell and Richard Stott, eds., *The Blair Years: Extracts from the Alastair Campbell Diaries* (New York: Knopf, 2007), 630.

48. As cited in Ricks, *Fiasco*, 54.

49. James Risen, "Prewar Views of Iraq Threat Are under Review by the CIA," *NYT* (May 22, 2003): A1.

50. E-mail from General Myers to the author dated August 28, 2007.

51. "Rumsfeld Sends Pentagon Planners Back to Drawing Board over Iraq," CNN.com (August 1, 2002).

52. Franks, *American Soldier*, 386–393. Franks has a tendency to skip over difficult issues throughout his book.

53. Ricks, "Timing, Tactics on Iraq War Disputed."

54. Fallows, "Blind into Baghdad," 10.

55. Woodward, *Plan of Attack*, 146; Franks, *American Soldier*, 389–390.

56. Michael R. Gordon, "A Prewar Slide Show Cast Iraq in Rosy Hues," *NYT* (February 15, 2007): A16.

57. Dana Milbank and Thomas E. Ricks, "Powell and Joint Chiefs Nudged Bush Toward U.N.," *WP* (September 4, 2003): A1.

58. DeYoung, *Soldier*, 400–401. "Powell was not the only one worried about the post-combat period. UK General Sir Mike Jackson commented, 'From the earliest stage, British concerns focused not just on itself but also what would happened afterwards—so-called Phase 4. At issue was not so much the number of troops needed to topple the regime as the number needed to maintain the peace afterwards.'" Mike Jackson, *Soldier: The Autobiography* (London: Bantam Press, 2007), 322.

59. Milbank and Ricks, "Powell and Joint Chiefs Nudged Bush toward U.N."

60. Karen DeYoung, "For Powell, a Long Path to a Victory," *WP* (November 10, 2002): A1.

61. Woodward, *Plan of Attack*, 155.

62. Brent Scowcroft, "Don't Attack Saddam," *Wall Street Journal* (August 15, 2002): A12.

63. Tenet, *At the Center of the Storm*, 315.

64. Jackson, *Soldier*, 335.

65. Tenet, *At the Center of the Storm*, 347.

66. Ibid.

67. "Future of Iraq Project," *Source Watch* (March 30, 2006).

68. Fallows, "Blind into Baghdad," 8.

69. Bremer also mentions the study in his memoirs. He claims he asked Ryan Crocker about it, since he had been "deeply involved" in it. According to Bremer, Crocker said it was not intended to provide a "practical plan for postwar Iraq." Instead, Crocker reportedly stated that its purpose was "to engage Iraqi-American thinking about their country's future after Saddam was ousted." Bremer states that once he had a chance to read the 15-volume study, he agreed. (Bremer, *My Year in Iraq: The Struggle to Build a Future of Hope* [New York: Simon and Schuster, 2006], 25). While the foregoing may be an accurate statement of Crocker's understanding of the plan, the bottom line is that Feith made sure that its findings were never incorporated into the Pentagon's plan for post-combat Iraq. Ironically, as much as the State Department's study was ignored in the U.S. government, General Jackson reports that the U.K. was placing a lot "of confidence in it" (Jackson, *Soldier*, 323).

70. David L. Phillips, *Losing Iraq: Inside the Postwar Reconstruction Fiasco* (New York: Westview, 2005), 122.

71. Isikoff and Corn, *Hubris*, 29. Emphasis added.

72. Tenet, *At the Center of the Storm*, 317.

73. Ricks, *Fiasco*, 71.

74. Ibid., 71–72.

75. George Packer, "War after the War," *New Yorker* (November 24, 2003): 59ff.

76. Charles A. Stevenson, *SECDEF: The Nearly Impossible Job of Secretary of Defense* (Dulles, VA: Potomac Books, 2006), 173.

77. "Three Retired Officers Demand Rumsfeld's Resignation," *WP* (September 25, 2006).

78. Isikoff and Corn, *Hubris*, 30.

79. As quoted in ibid., 44.

80. DeYoung, *Soldier*, 411.

81. As cited in DeYoung, *Soldier*, 418.

82. Tenet, *At the Center of the Storm*, 327.

83. Ibid., 328.

84. Ricks, *Fiasco*, 52.

85. Quoted in Tenet, *At the Center of the Storm*, 337.

86. Woodward, *State of Denial*, 91.

87. Isikoff and Corn, *Hubris*, 146–147.

88. Ibid., 149.

89. Ricks, *Fiasco*, 66.

90. Andrew Cockburn, *Rumsfeld: His Rise, Fall, and Catastrophic Legacy* (New York: Scribner, 2007), 168. In his *Foreign Affairs* article, General Myers claimed that General Newbold "never made his views known to the chairman or vice chairman for whom he worked directly." That is direct contradiction to Newbold's comment in *Time* that "I made no secret of my view that the zealot's rationale for war made no sense. And I think I was outspoken enough to make those senior to me uncomfortable." Since Pace was his direct superior, it would seem strange that Pace and Myers were not aware, or perhaps did not want to be aware, of Newbold's dissension. See Richard B. Myers and Richard H. Kohn, "The Military's Place," *Foreign Affairs* 86, 5 (September/October 2007): 148; and Greg Newbold, "Why Iraq Was a Mistake," *Time* (April 9, 2006), available at http://www.time.com/time/printout/0,8816,1181629,00.html.

91. According to one source, "Many of the present and former officials I spoke to were critical of Franks for his perceived failure to stand up to his civilian superiors. A former senator told me that Franks was widely seen as a commander who "will do what he's told." Seymour M. Hersh, "Offense and Defense. The Battle between Donald Rumsfeld and the Pentagon," *New Yorker* (April 7, 2003).

## Chapter 6. The Invasion of Iraq

1. As cited in Michael Isikoff and David Corn, *Hubris: The Inside Story of Spin, Scandal, and the Selling of the Iraq War* (New York: Crown, 2006), 197–198.

2. Thomas E. Ricks, *Fiasco: The American Military Adventure in Iraq* (New York: Penguin, 2006), 73.

3. Bob Woodward, *State of Denial: Bush at War, Part III* (New York: Simon and Schuster, 2006), 103. When Woodward interviewed Rumsfeld, he said he did not recall the conversation, making it clear just how unconcerned he was about Phase IV operations.

4. Ricks, *Fiasco*.

5. Bob Woodward, *Plan of Attack* (New York: Simon and Schuster, 2004), 232.

6. James Fallows, "Blind into Baghdad," *Atlantic Monthly* (January/February 2004): 15.

7. This officer requested to remain anonymous.

8. James Fallows, *Blind into Baghdad: America's War in Iraq* (New York: Vintage, 2006), 76.

9. Karen DeYoung, *Soldier: The Life of Colin Powell* (New York: Knopf, 2006), 429.

10. Woodward, *Plan of Attack*, 272.

11. Woodward, *State of Denial*, 112.

12. Ibid., 127.

13. Ibid.

14. Ibid., 123.

15. David L. Phillips, *Losing Iraq: Inside the Postwar Reconstruction Fiasco* (New York: Westview, 2005), 128.

16. Woodward, *State of Denial*, 129.

17. U.S. Senate Select Committee on Intelligence, *Prewar Intelligence Assessments About Postwar Iraq*, 110th Cong., 1st sess., May 25, 2007; Walter Pincus, "Analysts' Warnings of Iraq Chaos Detailed: Senate Panel Releases Assessments from 2003," *WP* (May 26, 2007): A1.

18. Walter Pincus, "Assessments Made in 2003 Foretold Situation in Iraq," *WP* (May 20, 2007): A6.

19. Steven R. Weisman, "The Saturday Profile: Ex-Powell Aide Moves from Insider to Apostate," *NYT* (December 24, 2005): A4.

20. Quoted in James P. Pfiffner, "Intelligence and Decision Making," *The Polarized Presidency of George W. Bush*, ed. George C. Edwards, III and Desmond S. King (New York: Oxford University Press, 2007), 218.

21. George Tenet, *At the Center of the Storm: My Years at the CIA* (New York: HarperCollins, 2007), 372.

22. Isikoff and Corn, *Hubris*, 177.

23. Ibid., 177–178.

24. Ibid., 181.

25. Thom Shanker and Eric Schmitt, "Rumsfeld Seeks Consensus Through Jousting," *NYT* (March 19, 2003): A1.

26. Peter W. Galbraith, *The End of Iraq: How American Incompetence Created a War Without End* (New York: Simon and Schuster, 2006), 90.

27. Ali Allawi, *The Occupation of Iraq: Winning the War, Losing the Peace* (New Haven, CT: Yale University Press, 2007), 97.

28. Thom Shanker, "New Strategy Vindicates Ex-Army Chief Shinseki," *NYT* (January 12, 2007): A13.

29. Ricks, *Fiasco*, 96–97.

30. Shanker, "New Strategy Vindicates Ex-Army Chief Shinseki."

31. Michael R. Gordon and Bernard E. Trainor, *Cobra II: The Inside Story of the Invasion and Occupation of Iraq* (New York: Pantheon, 2006), 103.

32. Rowan Scarborough, "Wolfowitz Criticizes 'Suspect' Estimate of Occupation Force," *WT* (February 28, 2003): A1.

33. Ricks, *Fiasco*, 100.

34. Shanker, "New Strategy Vindicates Ex-Army Chief Shinseki."

35. Dana Milbank, "Colonel Finally Saw Whites of Their Eyes," *WP* (October 20, 2005): A4.

36. See Larry Diamond, *Squandered Victory: The American Occupation and the Bungled Effort to Bring Democracy to Iraq* (New York: Times Books, 2005), 32.

37. Woodward, *State of Denial*, 140.

38. Rajiv Chandrasekaran, *Imperial Life in the Emerald City: Inside Iraq's Green Zone* (New York: Knopf, 2006), 31.

39. "Post-War Planning Non-Existent," Knight-Ridder (October 17, 2003).

40. Gordon and Trainor, *Cobra II*, 160.

41. Woodward, *Plan of Attack*, 339.

42. Woodward, *State of Denial*, 131.

43. Ricks, *Fiasco*, 122.

44. Michael R. Gordon, "The Strategy to Secure Iraq Did Not Foresee a 2nd War," *NYT* (October 19, 2004): A1.

45. Ibid. The idea that it was Rumsfeld pushing to off-ramp the First Cavalry Division was repeated several days later. Michael R. Gordon, "Criticizing an Agent of Change as Failing to Adapt," *NYT* (April 21, 2006): A18.

46. E-Mail from General Myers to the author dated August 27, 2007.

47. Gordon, "The Strategy to Secure Iraq Did Not Foresee a 2nd War."

48. Ibid.

49. "Remarks by Secretary of Defense Donald H. Rumsfeld," Transcript of Meeting at Council on Foreign Relations, New York, May 27, 2003, available at http://www.cfr.org/publication/5998/remarks_by_secretary_of_defense_donald_h_rumsfeld.htm.

50. Nicholas E. Reynolds, *Basrah, Baghdad, and Beyond: The U.S. Marine Corps in the Second Iraq War* (Annapolis, MD: U.S. Naval Institute, 2003), 111.

51. Andrew Cockburn, *Rumsfeld: His Rise, Fall, and Catastrophic Legacy* (New York: Scribner, 2007), 75; see also Ahmed S. Hashim, *Insurgency and Counter-Insurgency in Iraq* (Ithaca, NY: Cornell University Press, 2006), 19–20.

52. "Interview: James Fallows," *Frontline: The Invasion of Iraq* (January 28, 2004), available at http://www.pbs.org/wgbh/pages/frontline/shows/invasion/interviews/fallows.html.

53. Fallows, "Blind into Baghdad," 101.

54. Gordon, "The Strategy to Secure Iraq Did Not Foresee a 2nd War."

55. Woodward, *State of Denial*, 156.

56. Mark Fineman, Robin Wright, and Doyle McManus, "Washington's Battle Plan: Preparing for War, Stumbling for Peace," *LAT* (July 18, 2003): A1.

57. David Reiff, "Blueprint for a Mess," *NYT Magazine* (November 2, 2003): 28ff.

58. As quoted in Eric Herring and Glen Rankwala, *Iraq in Fragments: The Occupation and its Legacy* (Ithaca, NY: Cornell University Press, 2006), 4.

59. Ricks, *Fiasco*, 150. Colonel Alan King was head of civil affairs for the Third Infantry Division.

60. Gordon, "The Strategy to Secure Iraq."

61. Peter Slevin, "Baghdad Anarchy Spurs Call for Help," *WP* (May 13, 2006): A1.

62. Peter Slevin and Vernon Loeb, "Plan to Secure Postwar Iraq Faulted," *WP* (May 19, 2003): A1.

63. Vince Crawley, "Less is More," *Army Times* 63, 39 (April 21, 2003): 18.

64. Rajiv Chandrasekaran and Peter Slevin, "Iraq's Ragged Reconstruction," *WP* (May 9, 2003): A1.

65. George Packer, "War after the War. What Washington Doesn't See in Iraq," *New Yorker* (November 24, 2003): 58ff.

66. "Secretary Rumsfeld Town Hall Meeting, Baghdad, April 30, 2003," transcript available at http://www.defenselink.mil/Transcripts/Transcript.aspx?Transcript ID=2543.

67. See Allawi's discussion of Bremer's arrival in Iraq in Allawi, *The Occupation of Iraq: Winning the War, Losing the Peace,* 108–111. Or as Cockburn put it, "By the time Bremer left Iraq just over a year later there were few, either among the Iraqi or the Americans who dealt with him, who had a good word to say for him." Cockburn, *Rumsfeld,* 70. (Based on the writer's experience in the Foreign Service.) This was also his "corridor" reputation inside the State Department.

68. Ibid.

69. Slevin and Loeb, "Plan to Secure Postwar Iraq Faulted."

## Chapter 7. Winning the War, Losing the Peace

1. Thomas E. Ricks, *Fiasco: The American Military Adventure in Iraq* (New York: Penguin, 2006), 168–169. Ricks is correct in arguing that the military did not understand that it was not fighting a conventional war, but an insurgency. Rumsfeld could have had a major impact if he had pushed the military in the correct direction, but he began his litany—"things are getting better," "we had our problems, so do they," etc.

2. "Interview: Philip Zelikow," *Frontline: End Game* (February 6, 2007), available at http://www.pbs.org/wgbh/pages/frontline/endgame/interviews/zelikow.html. The problem, as Michael Gordon noted, was that General John Abizaid was CENTCOM and had an overall understanding of what was happening, but he was not involved in the day-to-day operations on the ground. As the direct field commander, it was General George W. Casey who, working with Rumsfeld, should have come up with a new approach for dealing with Phase IV as well as developing a new strategy, since the old one was clearly not working. "Interview: Michael Gordon," *Frontline: End Game* (January 11, 2007), available at http://www.pbs.org/wgbh/pages/frontline/endgame/interviews/gordon.html.

3. Ibid.

4. "Interview: Lieutenant Colonel Andrew Krepinevich (Ret.)," *Frontline: End Game* (January 10, 2007), available at http://www.pbs.org/wgbh/pages/frontline/endgame/interviews/krepinevich.html.

5. "Interview: Krepinevich," *Frontline: End Game.*

6. Ali A. Allawi, *The Occupation of Iraq: Winning the War, Losing the Peace* (New Haven, CT: Yale University Press, 2007), 110.

7. David L. Phillips, *Losing Iraq: Inside the Postwar Reconstruction Fiasco* (New York: Westview, 2005), 38.

8. Peter W. Galbraith, *The End of Iraq: How American Incompetence Created a War without End* (New York: Simon and Schuster, 2006), 122.

9. Ibid., 171.

10. George Tenet, *At the Center of the Storm: My Years at the CIA* (New York: HarperCollins, 2007), 423.

11. Galbraith, *The End of Iraq,* 125.

12. Bing West, *No True Glory* (New York: Bantam Dell, 2005), 22.

13. Rajiv Chandrasekaran, *Imperial Life in the Emerald City: Inside Iraq's Green Zone* (New York: Knopf, 2006), 233.

14. Larry Diamond, *Squandered Victory: The American Occupation and the Bungled Effort to Bring Democracy to Iraq* (New York: Times Books, 2005), 349n38.

15. Phillips, *Losing Iraq*, 163.

16. Allawi, *The Occupation of Iraq*, 124.

17. As cited in Lewis D. Solomon, *Paul D. Wolfowitz: Visionary Intellectual, Policymaker and Strategist* (Westport, CT: Praeger, 2007), 111.

18. Bob Woodward, *State of Denial: Bush at War, Part III* (New York: Simon and Schuster, 2006), 261.

19. Chandrasekaran, *Imperial Life in the Emerald City*, 70.

20. Tenet, *At the Center of the Storm*, 427.

21. Chandrasekaran, *Imperial Life in the Emerald City*, 70.

22. Ibid.

23. L. Paul Bremer, *My Year in Iraq: The Struggle to Build a Future of Hope* (New York: Simon and Schuster, 2006), 39.

24. Ibid. Interestingly, Woodward reported that Feith said that it was Bremer who had pushed both the de-Baathification order as well as one to disband the Iraqi Army. Woodward, *State of Denial*, 191.

25. Michael DeLong, *Inside CENTCOM: The Unvarnished Truth about the Wars in Afghanistan and Iraq* (New York: Regency, 2004), 123–124.

26. Allawi, *The Occupation of Iraq*, 151.

27. Thomas E. Ricks, "In Iraq, Military Forgot the Lessons of Vietnam," *WP* (July 23, 2006): A1. Emphasis in original.

28. Ibid. One of the interesting things about doing research for a book like this is to see how some writers do everything to present themselves in a favorable light. Reading Bremer, one comes away with the impression that there was minimal opposition to the order on the part of those in Baghdad; indeed, he suggests that they supported him. See Bremer, *My Year in Iraq*, 140–142.

29. Chandrasekaran, *Imperial Life in the Emerald City*, 71.

30. Phillips, *Losing Iraq*, 146.

31. Ricks, *Fiasco*, 161.

32. Tenet, *At the Center of the Storm*, 427. See also Chandrasekaran, *Imperial Life in the Emerald City*, 73.

33. DeLong, *Inside CENTCOM*, 124.

34. Chandrasekaran, *Imperial Life in the Emerald City*, 74.

35. Tenet, *At the Center of the Storm*, 428.

36. Robert Draper, *Dead Certain: The Presidency of George W. Bush* (New York: Free Press, 2007), 211.

37. See, "Letter from L. Paul Bremer to George W. Bush, May 23, 2003," *NYT* (September 4, 2007); "Letter from George W. Bush to L. Paul Bremer, May 23, 2003,"; and Edmund L. Andrews and Michael R. Gordon, "Envoy's Letters Counters Bush on Dismantling of Iraq Army," *NYT* (September 4, 2007): A1.

38. This was stated by a serving officer who asked to remain anonymous.

39. Woodward, *State of Denial*, 195.

40. James Fallows, "Why Iraq Has No Army," *Atlantic* (December 2005): 64.

41. Michael Gordon and Bernard Trainor, *Cobra II: The Inside Story of the Invasion and Occupation of Iraq* (New York: Pantheon, 2006), 481.

42. Richard Leiby, "Up in Arms in Baghdad," *WP* (May 9, 2003): A4.

43. Fallows, "Why Iraq Has No Army," 159.

44. Ibid.

45. Phillips, *Losing Iraq*, 153.

46. Chandrasekaran, *Imperial Life in the Emerald City*, 76.

47. Michael R. Gordon, "A New Commander, in Step with the White House on Iraq," *NYT* (January 6, 2007): A1.

48. Ricks, *Fiasco*, 164.

49. As cited in Ahmed S. Hasim, *Insurgency and Counter-Insurgency in Iraq* (Ithaca, NY: Cornell University Press, 2006), 27.

50. As cited in Woodward, *State of Denial*, 209.

51. Allawi, *The Occupation of Iraq*, 156.

52. Chandrasekaran, *Imperial Life in the Emerald City*, 77.

53. Bremer, *Iraq*, 68.

54. Fallows, "Why Iraq Has No Army," 65.

55. Mark Fineman, "Dissolving Iraqi Army Seen by Many as Costly Move," *LAT* (August 24, 2003): A1.

56. Phillips, *Losing Iraq*, 152.

57. Related to this writer by officers who were present at the time but have requested anonymity.

58. Mike Jackson, *Soldier: The Autobiography* (New York: Bantam Books, 2007), 341–342.

59. Andrew Cockburn, *Rumsfeld: His Rise, Fall, and Catastrophic Legacy* (New York: Scribner, 2007), 72.

60. Esther Schrader, "Senators Criticize Rumsfeld Over Instability Plaguing Iraq," *LAT* (May 15, 2003): A1.

61. "Remarks by Secretary of Defense Donald H. Rumsfeld," Transcript of Meeting at Council on Foreign Relations, New York, May 27, 2003, available at http://www.cfr .org/publication/5998/remarks_by_secretary_of_defense_donald_h_rumsfeld.html.

62. Greg Miller and Terry McDermott, "U.S. Defends Its Role in Iraq," *LAT* (July 1, 2003): A1.

63. Bremer, *My Year in Iraq*, 105–106.

64. Woodward, *State of Denial*, 234.

65. Esther Schrader, "U.S. Will Begin Rotation Plan on Iraq Deployment," *LAT* (July 24, 2003): A11.

66. Allawi, *The Occupation of Iraq*, 176.

67. Fallows, "Why Iraq Has No Army," 71.

68. Ibid., 72.

69. Ibid., 72–74.

70. Ibid., 68.

71. Bremer, *My Year in Iraq*, 156.

72. Ibid., 162.

73. Ibid., 167.

74. Ibid., 169.

75. Thomas E. Ricks and Vernon Loeb, "Iraq Takes a Toll on Rumsfeld: Criticism Mounts with Costs, Casualties," *WP* (September 14, 2003): A1.

76. Bremer, *My Year in Iraq*, 183.

77. Ibid., 184.

78. Ricks and Loeb, "Iraq Takes a Toll on Rumsfeld."

79. Donald H. Rumsfeld, "Beyond Nation-Building," *WP* (September 25, 2003): A33. The comparison is, quite frankly, silly. The creation of the police and the military in Germany were closely linked to Allied relations with the Russians. They had little to do with the Germans' Nazi past, which is what Rumsfeld seems to be trying to compare it to. The events were also sixty years apart.

80. Fallows, "Why Iraq Has No Army," 60.

81. Tyler Marshall, "U.S. General Says Iraqi Rebels Getting Stronger," *LAT* (October 3, 2003): A1.

82. Maura Reynolds, "Bush Reorganizes How Iraq Policy is Set," *LAT* (October 7, 2003): A5.

83. "No More Secretary Nice Guy," *NYT* (October 9, 2003): A36.

84. Bremer, *My Year in Iraq*, 191. The arrest warrant had been issued by the Iraqi government.

85. Ibid., 211.

86. Ibid., 203.

87. Woodward, *State of Denial*, 263.

88. Glenn Kessler and Mike Allen, "Rumsfeld: No Need for More U.S. Troops," *WP* (November 3, 2003): A1.

89. Woodward, *State of Denial*, 265.

90. Ibid., 277.

91. Bremer, *My Year in Iraq*, 245.

92. Ibid.

93. Woodward, *State of Denial*, 298.

94. Two former three-star generals who had served in high-level positions in Iraq both told me the same thing: that cultural and linguistic ignorance was the military's biggest problem in Iraq. I have also heard it repeated numerous times by officers at all levels. "We made mistakes, dumb mistakes and pissed the Iraqis off, not because we intended to but because we had no idea our actions or comments were offensive," is the way several officers put it.

95. Ricks, *Fiasco*, 308.

96. Thomas E. Ricks, "Rumsfeld's War Plan Shares the Blame," *WP* (August 25, 2004): A1.

97. "Rumsfeld Okayed Abuses Says Former U.S. General," Reuters (November 25, 2006).

98. Daniel Williams, "Top Pentagon Leaders Faulted in Prison Abuse," *WP* (August 25, 2006): A1.

99. Bradley Graham, "Huge Movement of Troops Is Underway," *WP* (January 9, 2004): A13.

100. Bradley Graham, "30,000 More Soldiers Approved by Rumsfeld," *WP* (January 29, 2004): A1.

101. Bradley Graham, "No Predictions for U.S. Role in Iraq," *WP* (February 20, 2004): A18.

102. Comment made by a serving officer who asked to remain anonymous.


*Chapter 8. Rumsfeld Is Fired*

1. Technically, Rumsfeld would submit his resignation. But in almost all cases, when the president "accepts" a resignation, it is assumed that it was requested and the individual was, in fact, fired.

2. David L. Phillips, *Losing Iraq: Inside the Postwar Reconstruction Fiasco* (New York: Westview, 2005), 199.

3. L. Paul Bremer, *My Year in Iraq: The Struggle to Build a Future of Hope* (New York: Simon and Schuster, 2006), 311.

4. Ibid., 60.

5. "Interview: Lt Col. Andrew Krepinevich (Ret.)," *Frontline: End Game* (June 19, 2007) available at: http://www.pbs.org/wgbh/pages/frontline/endgame/interviews/krepinevich.html.

6. Bing West, *No True Glory: A Frontline Account of the Battle for Fallujah* (New York: Putnam, 2005), 90. This is by far the best book to date on the battle for Fallujah, especially as seen from the standpoint of the Marines.

7. Ibid., 59.

8. Alissa J. Rubin, "The Fight for Iraq: Why America has Waged a Losing Battle in Fallouja," *LAT* (October 24, 2004): A1.

9. Rajiv Chandrasekaran, *Imperial Life in the Emerald City: Inside Iraq's Green Zone* (New York: Knopf, 2006), 274.

10. Ibid.

11. Bob Woodward, *State of Denial: Bush at War, Part III* (New York: Simon and Shuster, 2006), 297.

12. Chandrasekaran, *Imperial Life in the Emerald City*, 274.

13. Rubin, "The Fight for Iraq."

14. Chandrasekaran, *Imperial Life in the Emerald City*, 274.

15. Thomas E. Ricks, *Fiasco: The American Military Adventure in Iraq* (New York: Penguin, 2006), 332.

16. Ibid., 339.

17. Ibid., 341.

18. Ibid.

19. Bremer, *My Year in Iraq*, 334.

20. Ali A. Allawi, *The Occupation of Iraq: Winning the War, Losing the Peace* (New Haven, CT: Yale University Press, 2007), 277.

21. West, *No True Glory*, 114.

22. Ibid., 214.

23. Ibid.

24. Ibid., 156.

25. Ibid.

26. Woodward, *State of Denial*, 389.

27. One officer who had considerable experience in this context disagreed, noting that neither the ethnic nor the top–down building of an army was a problem in training the Iraqis. Officer's name withheld by request.

28. Thomas E. Ricks, "Dissension Grows in Senior Ranks on War Strategy: U.S. May be Winning Battles in Iraq But Losing the War, Some Officers Say," *WP* (May 9, 2004): A1.

29. Ricks, "Dissention Grows in Senior Ranks on War Strategy."

30. Ibid.

31. Ricks, *Fiasco*, 362.

32. Ricks, "Dissension Grows in Senior Ranks on War Strategy."

33. Woodward, *State of Denial*, 316–317.

34. Dana Priest and Thomas E. Ricks, "Growing Pessimism on Iraq," *WP* (September 29, 2004): A1.

35. William Hamilton, "Card Urged President to Replace Rumsfeld, Woodward Says," WashingtonPost.com (September 29, 2006).

36. "McCain Voices Lack of Trust in Rumsfeld," *NYT* (December 14, 2004): A14.

37. "Frist, McConnell Defend Rumsfeld," *Washington Times* (December 18, 2004).

38. Bremer, *My Year in Iraq*, 357.

39. "Pentagon Rejected Bremer's Call for Troops," Associated Press (January 9, 2006).

40. Esther Schrader, "Army Says it has Enough Troops for Three More Years," *LAT* (June 16, 2004): A10.

41. Ibid.

42. Mark Mazzetti, "U.S. to Cut Number of Overseas Bases: Some Forces will be Moved Closer to Global Hotspots," *LAT* (September 24, 2004): A12.

43. Mark Mazzetti, "Army will not Cut Iraq Combat Tours," *LAT* (October 27, 2004): A4.

44. Woodward, *State of Denial*, 312.

45. "The Conflict in Iraq," *LAT* (June 29, 2004): A1.

46. Allawi, *The Occupation of Iraq*, 288–289.

47. On May 2004, the CJTF-7 was replaced by Multinational Force Iraq (MNF-1), commanded by General Casey. See Eric Herring and Glen Rangwala, *Iraq in Fragments: The Occupation and its Legacy* (Ithaca, NY: Cornell University Press, 2006), 32.

48. "Interview: Gen. Jack Keane (ret.)," *Frontline: End Game* (June 19, 2007), available at: http://www.pbs.org/wgbh/pages/frontline/endgame/interviews/keane.html.

49. "Interview: Frederick Kagan," *Frontline: End Game* (June 19, 2007), available at: http://www.pbs.org/wgbh/pages/frontline/endgame/interviews/kagan.html.

50. Interview, Jack Keane.

51. Interview, Frederick Kagan.

52. Rubin, "The Fight for Iraq."

53. Allawi, *The Occupation of Iraq*, 338.

54. Ricks, *Fiasco*, 399.

55. Ibid.

56. Alissa J. Rubin and John Hendren, "Fallouja Toll Rises," *LAT* (November 12, 2004): A21.

57. Ricks, *Fiasco*, 399.

58. Fred Kaplan, "Rumsfeld vs. the American Soldier," *Slate* (December 8, 2004), available at http://slate.com/id/2110818/.

59. "Iraqi Legislative Election, January 2005," Wikipedia, available at: http://en.Wikipedia.org/Iraqi_legislative_election%2C_January_2005 (last accessed December 16, 2007).

60. Anthony Shadid and Steve Fainaru, "Building Iraq's Army: Mission Improbable," *WP* (June 10, 2005): A1.

61. Rowan Scarborough, "General Doubts Iraqis' Readiness," *WT* (July 23, 2005): A2.

62. Woodward, *State of Denial*, 428.

63. Ibid., 403, 404.

64. Ibid., 405.

65. Ibid.

66. Ibid., 470.

67. "Interview Philip Zelikow," *Frontline: End Game* (February 6, 2007) available at: http://www.pbs.org/wgbh/pages/frontline/endgame/interviews/zelikow.html.

68. According to Philip Zelikow, who was then a senior policy adviser to Secretary of State Rice, the idea for this new strategy came from a memo he sent to Rice on September 26, 2005, in which he suggested the adoption of the "clear, hold, and

build" policy. Ibid. According to Zelikow, General Casey was also upset "that . . . we were trying to articulate strategy; that was their job." Ibid.

69. Interview Philip Zelikow.

70. Ibid.

71. Allawi, *The Occupation of Iraq*, 436.

72. Ibid., 441.

73. "Interview: Michael Gordon," *Frontline: End Game* (June 19, 2007), available at: http://www.pbs.org/wgbh/pages/frontline/endgame/interviews/gordon.html.

74. Ibid.

75. Woodward, *State of Denial*, 444.

76. Ibid., 456.

77. See Major General Peter W. Chiarelli and Major Patrick R. Michaelis, "Winning the Peace: The Requirement for Full-Spectrum Operations," *Military Review* (July–August 2005): 4–17. See also, Kalev I. Sepp, "Best Practices in Counterinsurgency," *Military Review* (May–June 2005): 8–12; and Lieutenant Colonel Conrad C. Crane, (Ret.), "Phase IV Operations: Where Wars are Really Won," *Military Review* (May–June 2005): 27–36.

78. *The U.S. Army/Marine Corps Counterinsurgency Field Manual* (Chicago: University of Chicago Press, 2007).

79. Thom Shanker and David S. Cloud, "Pentagon to Raise Importance of 'Stability' Efforts in War," *NYT* (November 20, 2005): A14.

80. Fred Kaplan, "Do As I Say, Not as I DoD," *Slate* (December 2, 2005), available at: http://www.slate.com/id/2131376/.

81. Thomas E. Ricks, "Army Contests Rumsfeld Bid on Operation," *WP* (January 16, 2005): A6.

82. Andrew Cockburn, *Rumsfeld: His Rise, Fall, and Catastrophic Legacy* (New York: Scribner, 2007), 214.

83. Greg Newbold, "Why Iraq was a Mistake," *Time* (April 9, 2006).

84. David Margolick, "The Night of the Generals," *Vanity Fair* (April 2007): 246–251.

85. "Another General Joins Ranks Opposing Rumsfeld," CNN.com (April 13, 2006).

86. David Ignatius, "Replace Rumsfeld," *WP* (April 14, 2006): A17.

87. Cockburn, *Rumsfeld*, 215.

88. Noam Levey, "General: Appeals for More Troops Were Denied," *LAT* (September 26, 2006): A13.

89. Margolick, "The Night of the Generals."

90. David Ignatius, "Replace Rumsfeld," *WP* (April 14, 2006): A17.

91. Peter Baker and Josh White, "Bush Speaks Out for Rumsfeld," *WP* (April 15, 2006): A1.

92. "Text of Bush's Statement Expressing Support for Defense Secretary Rumsfeld," *WP* (April 14, 2006).

93. Mark Mazzetti and Jim Rutenberg, "Pentagon Memo Aims to Counter Rumsfeld Critics," *NYT* (April 16, 2006): A1.

94. Rowan Scarborough, "Generals Defend Rumsfeld," *WT* (April 15, 2006): A1.

95. Jim Rutenberg and Mark Mazzetti, "Rumsfeld Gets Robust Defense From President," *NYT* (April 15, 2006): A1.

96. "Debate Over Rumsfeld's Future Grows," *CBS News* (April 16, 2006).

97. Peter Spiegel, "Top General Disputes Criticism Against Rumsfeld," *LAT* (April 12, 2006): A4.
98. Solomon Moore, "Military Opposes Rumsfeld," *LAT* (April 20, 2006): A19.
99. Mazzetti and Rutenberg, "Pentagon Memo Aims to Counter Rumsfeld Critics."
100. Ibid.
101. Ibid.
102. Thomas L. Friedman, "Condi and Rummy," *NYT* (April 7, 2006): A25.
103. Ibid.
104. "Interview: Zelikow."
105. Interview, Frederick Kagan.
106. "Interview Michael Gordon," *Frontline: End Game* (June 19, 2007), available at: http://www.pbs.org/wgbh/pages/frontline/endgame/interviews/gordon.html.
107. Thomas E. Ricks, "Situation Called Dire in West Iraq," *WP* (September 11, 2006): A1.
108. Julian E. Barnes, "Rumsfeld Says Critics Appeasing Fascism," *LAT* (August 30, 2006): A1.
109. Julie Hirschfeld Davis, "Rumsfeld Derides Iraq War Critics," *Chicago Tribune* (August 30, 2006): A8.
110. "Democrats Urge Pentagon Changes," *WP* (September 5, 2006): A3.
111. William M. Welch, "Pentagon Extended Iraq Combat Tours for 3,800 Soldiers," *USA Today* (September 26, 2006): A1.
112. Amit R. Paley, "In Baghdad, A Force Under the Militias' Sway," *WP*, (October 31, 2006): A1.
113. Woodward, *State of Denial*, 426.
114. "Iraqi Forces Concern U.S. Commander," *WT* (October 16, 2006): A1.
115. "Interview: Michael Gordon," *Frontline: End Game* (June 19, 2007), available at: http://www.pbs.org/wgbh/pages/frontline/endgame/interviews/gordon.html.
116. "Military Papers: 'Rumsfeld Must Go,'" MSNBC.com (November 3, 2006).
117. Barry Schweid, "Conservatives Challenge Iraq Policy," Associated Press (November 4, 2006).
118. Peter Baker, "Embittered Insiders Turn Against Bush," *WP* (November 19, 2006): A1.
119. James Gerstenzang, "Bush Stands by Cheney, Rumsfeld," *LAT* (November 2, 2006): A11.
120. Lolita C. Baldor, "Rumsfeld Resignation Letter Omits 'Iraq,'" *WP* (August 15, 2007).
121. "Rumsfeld: Iraq Has Not Been Going Well Enough," CBSNews.com (November 9, 2006).
122. "Rumsfeld's Departure," *NYT* (November 9, 2006).
123. "Why Did Rumsfeld Fail," *Armed Forces Journal* (January, 2007), available at http://www.armedforcesjournal.com/2007/01/2410339.

*Conclusion*

1. E-mail to the author from General Myers dated August 28, 2007.
2. See James Dobbins, "Who Lost Iraq?" *Foreign Affairs* (September/October, 2007): 61–74.

3. Bob Woodward, *State of Denial: Bush at War, Part III* (New York: Simon and Schuster, 2006), 310.

4. Walter Pincus and Karen DeYoung, "Senators Debate Significance of Pentagon Report on Intelligence," *Washington Post* (February 10, 2007): A1.

5. Office of the Inspector General of the Department of Defense, *Report No. 07-INTELL-04, February 9, 2007,* "Review of Pre-Iraqi War Activities of the Office of the Under Secretary for Policy."

6. Fred Kaplan, "Challenging the Generals," *NYT* (August 26, 2007).

7. See, for example, Paul Yingling, "A Failure in Generalship," *Armed Forces Journal,* May, 2007, http://armedforcesjournal.com/2007/05/2635198; Ralph Peters, "General Failure," *USA Today* (July 24, 2007); Kaplan, "Challenging the Generals." Kaplan cites figures showing that in 2003, only 18 percent of the West Point Class of 1998 left the service. However, in 2006, when it was time for the class of 2001 to make the choice, 44 percent quit the army.

8. Kaplan, "Challenging the Generals."

9. Richard Myers and Richard H. Kohn, "Salute and Disobey: The Military's Place," *Foreign Affairs,* September/October 2007, 147–149.

10. Greg Newbold, "Why Iraq was a Mistake," *Time* (April 9, 2006), at http://www.time.com/time/printout/0,8816,118162,00.html.

11. Julian E. Barnes, "Army Rebuffs Rumsfeld Doctrine," *Chicago Tribune* (November 20, 2006): A1.

12. "The Army We Need," *Washington Post* (December 19, 2006): A28.

13. David Petraeus and James Amos, with a forward by John Nagl, *The US Army, Marine Corps, Counterinsurgency Field Manual* (Chicago: University of Chicago Press, 2007). I would like to thank John Nagl for providing me with a copy of this manual. LTC Nagl's introduction to the new counterinsurgency manual provides an excellent overview of the battle within the army to get the organization to realize the importance of counterinsurgency. "Forward to the University of Chicago Press Edition," Ibid., xii–xx. See also Thomas X. Hammes, *The Sling and the Stone: On War in the 21st Century* (St. Paul, MN: Zenith, 2006).

# Index